COLLOQUIAL ARABIC

It is generally supposed that a single language is spoken throughout the Arab world. But it is only written Arabic that is more or less common to the individual countries, and the spoken language can differ as widely as Spanish and Italian. This book has been prepared for those who wish to make everyday use of the living language of modern Egypt and for those who would like to add a colloquial Arabic to their knowledge of languages. Its subject is Cairene Arabic, the form of Egyptian colloquial Arabic spoken in Cairo which sets the standards for modern Egyptian usage. After working carefully through this book, the student should be able to carry on simple conversations fluently and accurately.

TEACH YOURSELF BOOKS

COLLOQUIAL ARABIC

T. F. Mitchell

Professor of English Language and General Linguistics.
University of Leeds

TEACH YOURSELF BOOKS
Hodder and Stoughton

First printed 1962
Eleventh impression 1983

This volume is published in the U.S.A.
by David McKay Company Inc.,
750 Third Avenue, New York, N.Y. 10017

ISBN 0 340 26519 1

Printed in Great Britain
for Hodder and Stoughton Educational,
a division of Hodder and Stoughton Ltd.,
Mill Road, Dunton Green, Sevenoaks, Kent
by Richard Clay (The Chaucer Press) Ltd., Bungay, Suffolk

ACKNOWLEDGMENTS

I am most grateful to the Shell Petroleum Company for generously allowing me to draw freely upon material contained in my *Introduction to Egyptian Colloquial Arabic* (Oxford, 1956).

My sincere thanks are also due to Dr. Mohamed Ahmed Abu Farag for his invaluable help in the preparation of Part IV.

T. F. M.

CONTENTS

I. THE LINGUISTIC BACKGROUND

There is a great deal in a name, sometimes a great deal of confusion. It is commonly supposed that *Arabic* designates a single language uniting in ties of mutual comprehension speakers from countries as widely separated as Iraq, Egypt, and Morocco, but this is not so. It is only *written* Arabic, that is the Classical language of the Koran and early literature and the grammatically similar neo-Classical or Modern Arabic of contemporary literature, journalism, broadcasting, and public address that is more or less common to the Arab world. Speaking and writing are essentially separate aspects of linguistic activity and the first has always preceded the second, both in the process of man's evolution and in the sequence by which the individual child acquires a complicated set of listening and speaking habits long before he sets hand and eye to paper. As a result of the normal processes of linguistic development, the colloquial Arabic which lives in the several Arab societies to-day and by which they mostly live, differs as widely between Arab countries as do those languages which nowadays go under the different names of Italian, Spanish, and Portuguese. Within the Arab world, the comparatively static and uniform written Arabic acts in a wholly desirable way as a kind of limited Esperanto, providing a means of communication between educated men of whatever nationality; as a spoken medium, it is an example of that paradox known to linguists as a *Schriftsprache* and might aptly be named *pan*-Arabic. The nearest contemporary European parallel to this use of a written language as a " control " for purposes of spoken communication is provided by the *Hochdeutsch* used between speakers of otherwise mutually unintelligible varieties of German, but a closer parallel is the historical one of Latin in the Middle Ages before the emergence of the several Romance languages. Even in English, of course, there are differences of grammar and vocabulary between the written and spoken language but the degree of such difference is far less than that between the artificial pan-Arabic and the living colloquial of any Arab country. Moreover, both written and spoken English are recognized in English-using societies as belonging to one living language and are both systematically taught and maintained by authority; colloquial Arabic, on the other hand, is largely ignored by its users and, what is more, unlike colloquial English, may not freely be written.

The educated Egyptian, then, uses pan-Arabic to talk, on as wide a range of topics as the present state and degree of unification of the written language allows, to equally literate Iraqis, Saudis, Moroccans, and even Europeans. No reasonable man, however, in whatever homogeneous society, is anxious to talk like a book, much less like a newspaper or a public orator, and the language that the same educated Egyptian uses on return to the bosom of his family or generally with his compatriots is quite other than that in which he addresses non-Egyptians. This second language is wholly Egyptian and it is exclusively with it that this book is concerned.

Egyptian Arabic is a vigorous, living language and, like all languages, which are inseparable from the men, women, and children who use them, it is, and has been over the many centuries of its evolution, subject to constant change. It is naïve to believe, as some do, that it is possible, let us say in the interests of Arab political and economic unity, to suppress all national forms of Arabic and to impose in their stead, either gradually or overnight, a new form of Arabic identical with or closely related to the present written language. What is needed in the present somewhat schizophrenic conditions is both development of pan-Arabic in order to increase its scope and at the same time the institution of *national* written languages. There are signs that an Egyptian written language is struggling to emerge; the dialogue of some playwrights, for example, is deliberately contrived to conform to both written and colloquial usage, but this is a half-measure at a time when nothing less is needed than the complete freedom in which, for example, a hypothetical thriller-writer is as much at liberty as Agatha Christie in England to include colloquial forms in his work and the educationist is able to write a grammar of English for use in Egyptian schools in which colloquial English is faced squarely by the colloquial Egyptian of the school-child's day-to-day experience. Egypt, favourably placed as she is culturally, politically, geographically, and demographically, and with the consciousness of "own language" that so many of her people enjoy, has a splendid opportunity to give the lead in this vital matter to the rest of the Arab world. The authoritative grammars, dictionaries, and other law-giving books must be written and compiled by Egyptians themselves, for they alone are masters of their own language.

Some may say that to do as has just been suggested would be to run counter to the ideal of Arab unity in the economic, political, religious, and cultural spheres, but surely such action would be to serve this ideal, for it is only by bringing differences out into the open that, when occasion demands, they can be avoided. Moreover, the parallel drawn above between pan-Arabic and Latin (now dead) is by no means a complete one, since vital factors are present in the modern situation which were absent in the Middle Ages. Pan-Arabic is not the prerogative of a single class of society, and not only is education to-day more widespread but the mass media and jet aircraft of the times make the world a small place indeed.

The question may reasonably be posed as to which form of Arabic the foreign learner should first be taught and the right answer in the current situation is undoubtedly pan-Arabic. But thereafter he may wish to learn one of the many living forms of Arabic and the question again arises, which? In the absence of any indication as to the particular country most likely to interest him, there can be no doubt about the answer. Egyptian films are seen and the Egyptian radio heard in every Arab country and Egyptians teach in schools from Kuwait to Libya; it is hardly surprising, therefore, that the Egyptian colloquial is much better known than any other. In addition, it has advanced further than other colloquials along the road to linguistic independence, for there exists a clearly recognizable norm to which educated Egyptian usage conforms. Standards are set in Egypt by the cultured classes in Cairo.

There are numerous forms of Egyptian colloquial Arabic, just as there are many dialects of English. Divergence may be considerable, as for example between Cairo, Qena in Upper Egypt, and the Bedouin area west of Alexandria, or it may be less marked as, say, between the towns and villages of the

Delta. Moreover, differences of educational standard and class correspond to speech differences in a single district. An educated Egyptian, however, has very definite ideas on what constitutes a "prestige" pronunciation, turn of phrase, etc., and the dominance of Cairo is not surprising, since the part played by capital cities in establishing a norm is well known. In England, London, as the centre of government, commerce, literature, law, etc., attracted in the past people from many parts of the country who helped fashion the dialect of English which was to become so widespread and which, in its present form, is spoken by most educated Englishmen to-day. It is, then, cultured Cairene Arabic that is the subject of this book.

Finally, a word of warning. In the present situation the student must be prepared to meet the attitude, common enough in European centres of learning, that written language, preferably literary, is alone worthy of study. The student of Arabic is as certain to encounter bigotry on the part of linguistically unsophisticated people—and how many of us are truly without prejudice in linguistic matters?—as he is to hear the dogmatic expression of views which, based on obsession with "Classical" and written form, are opposed to the statements of grammar and pronunciation made in this book. To such statements he should turn a deaf ear, concentrating rather on listening to what his informant is saying and how he is saying it. The pronunciation hints which follow are intended to help him to this end.

II. HINTS ON PRONUNCIATION

There is a minimum of phonetic courtesy to be achieved in learning to use any language; moreover, the advantages that proficiency in pronouncing Arabic confer on the English speaker are self-evident: among them, the respect of the Egyptian is not the least. The general hints contained in this book should suffice for practical purposes and provide a firm foundation on which to build a more detailed study of Egyptian pronunciation.

The system of writing used in the book is a transcription of colloquial pronunciation; it is neither a transliteration of Arabic written forms nor an orthography, which would require a constant shape for a given word, whatever its pronunciation in context. It is not, however, that kind of phonetic transcription which aims at representing as many features of consonant- and vowel-sound as possible, but rather one whose object is to suggest an acceptable pronunciation, with the minimum of frills and without losing sight of grammar and lexicon.

The transcription comprises the following consonant-letters, vowel-letters, and diacritics:

(*a*) *consonants*: **b, d, ḍ, f, g, h, ḥ, k, l, m, n, q, r, s, ṣ, t, ṭ, w, x, y, z, ẓ, ʕ, ʃ, ɛ, ɣ**
(*b*) *vowels*: **a, ɑ, e, i, o, u**
(*c*) *diacritics*: acute accent, hyphen, breve (˘)

Other consonant symbols, sporadically used and relating to loan-words in the colloquial, are included in the Addenda to the following section.

In the case of **ḍ, ḥ, ṣ, ṭ, ẓ, ʕ, ʃ, ɛ,** and **ɣ**, the letter-shape is strange and, with the exception of **ʃ** (= *sh* in *ship*), its strangeness relates to special pronunciation difficulty. In addition, it will be found that **q** and **x** are used with very different values from those associated with them in English orthography. Vowels occur both long and short; long vowels are shown by doubling the letter, i.e. long **a** by **aa,** long **i** by **ii,** etc. Capital letters are not used in the transcription.

PRONUNCIATION OF CONSONANTS

(*a*) Little difficulty is offered to English speakers by the sounds written with: **f** (as in English *film*), **b** (Eng. *bad*), **s** (Eng. *sit*), **z** (Eng. *zeal*), **ʃ** (Eng. *sheen*), **k** (Eng. *king*), **g** (Eng. *gear*), **m** (Eng. *mat*), **n** (Eng. *nap*), **w** (Eng. *win*), **y** (Eng. *yes*). **t** and **d**, too, do not present insuperable obstacles but care should be taken to ensure that the tongue is in contact with the teeth as well as with the ridge behind the teeth, since in most contexts it is exclusively with this ridge that contact is made in pronouncing the corresponding English sounds (cf. Eng. *tag* and *dam* and contrast Arabic **taag** *crown* and **damm** *blood*). **s, z, t, d** must always be distinguished from **ṣ, ẓ, ṭ, ḍ**.

(*b*) The following will require more careful attention:

ʕ: the glottal stop or catch. A common enough sound in English dialects, cf. a Cockney pronunciation of the *t*'s in *a bit o' butter*, and one which occurs frequently in Standard English pronunciation between words beginning and ending with a vowel, e.g. *Jaffa ʕorange, sea ʕeagle*, and also when we wish to give emphatic stress to a word beginning with a vowel, e.g. *it's ʕabsolutely ʕawful*. Arabic examples are: **ʕiktib!** *write!*, **ʕumm** *mother*, **ʕult** *I/you said*, **daʕiiʕa** *minute* (time), **ḥaʕʕ** *right*.

h: a sound which will not be found difficult when it begins a word or syllable as in **haat!** *bring, fetch!*, **muhimm** *important*, but one which must be carefully pronounced in the same way when, in an un-English way, it ends a word or syllable, e.g. **ʕabúuh** *his father*, **ʕáhwa** *coffee*; beware, however, of an English tendency to make **h** sound like **x** (see below) in these contexts. It sometimes helps in the early stages to put in an extra " ghost " vowel following **h**, i.e. **ʕáhəwa** (for **ʕáhwa**) and to aim at eliminating it gradually. In the speech of many educated Egyptians final **h**, e.g. **ʕabúuh**, is often not pronounced but the beginner is advised to practise its inclusion.

l: in almost all contexts the " clear " *l* of *leaf* as opposed to the " dark " *l* of *feel*. Imagine you are going to pronounce the word *leaf* but keep the tongue in the " l "-position, prolonging the sound and without uttering the " -eaf " portion; contrast the sound with that of the *l* at the end of *feel*. The pronunciation of Arabic **fiil** *elephant* and **milk** *property* in the manner of English *feel* and *milk* would be woefully inadequate. Most Irishmen, it may be noted, use the right kind of *l* in all English contexts: most Americans and Scots use the wrong kind even in *leaf*. An important exception to the general rule is that the "dark" *l* of *feel* is used in **ʕallάah** *God* and derivative forms as **ʕinʃάlla** *I hope*; **ʕa** of **ʕallάah** is elided if preceded by a vowel and, if this vowel is **i**, then **ll** is pronounced with the "clear" *l* of *leaf*; e.g. **ʕilḥámdu li-llάah** *praise be to God*.

r: English initial *r* in words like *rugged*, *rock*, and *rascal* will never do. The rolled Scottish *r* of *burn* is what is wanted. Many English people make the right kind of "r" in words such as *very* and *thorough*; if you do, try to isolate it in order to control it, if you do not, try to pronounce a very quick "d" in place of "r" in these words. Pay particular attention to the need to pronounce Arabic **r** when final: **ʕamíir** *prince* sounds nothing like *a mere*. A quick flip or tap of the tip of the tongue against the ridge behind the teeth is the basis of this sound and it is also the basis of the trilled or rolled "r", which consists of a number of intermittent taps and which is the sound of Arabic **r** when doubled (**rr**). The trilled "r" may take some time to master if the student cannot make it already, but with practice it will come, even if only after a month or so of perseverance. Arabic examples are: **raml** *sand*, **bard** *cold*, **bάrra** *outside*, **barr** *land, country*.

ṣ ẓ ṭ ḍ: so-called "emphatic" consonants, to be distinguished from "non-emphatic" **s, z, t, d** respectively. For the emphatics, the tongue must be broad (laterally expanded) and "thick", filling the mouth: for the corresponding non-emphatics, the tongue is narrow (laterally contracted) and "thin". The lateral expansion and contraction of the tongue may be practised when looking in a mirror. In addition, the front of the tongue is very much lower and the whole tongue much flatter in the mouth for the emphatics; for the non-emphatics the front of the tongue is raised and the back depressed much as it is for the pronunciation of the vowel **i** (see below): the difference is easily perceptible in moving from, say, the **t**-position to the **ṭ**-position and vice versa while maintaining the necessary contact at the teeth or junction of teeth and gums. It sometimes helps to practise hollowing the tongue from front to rear and to retain the hollowing when pronouncing the emphatics; the mirror is again helpful in this connection. The position of the lips is also important; for the emphatics, they are held neutral or slightly rounded and protruded: for **s, z, t, d** they are spread. It may be noted that **l** of **ʕalláah** (see above) is characterized by emphatic articulation.

The features described above combine to produce in the emphatics a characteristic "hollow" resonance; the hiss of **ṣ**, for example, is of much lower frequency, much more indeterminate than the high-frequency, clear-cut sibilance of **s**. In this particular case, it is also helpful to pronounce **ṣ** with considerable tension in the tongue and lips. Examples of difference between emphatic and non-emphatic are:

tiin *figs*	**ṭiin** *mud*
baat *he spent the night*	**baaṭ** *armpit*
seef *sword*	**ṣeef** *summer*
bass *only*	**baṣṣ** *he looked*
dall *he directed*	**ḍall** *he lost his way*
baɛd *after*	**baɛḍ** *some*
záayir *visitor*	**ẓáahir** *clear*
mafrúuz *selected*	**maḥfúuẓ** *learnt by heart*

x: not a difficult sound. Feel back along the roof of the mouth with the tip of the tongue until the *soft palate* is reached; the soft palate and the *uvula* (the extremity of the soft palate; it can be seen in a mirror, hanging down at the extreme back of the mouth) must be made to vibrate for **x** as, for example, when breathing out heavily during snoring. It is much the same sound as in Scottish *loch* or *och aye* and German *achtung*. Arabic examples are **xáʃab** *wood*, **baxt** *luck*, **muxx** *brains*. More practice may be necessary when the sound occurs before or after **i** (or **ii**), e.g. **baxiil** *miser, miserly*, **xigil** *he was ashamed, confused*.

ɣ: **x** with the vocal cords vibrating, that is to say with the buzzing introduced into **x** that is made when passing from **s** to **z**, i.e. **sss-zzz, xxx-ɣɣɣ**. If difficulty is encountered, "dry gargling" should do the trick. **ɣ** is also the familiar sound of French "r" in Paris and Northern France. Examples are **ɣafíir** *watchman*, **ṣuɣáyyar** *small*, **ʃuɣl** *work*, **riɣíif** *loaf*.

q: a sound made in a somewhat similar manner to **k** but of very different acoustic impression, made in fact in the same place as **x** and **ɣ**, at the uvula. Make a **k** as far back as possible; again the mirror is of some help. This sound is used by educated speakers for "classicisms" in the colloquial; used in the right places, it is perhaps the most important single sign of educated speech. Examples are **qárya** *village*, **ʕilqurʕáan** *the Koran*, **ḥuqúul izzéet** *the oilfields*.

q is a "Classical" sound to which colloquial **ʕ** usually corresponds; there is, however, no simple equation classical **q** = colloquial **ʕ**. Words keep habitual company with other words and their total associations with particular contexts and styles of discourse. No doubt **ʕadíima** and **qadíima** are in some sense the "same word" in **fi máṣr ilʕadíima** *in Old Cairo* and in **f-ilʕuṣúur ilqadíima** *in olden times* but it would be quite wrong to substitute one form for the other and the difference between the forms is charged with meaning.

ḥ: a sound articulated (like **ʕ**) in the pharynx, the throat region above the windpipe; to master it, it is necessary to "get the feel" of this region. Look in a mirror and see what happens to the Adam's apple when one swallows; it will be seen to rise considerably and then descend again to its position of rest: if an attempt is made to keep it at the top of its run instead of allowing it to descend, the discomfort felt will be in the region in which it is necessary to make **ḥ**. To pronounce **ḥ**, adopt a posture as if about to retch, then release the tension in the pharynx just sufficiently to allow egress of air from the lungs; the result should be a satisfactory **ḥ**. Try to make the root of the tongue fill the throat for the sound, which, it must be emphasized, is not in the least like **x** or **h** and must at all times be clearly distinguished from them. It is quite possible to make a sound which combines features of **ḩ** and **x** and this is often a stage through which the beginner passes on the way to mastery of **ḩ**. Examples are: **ḩáaga** *thing*, **ḩilw** *sweet, nice*, **naḩl** *bees*, **ráḩḩab** *to welcome*, **riiḩ** *wind*, **malḩ** *salt*.

ɛ: the voiced sound corresponding to **ḩ**, i.e. as **ɣ** is to **x** (see above) so **ɛ** is to **ḩ**. Follow carefully the instructions for **ḩ** and simply introduce the necessary buzz of voice; do not do anything else. It has to be remembered that the tongue is made up of many muscles and is capable of movement in its parts as well as in its whole, so that it is quite possible for the root of the tongue in the pharynx to be correctly disposed for **ɛ** (and **ḩ**) and for the front of the tongue to perform unwanted action; when practising, therefore, open the mouth fairly wide and keep the part of the tongue visible in a mirror flat on the floor of the mouth. Having mastered the basic sound by following the above instructions, the student is likely to experience difficulty in controlling these two sounds in context, in "turning them on and off" at the right moments in the stream of speech; it is quite possible to imbue speech with the sound of **ɛ** throughout—the effect is somewhat "strangled". Such an effect is unfortunate in Arabic and in the early stages practice in "turning on and off" will be necessary, especially after vowels but also before vowels to some extent; practice the sound, therefore, intervocalically, short and long, i.e. **aa-ɛ-aa, aa-ɛ-uu, aa-ɛ-ii, uu-ɛ-aa, uu-ɛ-uu, uu-ɛ-ii, ii-ɛ-aa, ii-ɛ-uu, ii-ɛ-ii, a-ɛɛ-aa, a-ɛɛ-uu, a-ɛɛ-ii**, etc. Finally, beware of a common tendency to confuse **ɛ** with **ʕ**. Arabic examples are: **ɛáada** *custom, habit*, **ɛádad** *number*, **ɛeen** *eye*, **ɛiid** *festival*, **ɛumr** *life, age*, **baɛdéen** *afterwards, later*, **buɛd** *distance*, **sábɛa** *seven*, **sabɛíin** *seventy*, **báɛat** *he sent*, **gaɛáan** *hungry*, **biɛíid** *far*, **buɛáad** *far* (plural), **láaɛib** *player*, **záɛɛaʕ** *he shouted*, **dáfaɛ** *he paid*, **wiʕiɛ** *he fell*, **niɛnáaɛ** *mint*, **sabɛ** *lion*.

Doubled consonants

Any Arabic consonant may be doubled. Except when final, a doubled consonant must be pronounced at least twice as long as its single counterpart and is characterized by greater muscular tension in the articulating organs It is infinitely preferable to pronounce a doubled consonant occurring between vowels extremely long rather than not long enough; many English speakers do not pronounce doubled consonants with sufficient length when they occur at some distance from the accented syllable, e.g. **naʃʃalíin** *pickpockets* (sing. **naʃʃáal**). The contrary tendency is also observable among English speakers, who often pronounce a single consonant too long when it occurs after a short stressed syllable, as **t** and **s** in **kátaba** *clerks*, **kásar** *he broke*. Consonants which are pronounced long occur in English at the junction of words or of affixes and words; for example, *black king* (contrast *blacking*), *misspelt*, *unnecessary*, but, of course, the double letters of English spelling in such words as *better* and *butter* are pronounced as single sounds. The single-double distinction is a very important feature of Arabic and the **ss** of **kássɑr** *he smashed*, for example, must always be pronounced considerably longer than **s** in **kásɑr** *he broke*. Other examples are **ʕissámak** (*the*) *fish*, **ʃaɣɣáal** *hardworking*, **dáffaʕ** *he charged* (*money*), **fáḍḍɑ** *silver*, **ʃayyalíin** *porters*, **bɑṣṣ** *he looked*, **muhímm** *important*. Doubled consonants are usually pronounced shorter when final.

Addenda

(*a*) The sound written *v* in English sometimes occurs for **f** in the transcription, e.g. **lɑfẓ** *pronunciation*, but has no independent status except in very rare loan-words such as **se(e)rv** *service* (*tennis*), **vitíss** *gear-lever*; it has not, therefore, been included above. Similar remarks apply to the sound written generally as *p*, which sometimes occurs for transcribed **b**, e.g. **yóom issábt** *Saturday*, but again has no independent status except in loans, e.g. **piláaj** *seaside resort*. Less sophisticated speakers tend to replace **v** and **p** in such loans with **f** and **b** respectively, e.g. **balf** *valve*, **bíiba** *pipe*. **j**, as in English *jeep*, also occurs in loan-words, e.g. **jakétta** *jacket*, **jóoki** *jockey*, **julúuji** *geologist*.

(*b*) The sounds of English *th* in (i) *thin* and (ii) *then* belong to a "Classical" pronunciation of Arabic and occur sporadically when reading written language aloud. Examples occur in the book and the symbols used are as follows: **θ** (as *th* in *thin*), **ð** (as *th* in *then*). An emphatic counterpart of **ð**, symbol **ð̣**, also occurs in this style of pronunciation.

PRONUNCIATION OF VOWELS

General

Of the six vowels (**a, ɑ, e, i, o, u**), three (**i, e, a**) are articulated in the front of the mouth and three (**ɑ, o, u**) in the back: the tongue becomes flatter in the mouth or at a greater distance from the roof of the mouth as it moves from **i** through **e** to **a** and, conversely, moves towards the roof of the mouth in the back series from **ɑ** through **o** to **u**; the degree of opening, measurable roughly by the distance between the top and bottom teeth, is greatest for the open vowels (**a, ɑ**) and least for the close vowels (**i, u**). The lips are spread for **i** and **e**, neutral for **a** and **ɑ**, rounded for **o** and (especially) **u**.

Vowel-length

Vowels occur both short and long; when pronouncing a long vowel, give it at least twice the length given to its single counterpart; cf., for example, **ṣádaf** *sea-shells* and **ṣáɑdif** *he chanced upon*.

Two principal rules govern the occurrence of long vowels:

(1) they occur only in prominent or stressed syllables, cf. **máasik** *holding* but **masíkhum** *holding them*;

(2) they do not occur in closed syllables, i.e. type CVVC, where C = consonant and VV = long vowel, unless the syllable is final, cf. **manadíil** *handkerchiefs* but **manadílha** *her handkerchiefs*.

Note

It will be seen that if a vowel is pronounced short, then it is written short, even where grammar and lexicon would suggest a long vowel.

Contrary to rule (1), long vowels sometimes occur in non-prominent syllables in loans from written Arabic, e.g. **ʕadátan** or **ʕaadátan** *usually*, **ʕilqɑhíra** or **ʕilqɑɑhíra** *Cairo*. The vowel in such cases is not as long as in prominent syllables (cf. **ʕáamil** *workman*) but is distinctly longer than the short counterpart. This possibility of incremental length has been indicated where appropriate in the transcription by the use of brackets, i.e. **ɛa(a)dátan, ʕilqa(a)híra.** Loans from the written language also account for a few exceptions to rule (2). Most educated speakers make a difference of vowel-length between **ɛámmi** *my uncle* and **ɛáammi** *ignorant* (a "learned" form) and also between **ɛamm** *uncle* and **ɛaamm** *public, general* (cf. **ɛaam** *year*); in neither **ɛáammi** nor **ɛaamm** is the vowel pronounced as long as in, say, **ɛáamil,** where it occurs in an open syllable. Again, contrary to rule (2), a vowel which is generally short and corresponds to a long vowel in related forms is sometimes pronounced very long when the word containing it is singled out for special emphasis, e.g. **di ɣáalya giddan !** *that's terribly dear !,* cf. the more usual **ɣálya** (masc. **ɣáali**). Taking the language as a whole, however, exceptions to both rules are extremely rare.

Finally, it may be noted that the style of utterance on which the transcription in this book is based is *slow colloquial*; in *rapid* style, vowels are commonly pronounced long only before a pause.

Vowel-quality

In English we "slur" the vowel-sounds in the majority of syllables which are non-prominent or unstressed. Consider the vowels italicized in "th*e* Queen *o*f Engl*a*nd" or "fr*o*m head t*o* foot". This must be avoided at all costs in Arabic; each vowel should be clearly pronounced, each syllable given its due rhythmic weight. For this among other reasons, do not try to speak too rapidly at first—the formation of good habits early on will save a lot of trouble later. Vowels will now be considered in turn from the point of view of the quality to be associated with them.

a : between the vowel sounds of "Standard" English *hat* and *hurt* or *had* and *herd.* Try to isolate the vowel in *had* and then make it sound a little like the vowel in *herd*; if the complete word *hat* is taken as a starting-point and made to sound something like *hurt* without going the whole way, the result should be an acceptable rendering of the Arabic **haat !** *fetch, bring !* Other examples are: **dáras** *he studied,* **baab** *door,* **kátaba** *clerks,* **kitáaba** *writing.* Remember to beware of any tendency to "slur", for example in the second or third syllable of **kátaba.**

ɑ: when short and in a closed syllable, between the vowels of "Standard" English *hut* and *hot*; when in an open syllable or when long, as the vowel of English *heart.* **ɑ** occurs especially in the vicinity of the emphatic consonants, e.g. **ṣɑff** *row, line,* **ruṣɑ́ɑṣ** *lead* (*metal*), **ḍɑ́rɑb** *he hit,* **fɑ́ḍḍɑ** *he emptied*; *silver,* **ḥɑ́ɑḍir** *certainly,* **bɑɑṭ** *armpit,* **bɑṭn** *stomach,* **ẓɑnn** *he thought, believed,* **mɑẓbúuṭ** *exact*(*ly*). The vowel also commonly occurs in association with **r,** e.g. **rɑff** *shelf,* **rɑɑḥ** *he went,* **rɑ́ɑgil** *man,* **ḥúfrɑ** *hole,* **bɑ́rrɑ** *outside,* **bɑrrɑ́ɑd** *fitter,* **nɑɑr** *fire,* but contrast the occurrence of **a** in, say, **ráayiḥ** *going,* **ráagiʕ** *returning,* **bard** *cold,* **wárra** *he showed,* **firáan** *mice.* **ɑ** is also regularly associated with **q,** e.g. **qɑ́ryɑ** *village,* **ʕilqɑ(ɑ)híra** *Cairo,* **ʕaqsáam** (*administrative*) *departments.* It is not essential for the vowel immediately to precede or follow **ḍ, ṣ, ṭ, ẓ, r,** or **q**; cf. **mɑ́ṭbɑx** *kitchen,* **xɑ́ɑliṣ** *very, completely,* **lɑfẓ** *pronunciation,* **ṭurumbɑ́ɑt** (*petrol*) *pumps,* **ʃɑrɑbɑ́ɑt** *socks,* **mɑbrúuk** *congratulations!,* **ʕilqurʕɑ́ɑn** *the Koran.* The consonant context, moreover, is not an infallible guide to the quality of an associated open vowel, cf., for example, **hɑ́bhɑb** *it barked,* **mɑ́yyɑ** *water,* etc., and numerous loans from foreign languages, as **lɑ́mbɑ** *lamp,* (**sámak**) **bɑkɑlɑ́ɑ** *cod*; cf., too, **ʕámar** *he ordered* but **ʕɑ́mɑr** *moon.* Moreover, back vowels may be used with non-emphatic consonants which themselves must be clearly differentiated from emphatic counterparts, e.g. **xɑ́ddɑr** *he anaesthetized* but **xɑ́ḍḍɑr** *he trimmed* (*hair*); *watered* (*seedlings*); although the vowel in the first syllable of **xɑ́ḍḍɑr** tends to be nearer than its counterpart in **xɑ́ddɑr** to the vowel of English *hot,* nevertheless both these Arabic vowels are back vowels and to be distinguished not so much from each other as both of them from **a,** cf. **ʕándah** *I call,* **lukɑ́ndɑ** *hotel,* **ʕɑ́nḍɑf** *cleaner.*

The distribution of **a** and **ɑ** varies between men and women (see below), to some extent also between individuals, and notably between dialects. Cairene **xaaf** *he was afraid,* for example, corresponds to **xɑɑf** in Upper Egypt. A "Classical" pronunciation anywhere in the country conforms to the practice of Al-Azhar Mosque and University in Cairo and requires **ɑ** in association with **x** and **ɣ**, and also invariably with **r**, e.g. **xɑɑl** (*maternal*) *uncle*, **ɣɑ́ɑyib** *absent*, **fi(i)rɑ́ɑn** mice. Thus, a man using his "Classical" style at an appropriate time may be heard to say **xɑ́ɑdim** but will certainly use **xáadim** *servant* on normal colloquial occasions.

The difference **ɑ** : **a** (usually in association with the consonantal distinction emphatic : non-emphatic) tends to relate to difference between the speech of men and women respectively. **garráah̡** *surgeon*, for example, is typically a woman's form, to which **gɑrrɑ́ɑh̡** would usually correspond in men's speech.

e: a vowel approximately mid-way between the vowels in *bet* and *beet*. Pronouncing the vowel of English *bit* energetically and with spread lips usually produces the right result. The sound is common enough in English dialects, for example in Devon and Southern Ireland. Take care not to pronounce **e** like the "ay" sound in *day* or *bait*. Examples: **beet** *house*, **beeḍ** *eggs*.

When short, **e** is difficult to distinguish from short **i** in the speech of many people, especially in rapid style (cf. **bétna** *our house* and **bítna** *we spent the night*), but most educated speakers appear to make a slight difference and even in dialects where no distinction is made it would for most purposes be desirable to retain the transcribed difference between **bétna** and **bítna** in order to facilitate identification of the forms.

i: when short, as in English *bit*, e.g. **bint** *girl, daughter*; when long or final, approximately as in English *beet* but with more tension in the tongue and greater spreading of the lips, e.g. **ʃiil** *remove !*, **tamálli** *always*. An example which illustrates both qualities is **kibíir** *big, old*. Before **-yya**, the vowel tends towards the quality of **e**, e.g. in **mɑsríyya** *Egyptian* (fem.).

ii, pronounced short in accordance with the rules of vowel-length, tends nevertheless to retain the quality described for **ii**, not non-final **i**; the qualities of **ii** and **i** in **ʃiil** *remove* (masc.) *!*, **ʃílhum** *remove* (masc.) *them !*, **ʃíili** *remove* (fem.) *!*, **ʃillih** *remove* (fem.) *it* (masc.) *!*, are substantially the same.

o: between the vowels in *hawk* and *hook*. Pronounce the vowel of *hawk* with greater rounding and protrusion of the lips and an acceptable **o** should result. The sound is again common enough in English dialects, but neither the usual *o* of *no* nor the *ow* of *now* will do at all. Examples: **fooʕ** *above, upstairs, on top,* **miṣóogar** *registered.*

As between **e** and **i**, the difference between short **o** and **u** (see below) is greatly reduced in the speech of some, especially in rapid style.

u: when short, as in English *put*, e.g. **kútub** *books*; when long or final, approximately as *oo* in *food* but with greater tension and stronger rounding and protrusion of the lips, e.g. **ʃuuf** *see!*, **yínsu** *they forget.* **duxúul** *entrance, entry,* illustrates both qualities. Before **-wwa**, the vowel tends towards the quality of **o**, e.g. in **húwwa** *he, it.*

Like **ii** (see above), **uu** may be regularly shortened in accordance with the rules of vowel-length, e.g. **ʃuuf** but **ʃúfha** *look at her!* In parallel with **ii**, **u** in **ʃúfha** may be pronounced as **uu** in **ʃuuf**, but equally, and in contrast with the usual practice concerning **ii**, **u** may be pronounced with the quality described for short non-final **u** above.

Diphthongs

A diphthong is a combination of two vowel sounds in the same syllable. English contains many diphthongs (cf. the pronunciation of *bay, by, boy, bough, bow* (ribbon), also *bear, beer,* and *boor*) and is sharply differentiated from Arabic in this respect. Diphthongization may occur notably in Egyptian Arabic when, following a vowel (especially **a** and **ɑ**), **y** and **w** are either final or precede another consonant, circumstances in which they are often pronounced respectively as final **i** and **u**. As diphthongal elements, however, **y** and **w** should not be pronounced "lazily" as in the typical southern English pronunciation of, say, *hay* and *how* but, on the contrary, with energy and perceptible tension in the articulating organs; at the same time seek to make **y** as much as possible like the *y* of *yes* and to pronounce **w** with strong lip-rounding and protrusion—indeed, with many speakers, the sounds are so characterized by such features as to be consonantal rather than vocalic. Examples: **law** *if,* **mawgúud** *present,* **yíwṣɑl** *he arrives,* **ʃaay** *tea,* **ṭɑyyáɑr** *aeroplane.*

THE PROMINENT SYLLABLE

Turning now to the diacritica of the transcription, and first to the acute accent, we find that just as in English words, e.g. *phótograph, photógrapher, photográphic,* a given syllable stands out to the ear above the others, the first, second, and third syllables respectively in the examples, so Egyptian Arabic words contain a similarly prominent (*or* accented *or* stressed) syllable. In contrast with English, however, the facts concerning the placing of this syllable can be formulated within a few rules, since prominence in Egyptian Arabic depends on the structure of the word in terms of its constituent syllables. Taking every syllable to begin with a consonant and to contain a vowel, there are five syllable types: CV, CVC, CVV, CVVC, CVCC (C = consonant, V = vowel, VV = long vowel); e.g. **maẓbúuṭ** CVC-CVVC, **katábt** CV-CVCC, **manadíil** CV-CV-CVVC, **ʕáabil** CVV-CVC, **kátab** CV-CVC, **kátabit** CV-CV-CVC. CVV rarely occurs final except in loan-words and as a variant possibility for CVVh, where **-h** is the third person singular masculine pronominal suffix; it will be remembered that vowel-length and prominence are concomitant and that, therefore, any CVV syllable is by definition prominent.

The following rules show how prominence depends on the quantitative syllabic pattern of the whole word:

(1) If the ultimate syllable is long (CVVC, CVCC), that syllable is always prominent, e.g. **fanagíin** *cups*, **fihímt** *I/you understood*, **ḍarabúuh** (or **ḍarabúu**) *they hit him*. CVV must be considered long in ultimate position in loans such as **tintiraríi** *dyer's, cleaner's*.

(2) If the ultimate syllable is not long (CV, CVC), then, in relation to the pattern of remaining syllables, either the penultimate or the antepenultimate syllable is prominent as follows:

(*a*) If both the penultimate and antepenultimate syllables are short (CV), e.g. **kátaba** *clerks*, **kátabit** *she wrote*, and, in the case of words of four or five syllables, the pre-antepenultimate is not a further short syllable, e.g. **ʕinkásarit** *it* (fem.) *was broken*, then the antepenultimate is prominent;

(*b*) in all other cases, i.e. in the overwhelming majority of

Egyptian words, the penultimate syllable is prominent, e.g. **muʕállim** *teacher*, **maknása** *broom*, **dáawa** *he treated, cured*, **ʕitwágad** *it was found*, **mahiyyíti** *my pay*, **fihmúuha** *they understood her*, **ḍarabítu(h)** *she hit him*. It will be seen that whereas the operative distinction in relation to the ultimate syllable was between *long* and *not long*, the distinction that has to be made in respect of other positions is in terms of *short* and *not short*; the difference in prominence between **ḍárabit** and **ʕinkásar**, **ḍarabítu(h)** and **ʕinkásarit**, relates to the difference between short (CV) and not-short (CVC) in the first syllables.

Notes

(*a*) It will have been clear from the examples given that the rules of prominence apply to suffixed and unsuffixed forms alike.

(*b*) There are two exceptions to the rules, both of which concern the pattern CVCVCV(h) which, in contrast with usual antepenultimate prominence, has the penultimate prominent in:

(i) The third person singular feminine perfect of weak verbs of the **ráma**-type when associated with a vowel-beginning pronominal suffix, e.g. **rámit** + **u(h)** = **ramítu(h)** *she threw it*;

(ii) the plural forms **ḍubúʕa** *hyenas*, **subúʕa** *lions*, **dukúra** *males*, **libísa** *underpants*, **ɣiríba** *crows*, **ḥiṣína** *horses*, in which the rare sequence of close vowels (**u-u** and **i-i**) in the first two syllables is associated with penultimate prominence and which thus contrast with, say, **kátaba** *clerks*, **búxala** *misers*, **ʕínaba** *grape*, etc. This pattern is commoner in other dialects than in Cairene and in the case of **i-i** the alternative forms **ʕilbísa**, **ʕiɣríba**, **ʕiḥṣína**, are, in fact, more usual than the forms given.

(*c*) Although on the face of things **xamast** in the numeral-noun construction illustrated by **xámast iyyáam** *five days* contains a long final syllable which is non-prominent, it will be found at the appropriate place in the grammatical section that there are a number of special features about this type of grammatical structure and that the **-t** of

xamast, arbitrarily allotted to the numeral, is in fact a feature of the whole complex.

(*d*) It frequently happens, of course, that in phrases and sentences a word is pronounced without prominence in relation to adjoining words. Standing alone, both **kitáab** *book* and **faríid** *Fareed* (proper name) have their prominent syllable, but in **kitab faríid** *Fareed's book* it is possible for the prominent syllable of the second word only to stand out; no long vowel appears in a non-prominent syllable, it will be remembered, hence **kitab.**

ELISION

Elision concerns the omission under certain conditions of the short vowels **i** and **u**, on the one hand, and of **ʕ** (with or without an accompanying vowel),[1] on the other. Where elision of a vowel ± **ʕ** occurs at the junction of words or of a particle and a word, the feature has been marked in the writing by a hyphen.

1. *Elision of short* **i** *and* **u**

The close vowels **i** and **u** differ in status as syllable-makers from the open vowels **a** and **ɑ**; in parallel contexts, **i** and **u** are elided, **a** and **ɑ** are not. Contexts of elision of **i** and **u** may be subdivided according to whether elision is within the word or at a word-junction. It is only the latter that is indicated by the hyphen in the transcription.

(*a*) *Intra-word*

Elision relates exclusively to suffixation and, strictly speaking, is a term of comparison between suffixed and unsuffixed forms. The conditions necessary for the elision in a suffixed form of a short vowel present in the final syllable of the corresponding unsuffixed form are:

(i) The suffix must begin with a vowel;

(ii) the final syllable of the unsuffixed form must be of structure -CiC or -CuC;

(iii) the penultimate syllable of the unsuffixed form must be open, i.e. CV- or CVV-.

Examples:

ɛáawiz (m.s.) + **a** = **ɛáwza** *wanting* (f.s.), **ʕáabil** *he met* + **u** = **ʕáblu** *they met* or *he met him*, **yáaxud** *he takes* + **u**

[1] Never of the **ʕ** which corresponds to Classical **q.**

= **yáxdu** *they take* or *he takes it*, **wiḥiʃ** (m.s.) + **a** = **wiḥʃa** *unpleasant* (f.s.), **fihim** *he understood* + **it** = **fihmit** *she understood*, **yitwigid** *it is found* + **u** = **yitwigdu** *they are found.*

Contrast the facts when the suffix begins with a consonant, e.g. **ʕáabil** + **hum** = **ʕabilhum** *he met them.*

Contrast, too, the non-elision of open vowels in comparable contexts, e.g. **ḍárab** *he hit* + **it** = **ḍárabit** *she hit*, **ʕitwágad** *it was found* + **u** = **ʕitwágadu** *they were found.*

Finally, contrast the case of non-elision when the penultimate syllable of the unsuffixed form is closed (CVC), e.g. **fáhhim** *he explained* + **u** = **fahhimu** *they explained* or *he explained to him.*

Exceptions:

(i) Final -CuC in the unsuffixed form is comparatively rare and **u** is not elided in the case of the pattern CuCuC, cf. **kútub** *books* + **u(h)** = **kútubu(h)** *his books.*

(ii) **i** of the suffix **-it** (3rd pers. sing. fem. perfect tense) is never elided when a further suffix is added, cf. **kátabit** + **u(h)** = **katabitu(h)** *she wrote it*, **rámit** + **u(h)** = **ramitu(h)** *she threw it.* Contrast, for example, **ʕáalit** + **u(h)** = **ʕalitu(h)** *she said it* with **ʕáabil** + **u(h)** = **ʕáblu(h)** *he met him.* Contrast, too, **-i-** of the suffix **-it** of the feminine noun in construct, which, in contrast with the **i** of the verbal suffix, is regularly elided, e.g. **tigáara** + **u(h)** = **tigártu(h)** *his business* (not ***tigaritu(h)**; cf. **tigarithum** *their business*).

(iii) Elision is not a feature of the "Classical" language and is accordingly absent from "classicisms" in the colloquial. This is particularly noteworthy with participial forms; educated speakers will prefer, for example, **munfáɛil** (m.s.)/ **munfáɛila** (f.s.)/**munfaɛiliin** (pl.) *angry, upset*, to the less sophisticated **minfiɛil/minfiɛla/minfiɛliin.**

(*b*) *Inter-word* (word-junctions)

The ability to link in one syllable as a result of elision the end of one word and the beginning of the next is absolutely essential to the attainment of fluency in the language and considerable attention should therefore be paid to the feature of elision from the beginning.

A vowel appearing elsewhere in an initial (short) syllable of a word is elided when

(i) the syllable in question is of type Ci- or Cu-;

(ii) the syllable is non-prominent;
(iii) the preceding word ends in a vowel.

Examples:

ʕinta + **tiɛibt** = **ʕinta-tɛíbt** *you are tired,* **ʕana** + **fihimt** = **ʕana-fhímt** *I understood,* **ʕiddiini** + **huduumak** = **ʕiddíini-hdúumak** *give me your clothes,* **ʕabu** + **ḥuseen** = **ʕabu-ḥséen** *Husein's father.*.

Contrast once again the non-elision of open vowels in parallel contexts, e.g. **ʕinta katábt** *you wrote,* **ʕana ḍarábt** *I hit,* **ʕiddíini ʃaráabak** *give me your socks,* **ʕabu faríid** *Fareed's father.*

Contrast, too, the case when the initial syllable is prominent, e.g. **ʕabu ɛúmar** *Omar's father,* **fáḍḍa ɛílabu(h)** *he emptied his boxes.*

Notes

(*a*) Elision also concerns the vowel of particles, notably of **fi** *in,* **bi** *by, with,* **li** *to, for,* and **wi** *and,* as well as that of the verbal prefix **bi-**, e.g. **ʕiʃtaréetu-b káam?** *How much did you buy it for?,* **huwwa-f máṣr** *he's in Cairo,* **huwwa-byílɛab** *he's playing.*

(*b*) In emphatic utterance which is characterized by the deliberate enunciation of each syllable, elision will not occur; compare **yáa xuṣáara** uttered in this way with the more usual **ya-xṣáara!** *what a pity!*

(*c*) Although the vowel **u** is elided as expected in, say, **ɛandi** + **ḥumaar** = **ɛándi-ḥmáar** *I have a donkey,* nevertheless **ḥ** is often pronounced with the lips rounded as for **u.**

(*d*) Contrary to rule, **a** is elided in a few common forms in which **ḥ** or **ɛ** follows the vowel, e.g. **ʃufti** + **maḥammad** = **ʃúfti-mḥámmad?** *did you* (fem.) *see Mohamed?,* **ma** + **maɛiiʃ** = **ma-mɛíiʃ** *I haven't* (*got*) *any.*

2. *Elision of* ʕ

In principle, utterance in Arabic may not begin with (i) a vowel or (ii) two consonants. Initial ʕ is often no more than a means of obviating these inadmissible features and, as might be expected, is frequently elided when the word to which it belongs no longer begins the utterance.

There are two major subdivisions of the contexts in which ʕ is elided when no longer initial; following a consonant and following a vowel. It should perhaps be noted that if a pause is made before the word in which the consonant is initial, then notwithstanding any of the rules given subsequently, ʕ is not elided.

(a) Preceded by a consonant

ʕ is very commonly elided when following a consonant unless the word with which it is associated elsewhere is singled out for emphasis. Thus **ʃúγl ibnak** *your son's work* is a commoner form than **ʃúγli ʕibnak**, which might, however, be used to mark a contrast, say with **ʃúγlak inta** *your work*; again, **ʢamalt éeh ?** *what have you done ?* is doubtless more frequent than **ʢamálti ʕéeh ?**, which may be used to indicate surprise, indignation, sarcasm, etc. A word like **ʕábadan** *ever, never*, is hardly, if ever, used other than emphatically and as a result ʕ is very rarely elided. Generally speaking, elision is more frequent in the speech of less educated people; the most important categories and forms involving elision of ʕ in educated usage are as follows:

(i) 1st pers. sing. imperfect tense (e.g. **ʕáktib** *I write*); imperative forms (e.g. **ʕiktib** *write !*); the perfect tense of derived forms of the verb (e.g. **ʕitbáʢat** *it was sent*, **ʕiftákar** *he thought*, **ʕistáʢlim** *he inquired*); verbal nouns of the derived forms (e.g. **ʕistiʢláam** *inquiry*, **ʕintixabáat** *elections*).

(ii) More particular forms as follows: the article **ʕil**; the pronouns **ʕána** *I*, **ʕinta** *you* (m.s.), **ʕinti** *you* (f.s.), **ʕintu** *you* (pl.), and **ʕiḥna** *we*; the nouns of relationship **ʕabb** *father*, **ʕumm** *mother*, **ʕibn** *son*, **ʕaxx** *brother*, **ʕuxt** *sister*; the "deictics" **ʕaho/ʕahe/ʕahum** and **ʕáadi** *there is/are*; the interrogative particles **ʕeeh** *what*, **ʕímta** *when*, **ʕánhu** *which*; the phrase- and clause-introducing particles **ʕilli** *that (relative), which (ditto)*, and **ʕinn** *that (conjunctive)*; a few common nouns such as **ʕism** *name*.

(iii) ʕ is variously elided or not in the comparative form of adjectives (e.g. **ʕil** + **ʕakbar** = either **lákbar** or **ʕilʕákbar** *the bigger, biggest*) and in one or two broken plural patterns of nouns, notably **ʕaCCaaC** (e.g. **ʕil** + **ʕayyaam** = either **ʕilʕayyáam** or **liyyáam** *the days*, also **ʕiʕfáal ilʕabwáab** or **ʕiʕfáal libwáab** *the locks of the doors*). On balance, educated practice tends towards non-elision; this is also particularly true of (noun) patterns which contain only two consonants other than ʕ, e.g. **ʕizn** *permission* (contrast **ʕibn** and **ʕism** above), **ʕakl** *food*, **ʕúgra** *rate, hire*, **ʕamíin** *trustworthy*, **ʕasáami** *names*, **ʕagáaza** *leave*, **ʕasáasi** *basic*, **ʕiḥáala** *retirement*, **ʕiṣáaba** *injury*, **ʕizáaza** *bottle*; ʕ is far better not elided in these forms.

Notes

(*a*) ʕ is not elided when it is the initial radical (see below) of certain verbal forms, e.g. **ʕámar** *he ordered*, **ʕáxxar** *he delayed*.

(*b*) ʕ is similarly retained in the quadriliteral form (see below) **ʕárnab** *rabbit*.

(*c*) ʕ of **ʕeeh** is not elided following **h** in **fiih ʕéeh?** *what is there?, what's going on?*, nor after **yy** in **záyyi ʕéeh?** *such as?*

(*d*) ʕ corresponding to "Classical" **q** is never elided, e.g. **ʕifl** *lock*, **ʕirʃ** *piastre*.

(*e*) Elision of ʕ which is not accompanied as below by the elision of a vowel is not marked in the transcription except by the omission of ʕ.

(*b*) *Preceded by a vowel*

When a vowel precedes, not only may ʕ be elided as indicated above but so, too, under certain conditions, may the preceding or following vowel. Contexts are broadly divisible into those in which the vowels flanking ʕ are the same and those in which they are different.

Same vowels.—Except under conditions of strong stress, one of the vowels is elided together with ʕ, e.g. **ʕinta** + **ʕaḥmar** = **ʕint-áḥmar** *you are red*, **fi** + **ʕiidu(h)** = **f-iidu(h)** *in his hand* (in the transcription, the first vowel has regularly been omitted); the forms **ʕinta ʕáḥmar** and **fi ʕiidu(h)** occur when special emphasis is given to **ʕáḥmar** and **ʕiidu(h)**. From the single sentence **ʕana ɛawz-áakul** *I want to eat*, it will be noticed, it cannot be said whether a man or a woman is speaking since **ɛaawiz** + **ʕaakul** and **ɛawza** + **ʕaakul** may both give the same result.

Different vowels.—Some subdivision is necessary under this heading. Generally speaking, when the vowels preceding and following ʕ differ, both vowels and ʕ remain, e.g. **ʕismåha ʕéeh**? *what's her name?*, **biyiɛmílu ʕéeh**? *what are they doing?* The following contexts, however, and especially the vowel **i**, need special notice:

-V ʕi-

ʕi is elided whatever the vowel that precedes, e.g. **da** + **ʕilli** + **ʕinta** + **ɛawzu(h)** = **dá-ll-inta ɛáwzu(h)** *that's what you want*, **ʕissana** + **ʕilli** + **ḟaatit** = **ʕissána-lli ḟáatit** *last year*, **ʃuufu** + **ʕilli** + **ʕuddamku** = **ʃúufu-lli ʕuddámku** *look* (pl.) *who's in front of you*, **ʕana** + **ʕiddethaalu(h)** = **ʕana-ddetháalu(h)** *I gave it* (f.) *to him*.

-i ʕa-

-i, as well as **ʕ**, is elided before **a** or **-ɑ**, e.g. **bi** + **ʕaktib** = **báktib** *I write, am writing*, **naawi** + **ʕaruuḫ** = **náaw-arúuḫ** *I intend going*, **xalliini** + **ʕɑrɑwwɑḫ** = **xallíin-ɑrɑ́wwɑḫ** *let me go home*, **ɛali** + **ʕafandi** = **ɛál-afandi** *Ali Efendi*.

-a ʕu-

A rare junction, frequent only in the vocative context and treated in the manner of **-a ʕi-**, i.e. with elision of **ʕu-**, cf. **ya** + **ʕumm** in **yɑ́-mmŭ kalsúum**! (*O*) *Umm Kalsum!*; notice the back quality of the open vowel, at any rate in men's speech—**yɑ́-xti** (= **ya** + **ʕuxti**) (*O*) *my sister!* usually corresponds in the pronunciation of men to **yá-xti** in that of women.

Notes

(*a*) **ʕɑllɑ́ɑh** *God* is treated exceptionally, **ʕɑ** being elided after any vowel, e.g. **li** + **ʕɑllɑɑh** = **li-lláah** *to God*, **yɑrḫamkumu** + **ʕɑllɑɑh** = **yɑrḫámkumu-llɑ́ɑh** *may God have mercy on you*. In passing, it may be noted that, in spite of appearances, **yɑrḫamkumu** is not an exception to the rules of prominence which have been given; **yɑrḫámkumu-llɑ́ɑh** is a borrowing from the Classical language and the apparently word-final **u** does not belong to the first word but is a feature of the junction.

(*b*) The special treatment of the noun plural pattern ʕaCCaaC in rather less educated speech has been already noted under 2 (*a*) (iii) above (cf. **liyyáam** as a variant of **ʕilʕayyáam** *the days*) and is also relevant in the present context. The elision of **ʕa-** (cf. **ʕalláah** above) may be encountered in, say, **fi** + **ʕafraan** = **fi-fráan** *in ovens*, to which **fi ʕafráan** more generally corresponds in educated usage.[1]

(*c*) The hyphen in the transcription marks the elision of a vowel (± ʕ); it is not specifically intended to mark the place at which the vowel occurs in corresponding contexts of non-elision (cf. **ʕana-f xidmítak** *I'm at your service* = **ʕana** + **fi**, etc., **huwwa-byilʕab** *he's playing* = **huwwa** + **biyilʕab**) but does so incidentally in the case of elision of (vowel + ʕ) or (ʕ + vowel).

(*d*) Notice the regular elision of **i** but retention of **ʕ** in **ʕabu** + **ʕimaam** (proper name) = **ʕabu-ʕmáam** *Imam's father.*

(*e*) In disyllabic forms (notably **ʕílli**) in which **ʕi** is initial in the prominent syllable in contexts of non-elision, **ʕi** may be elided according to rule but the prominence associated with the syllable may remain to mark the junction with a preceding vowel-ending form, e.g. **ʕaná-lli ḥarúuḥ** *I'm the one who'll go* = **ʕána** + **ʕílli** + **ḥarúuḥ**.

(*f*) The prepositional particles **min** *from* and **ʕála** *on* require special notice in the matter of elision when they precede a noun prefixed with the definite article; not essentially but extremely commonly, the total portions **-in** and **-la** of the particles are elided, e.g. **m-ilmáktab** *from the office* = **min** + **ʕilmaktab**, **ʕa-ṭṭarabéeẓa** *on the table* = **ʕala** + **ʕiṭṭarabeeẓa**.

THE "EXTRA" OR ANAPTYCTIC VOWEL

Three successive consonants are inadmissible in Egyptian Arabic. Such successions could potentially occur when a word ending in two consonants is followed by a consonant-beginning word or suffix, but the pattern is avoided by the introduction of an "extra" vowel between the second and third consonants; this vowel, often pronounced very short but which may equally be the vowel of a prominent syllable according to the rules of prominence, is written in the transcription with the breve sign,

[1] **fi-fráan** should perhaps be related to a form **ʕifráan** rather than **ʕafráan**.

i.e. ĭ, ă, ŭ. In the vast majority of contexts the quality to be associated with this vowel is that of short non-final **i** as already described; preceding the pronominal suffixes, however, the vowel is regularly **ŭ** (before **-ku(m)** and **-hum**) and **ă** or **a** (before **-ha**).

Examples:

bintĭ maḫmúud *Mahmoud's daughter*, **ma fiʃ ḫáddĭ-hnáak** *there's nobody there*, **ma rúḫtiʃ** *I didn't go*, **ʕultílu(h)** *I said to him*, **ḫaʕʕŭhum** *their right*, **ʃuftăha** *I/you saw her*. **ŭ** occurs sporadically in other contexts, e.g. after **ʕumm** in, say, **yú-mmŭ kalsúum** (*O*) *Umm Kalsum!*

CONCLUSION

The pronunciation of isolated sounds and words, however useful, is only half the battle. The stringing together of words and phrases into the sentences required for speech purposes needs constant practice from the outset. Moreover, as to some extent we have seen, the sentence brings out features of pronunciation not apparent with the word in isolation but which must be observed if accuracy and fluency are to be achieved. The secret of success is constant practice. Learning by heart, with the aid of an Egyptian, not too great a number of the sentences which are given in this book will help considerably, for it is surprising how little material is necessary in order to exhaust the difficult sequences which occur in a language. Insist with the Arabic speaker on the need for patience and careful correction, then listen to and repeat each phrase and sentence over and over again, trying to remember every detail, including the rise and fall of the speaker's voice. Imitate him slavishly and do not feel embarrassed about it; the chances are that the more outlandish you sound to yourself, the nearer you are to the mark. Practice must include as much listening for the sake of listening as possible, for not only must the tongue be trained to utter Arabic but also the ear to catch what is going on in the language.

III. GRAMMAR

ROOTS AND RADICALS

Perhaps the most striking characteristic of all forms of Arabic is that the great majority of words are built on a framework of three consonants and that by ringing the changes with affixes, vowel-differences, etc., on a given base it is possible to obtain a great variety of related forms, e.g. on base **k-t-b**, the series **kátab** *he wrote*, **yíktib** *he writes, will write*, **káatib** *clerk*, **kátaba** *clerks*, **kitáab** *book*, **kútub** *books*, **maktúub** *written*, **máktab** *office, desk*, **maktába** *library*, etc. The base, **k-t-b** in the example, is called the *root* and each consonant of the root a *radical*. The terminology is equally applicable when bases are of more or less than three consonants.

Many such patterns as those illustrated in the preceding paragraph are grammatically specialized, cf. for example, the characteristic prefixes **ma-** and **mu-**, the presence of vowel **i** or **a** in the second syllable and, in some cases, of a suffix **-a**, in the so-called nouns of place and instrument, e.g. **máglis** (pl. **magáalis**) *council, council-room* (root **g-l-s**), **maʕáṣṣ** (pl. **maʕaṣṣáat**) *scissors, shears* (root **ʕ-ṣ-ṣ**), **muftáaḥ** (pl. **mafatiiḥ**) *key* (root **f-t-ḥ**), **maknása** (pl. **makáanis**) *broom* (root **k-n-s**).

NOUNS AND ADJECTIVES

GENDER AND NUMBER

Gender and number are important because they relate not only, indeed not so much to the form of individual nouns, adjectives, verbs, etc., as to their agreement when occurring together. At present nouns and adjectives only will be dealt with but differences of gender and number are equally important elsewhere, notably in respect of verbs, pronouns, and demonstratives.

Two genders have to be distinguished, masculine and feminine. As a rule final **-a** (or **-ɑ**) [1] marks a noun or adjective as feminine singular, whether or not there exists a corre-

[1] Variation between the open vowels **-a** and **-ɑ** is a purely phonetic matter.

sponding masculine form. Examples, masculine form first: **málik-málika** *king-queen*, **kibíir-kibíira** *big, old*, **ʕagnábi-ʕagnabíyya**[1] *foreign(er)*, **máktab-maktába** *desk, office-library, stationer's*, **kitáab** (m.) *book*, **ʃírka** (f.) *company*. The commonest exception to the rule that final **-a/-ɑ** is a feminine sign is provided by the plural forms of many nouns, for example **riggáala** *men*, **rúyasa** *supervisors*; there are, too, a few invariable adjectives ending in **-a/-ɑ**, of which **ɛítra** *clever* is an example. Conversely, some nouns which do not end in **-a/-ɑ** are none the less feminine; these include (i) words of female-sex reference, e.g. **sitt** *woman, lady*, **bint** *girl, daughter*, **fáras** *mare*, (ii) names of towns and countries, e.g. **maṣr** *Cairo*, **ʕissuwées** *Suez*, **libnáan** (*the*) *Lebanon*, (iii) some parts of the body, viz. **ʕiid** *hand*, **rigl** *leg*, **widn** *ear*, **ɛeen** *eye*, **raas** *head*, **daʕn** *chin*, **baṭn** *stomach*, (iv) some miscellaneous nouns, including **ʕarḍ** *earth, floor*, **naar** *fire*, **ʃams** *sun*, **márkib** *ship*, **bálad** *town*, **filúus** *money*.

With a few extremely rare exceptions provided by "classicisms" in educated colloquial usage, gender distinction relates to the singular only in Egyptian Arabic. There is thus, for example, only one (common) plural form **rufayyaɛíin** *thin* corresponding to **rufáyyaɛ** (masc. sing.) and **rufayyáɛa** (fem. sing.). Generally speaking, such a threefold differentiation of forms as **rufáyyaɛ-rufayyáɛa/rufayyaɛíin** is characteristic of adjectives rather than nouns, but certain forms in Arabic are used both nominally and adjectivally.

There are two types of plural formation relating to both nouns and adjectives. These are

(i) straightforward addition of certain suffixes to the singular;
(ii) *internal* difference in relation to the singular, e.g. **ṣaḥn/ṣuḥúun** *plate/s, saucer/s*, **kibíir/kubáar** *big (one/s)*.[2]

Plurals of the second type, traditionally known as "broken" plurals, are very numerous.

Plural by suffix

The plural suffixes are **-iin**, **-aat/-ɑɑt** and, to a lesser extent, **-iyya**. These are distributed as follows:

[1] If the masculine ends in **-i**, then a corresponding feminine form ends in **-iyya** or **-ya**.

[2] The fact of internal difference does not exclude the possibility of further difference *external* to the root, cf. **suʕáal/ʕasʕila** *question/s*.

(*a*) **-iin** is used for the plural of

(i) nouns and adjectives of the pattern illustrated by **sawwáaʕ-sawwáaʕa/sawwaʕíin** *driver/s*, **kaddáab-kaddáaba/kaddabíin** *liar/s*, **malyáan-malyáana/malyaníin** *full*;

(ii) active and passive participles (see below), as **ɛáarif-ɛárfa/ɛarfíin** *knowing*, **maftúuḥ-maftúuḥa/maftuḥíin** *open(ed)*;

(iii) adjectives of the pattern of **kuwáyyis-kuwayyísa/kuwayyisíin** *nice, good*, **ʕuṣáyyar-ʕuṣayyára/ʕuṣayyaríin** *short*;

(iv) most derivative nouns and adjectives of which the singular is characterized by a suffix **-i** or **-aani**, e.g. **ʕasbáani-ʕasbaníyya/ʕasbaniyyíin** *Spaniard/s, Spanish*, **díini-diníyya/diniyyíin** *religious*, **barráani-barraníyya/barraniyyíin** *outer, exterior*.

(*b*) **-aat/-aat** is suffixed to nouns having only one singular form which is characterized for the most part by final **-a/-a**. The use of **-aat/-aat** is distributed among

(i) a number of patterns in which the final radical is preceded in the singular by the long vowel **-aa/-aa**; **ḥáaga/ḥagáat** *thing/s*, **ḥisáab/ḥisabáat** *account/s, bill/s*, **ʃaháada, ʃahadáat** *certificate/s*, **ʃammáaɛa/ʃammaɛáat** *(clothes-)hanger/s*;

(ii) many loan-words, e.g. **duséeh/dusehéat** *file/s*, **ʕutubíis/ʕutubisáat** *bus/es*, **baskalítta/baskalittáat** *bicycle/s*;

(iii) nouns of the pattern CVCVCV, where V = **a/a**, e.g. **báraka/barakáat** *blessing/s*, **ḥáʃara/ḥaʃaráat** *insect/s*;

(iv) nouns which in the singular end in **-iyya**, e.g. **ḥanafíyya/ḥanafiyyáat** *tap/s*, **masʕulíyya/masʕuliyyáat** *responsibility/-ies*;

(v) certain **m**-prefixed patterns, with gemination of the second radical and final **-a/-a**, e.g. **mixádda/mixaddáat** *pillow/s*, **magálla/magalláat** *magazine/s*;

(vi) the "counted" or "little plural" form of collective nouns (see below), e.g. **búṣal** *onions* (coll.)/**baṣaláaya** *an onion*/**baṣaláat** *3–10* or *a few onions*;

(vii) verbal noun plurals (see below), e.g. **ʕistiɛráaḍ/ʕistiɛraḍáat** *parade/s.*

(*c*) **-iyya** is used for the plural of

(i) those nouns of trade or occupation which are characterized in the singular by a suffix **-gi** or, less often, **-i**, e.g. **makwági/makwagíyya** *laundryman/-men*, **ɛarbági/ɛarbagíyya** *gharry-driver/s*, **makaníiki/makanikíyya** *mechanic/s*;

(ii) certain military and police ranks, e.g. **ʃawíiʃ/ʃawiʃíyya** *sergeant/s*, **ʕumbáaʃa/ʕumbaʃíyya** *corporal/s.*[1]

"Broken" plural

Although there is considerable regularity of correspondence between singular and plural patterns, it is nevertheless not always possible to forecast from singular to plural or vice versa. Both singular and plural forms of nouns and adjectives should, therefore, be learned as they are met. The following are common plural patterns (C = consonant):

(i) ʕaCCáaC and ʕiCCáaC: **ʕálam/ʕiʕláam** *pen/s, pencil/s*, **ʃakl/ʕaʃkáal** *shape/s*, **loon/ʕalwáan** *colour/s*;

(ii) CuCúuC and CiCúuC: **ṣaḥn/ṣuḥúun** *plate/s, saucer/s*, **beet/biyúut** or **buyúut** *house/s*;

(iii) CíCaC and CúCaC: **ɛílba/ɛílab** (*small*) *box/es*, **ʃánṭa/ʃúnaṭ** *bag/s, briefcase/s*;

(iv) CuCáaC: **kibíir/kubáar** *big, old*, **ṭawíil/ṭuwáal** *long, tall*;

Note

This is the pattern of certain common adjectives, with the feminine singular formed in the usual way with **-a.**[2]

(v) CuCCáaC: **ɛáamil/ɛummáal** *workman/-men*, **ʃáaṭir/ʃuṭṭáar** *clever, intelligent*;

Note

Nouns and adjectives of pattern (v) are always of personal reference. The singular form is as that of the active participle of the simple verb-form (see below).

(vi) CúCaCa: **ʃaríik/ʃúraka** *partner/s*, **xaṭíib/xúṭaba** *orator/s*;

[1] The names of most such ranks have recently been modified ("arabicized") by decree.

[2] Phonetic variation between **-a** and **-ɑ** is henceforth taken as read and **-a** is used to symbolize an open vowel generally.

Note

This pattern, in contrast with (v), is of nouns only and is again exclusively of personal reference. The pattern CuCaCáaʕ, e.g. **xuṭabáaʕ**, is sometimes used by educated speakers.

(vii) CaCáaCi: **kúrsi/karáasi** *chair/s*, **ʃákwa/ʃakáawi** *complaint/s*, **ṣiníyya/ṣawáani** *tray/s*;

(viii) ʕaCCíCa and ʕiCCíCa: **suʕáal/ʕasʕíla** *question/s*, **gawáab/ʕagwíba** *answer/s*, **sábat/ʕisbíta** *basket/s*;

(ix) CaCáaCiC: **máktab/makáatib** *office/s, desk/s*, **gárdal/garáadil** *bucket/s*, **márkib/maráakib** *ship/s*, **sitáara/satáayir** *curtain/s*, **ginéena/ganáayin** *garden/s*;

(x) CaCaCíiC: **fingáal/fanagíil** (or **fingáan/fanagíin**) *cup/s*, **ṭarbúuʃ/ṭarabíiʃ** *tarboosh/es*, **mandíil/manadíil** *handkerchief/s*, **fanúus/fawaníis** *lamp/s*, **niʃáan/nayaʃíin** *medal/s, decoration/s*.

Note

Singular patterns containing four consonants regularly correspond to one of the plural patterns (ix) or (x), depending on the length of the vowel between the third and fourth consonants of the singular, viz. short vowel—(ix), long vowel—(x). Singulars containing three consonants with a long vowel between the second and third, and with the ending -a, correspond to plurals of pattern (ix). Etymologically, the singular type illustrated by **fanúus** and **niʃáan** under (x) relates to forms containing a long vowel in the first syllable, i.e. **faa-** and **nii-**.

Addenda

(i) The following are examples of frequently occurring nouns for which the type of singular-plural relationship is comparatively rare: **gámal/gimáal** *camel/s*, **gábal/gibáal** *mountain/s*, **wálad/wiláad**, or **ʕawláad** *boy/s, son/s, young man/men*, **kitáab/kútub** *book/s*, **madíina/múdun** *city/-ies*, **saʕf/ʕúsʕuf** *ceiling/s*, **ṣaṭḥ/ʕúṣṭuḥ** or **ṣuṭúuḥ** *roof/s*, **raas/ruus** *head/s*, **sána/siníin** or **sanawáat** *year/s*, **ráagil/riggáala** *man/men*, **duktúur/dakátra** *doctor/s*.

(ii) In some cases a given singular form may correspond to more than one plural, e.g. **gawáab** *answer*; *letter*/**ʕagwíba** *answers*; **gawabáat** *letters*, **másal** *proverb, saying; example/* **ʕamsáal** *proverbs*; **ʕamsíla** *examples*, **líɛba** *game; toy/* **ʕalɛáab** *games*; **líɛab** *toys*.

(iii) A few nouns form their plural by the straightforward addition of a suffix **-aan**, e.g. **ḥeeṭ/ḥeṭɑ́ɑn** *wall/s*, **ɣeeṭ/ɣeṭɑ́ɑn** *field/s*. This suffix also appears in association with internal difference of the " broken " type, e.g. **fɑɑr/firáan** *mouse/mice*, **gɑɑr/giráan** *neighbour/s*, **toor/tiráan** *bull/s*, **ɣazáal/ɣizláan** *gazelle/s*, **ʕamiiṣ/ʕumṣɑ́ɑn** *shirt/s*.

(iv) Nouns of relationship are often of special shape. The most important are **ʕabb/ʕabbaháat** *father/s*, **ʕumm/ʕummaháat** *mother/s*, **ʕaxx/ʕixwáat** *brother/s*, **ʕuxt/ʕixwáat** *sister/s*, **ʕibn/ʕabnáaʕ** *son/s*, **bint/banáat** *daughter/s*, **ɛamm/ʕaɛmáam** (*paternal*) *uncle/s*, **ɛámma/ɛammáat** (*paternal*) *aunt/s*, **xaal/xiláan** (*maternal*) *uncle/s*, **xáala/xaláat** (*maternal*) *aunt/s*, **gidd/gudúud** *grandfather/s*, **gidda/giddáat** *grandmother/s*. Note **ʕíbnĭ ɛámm/xáal** (*male*) *cousin* and **bíntĭ ɛámm/xáal** (*female*) *cousin*.

Dual

The distinction already made between singular and plural will be familiar enough to those with a " western " linguistic background. It is also necessary, however, under the general heading of *number* to distinguish other categories, the most important of which is *dual*. Unlike singular and plural, dual relates to nouns only. Dual nouns are characterized by the suffix **-een**, e.g. **betéen** *two houses*, **kitabéen** *two books*. When compounded with any suffix, feminine nouns which elsewhere end in **-a** contain **-t-** in place of **-a**, e.g. **ṭɑrɑbeeẓɑ** *table* + **een** = **ṭɑrɑbeẓtéen** *two tables*. **-t-** is preceded by the vowel **i** (similar in function to **ĭ**) when otherwise a sequence of three or more consonants would result, e.g. **ʃírka** *company* + **een** = **ʃirkitéen** *two companies* (cf. elsewhere below, say, **ɛɑrɑbíyya** *car* + **na** = **ɛɑrɑbiyyítna** *our car*, **tigɑ́ɑrɑ** + **na** = **tigɑrítna** *our business*).

Nouns of personal reference, with the exception of nouns of relationship, do not occur with the suffix **-een** but are associated with the numeral **ʕitnéen** *two*. Thus, **ʕitnéen sawwaʕíin/ɛasáakir/muɛallimíin/ɛɑrbagíyya/ɛummáal/ʃúrɑkɑ** *two drivers/soldiers/teachers/gharry-drivers/workmen/partners*, but **ʕaxxéen/ʕuxtéen/waladéen/bintéen/rɑgléen/mɑrɑtéen** *two brothers/*

sisters/boys (or *sons*)/*girls* (or *daughters*)/*men* (or *husbands*)/ *women* (or *wives*).

The dual form of nouns relating to certain parts of the body occurring in pairs will correspond to an English plural in translation, e.g. **rigléen** *legs,* **ʕidéen** *hands,* **ʒenéen** *eyes.*

Collectives

With regard to certain nouns, termed *collectives,* it is sometimes necessary to distinguish between *five* categories of number. The form **ʃágara**[1] *tree,* for example, is regularly related to **ʃágar** (*a lot of*) *trees, trees* (*in general*) by the addition of the (feminine) suffix **-a**; equally relatable to **ʃágar,** by the addition of **-aat,** is **ʃagaráat** (*a few*) *trees,* a form which occurs most commonly in association with a numeral form from "3" to "10". Threefold differentiation of the type **ʃágar/ʃágara/ʃagaráat** is characteristic of all collectives, but in the case of **ʃágar,** there is not only the regular dual form **ʃágara + een = ʃagartéen** *two trees,* but also the broken plural form **ʕaʃgáar** (*different kinds of*) *trees* to be considered. The designation *singulative* is more appropriate than *singular* to the form **ʃágara,** and **ʃagaráat** may be termed the *counted* or *little plural* form. Thus, *in toto* we have **ʃágar** (collective), **ʃágara** (singulative), **ʃagartéen** (dual), **ʃagaráat** (counted or little plural), **ʕaʃgáar** (plural or big plural). The majority of collectives, however, lack a (big) plural form. The little plural is characterized by the suffix **-aat** (rarely **-ayaat**) but the singulative suffix is frequently **-aaya,** not **-a**; cf., for example:

Collective	*Singulative*	*Little plural*
xoox *peaches*	**xóoxa**	**xoxáat**
lamúun *lemons*	**lamúuna**	**lamunáat**
burtuʕáan *oranges*	**burtuʕáana**	**burtuʕanáat**
básal *onions*	**básala** *or* **baṣaláaya**	**baṣaláat**
gáẓar *carrots*	**gáẓara** *or* **gaẓaráaya**	**gaẓaráat**
baṭáaṭiṣ *potatoes*	**baṭaṭṣáaya**	**baṭaṭṣáat**
ʕúuṭa *tomatoes*	**ʕuṭáaya**	**ʕuṭáat** *or* **ʕuṭayáat**

The singulative and little plural forms of certain collectives are characterized not by the suffixation of **-a**(**aya**) and **-aat** but

[1] Or **ʃágara.**

by the association of the collective form with one of the specific words **ḥabbáaya/ḥabbáat, ḥítta/ḥítat, lúʔma/lúʔam, raas/ruus, ṣubáaʕ/ṣawáabiʕ**, i.e.:

faṣúlya *beans*	**ḥabbáayit faṣúlya**	**ḥabbáat faṣúlya**
bisílla *peas*	**ḥabbáayit bisílla**	**ḥabbáat bisílla**
súkkar *sugar*	**ḥíttit súkkar**	**ḥítat súkkar**
láḥma *meat*	**ḥíttit láḥma** [1]	**ḥítat láḥma**
ʕeeʃ *bread*	**lúʔmit ʕéeʃ**	**lúʔam ʕéeʃ**
toom *garlic*	**ráas toom** [2]	**rúus tóom**
sugúʔʔ *sausages*	**ṣubáaʕ sugúʔʔ**	**ṣawáabiʕ sugúʔʔ**

The dual is formed on the appropriate special word, e.g. **ḥittitéen súkkar** *two lumps of sugar.*

GENDER AND NUMBER CONCORD

Singular patterns

The following examples illustrate the typical noun-adjective sequence, in which the adjective follows the noun:

Masculine	*Feminine*
béet kibíir *a big house*	**ginéena-kbíira** *a big garden*
ʔamíiṣ wísix *a dirty shirt*	**maʔláʔa wísxa** *a dirty spoon*
ráagil ṭawíil rufáyyaʕ *a tall, thin man*	**sítti ṭawíila-rfayyáʕa** *a tall, thin woman*

These examples illustrate the most frequent pattern of concord, in which it will be seen that gender difference relates to the presence or absence of final **-a**, especially in adjectival forms.

The sequence of noun preceding adjective will be familiar to those with experience of, say, the Romance languages; less familiar will be the fact that in order to get concords right in Egyptian Arabic, it is necessary to know the sub-class of both the noun and adjective involved. Thus, in contrast with the adjectives in the examples above, adjectives of origin and nationality, which end in **-i** (masc.) and **-iyya** (fem.), show gender distinction only when the preceding noun is a noun of personal reference. **siggáada ʕaríiḍa** *a wide carpet* is like **maʔláʔa wísxa** in the feminine example above but only **siggáada**

[1] *A slice* or *piece of meat.*
[2] *A clove of garlic.*

ɛágami *a Persian carpet* is possible, not ***siggaada ɛagamiyya**; conversely, in association with a noun of personal reference, the adjectival form in **-iyya** must be used where appropriate, e.g. **sítti ɛagamíyya** *a Persian lady.*

Certain adjectives of colour, similarly formed by the addition of a suffix **-i,** for the most part to a noun of material reference, are wholly invariable, e.g. **búnni** *brown, coffee-coloured,* **ruṣáaṣi** *grey* (lit. *leaden, lead-coloured*), **rumáadi** *grey* (lit. *ashen, ash-coloured*), **banafsígi** *purple,* **burtuʕáani** *orange(-coloured),* **fáḍḍi** *silver(-coloured), silvery,* **dáhabi** *gold(en),* **lábani** *pink* (lit. *milky*).

Other forms, appearing elsewhere as nouns, are used as invariable adjectives of material, e.g. **sáaɛa dáhab** *a gold watch,* **ɛúmla fáḍḍa** *silver coins,* **ṭarabéeẓa xáʃab** *a wooden table,* **ʃánṭa gild** *a leather bag,* **béeʃa dantílla** *a lace veil,* **ʃarabáat ṣúuf** *wool(len) socks.* Other noteworthy invariable forms are **sáada** *plain* and **ɛítra** *clever* as in, for example, **ráagil ɛítra** *a clever man.*

Knowledge of the nominal and adjectival classes concerned is also necessary when more than one adjective follows the noun, in order to place the adjectives in the correct order. When the noun is of personal reference, the position of the adjectives is immaterial; we may say, for example, either **ráagil ṭawíil ingilíizi** or **ráagil ingilíizi ṭawíil** *a tall Englishman,* but in association with other classes of noun, an adjective of origin must immediately follow the noun, e.g. **ʕissiggáada lingilíizi-lɛaríiḍa** *the wide English carpet,* unless there is also present an adjective of material, in which case the latter immediately follows the noun and immediately precedes an adjective of origin, e.g. **siggáada ṣúuf ingilíizi** *an English wool carpet,* **ʃáal ḥaríir híndi-kbíir** *a large Indian silk scarf.* Examples containing adjectives of material but not adjectives of origin are **karaváṭṭa**[1] **ḥaríir zárʕa** *a blue silk tie,* **fustáan ṣúuf xafíif** *a light woollen dress.* In the earlier examples above, viz. **ráagil ṭawíil rufáyyaɛ** and **sítti ṭawíila-rfayyáɛa,** the adjectives are neither of origin nor of material and therefore their sequential order is immaterial. It may be noted in passing that somewhat similar positional variation in association with other differences is observable in English, as between, say, *hard black eyes, black silk stockings, jet-black hair, a black, glowering look.* The particle **wi** *and* in Arabic often corresponds to the comma of the last

[1] **Or karafítta.**

English example, cf. **ʔóoḍa háwya-w wásɛa** *a large, airy room* (lit. *airy and spacious*).

There is in Arabic a special regular paradigm of nouns and adjectives of colour (excluding the invariable forms in **-i** noted above) and physical defect. Examples are **ʔáḥmar** (m.s.)-**ḥámra** (f.s.)/**ḥumr** (pl.) *red*, **ʔáxḍar-xáḍra/xuḍr** *green*, **ʔáṭraʃ-ṭárʃa/ṭurʃ** *deaf*, **ʔáxraṣ-xárṣa/xurṣ** *dumb*, etc. **ʔíswid-sóoda/suud** *black*, **ʔábyaḍ-béeḍa/biiḍ** *white*, **ʔáɛwar-ɛóora/ɛuur** *one-eyed*, **ʔáɛma-ɛámya/ɛumy** *blind* are somewhat irregular and it may help in learning them to realize that **ee** and **oo** usually correspond to Classical Arabic **ay** and **aw** respectively and **ii** and **uu** to the pronunciation of *iy* and *uw*. In certain contexts and notably in combination with **fáatiḥ/fátḥa/fatḥiin** *light* and **ɣáamiʔ/ɣámʔa/ɣamʔiin** *dark*, adjectives of colour of this special pattern are used in the masculine singular form even when the noun they accompany is feminine, e.g. **karafítta ʔáḥmar fáatiḥ** *a light red tie*, **bádla ʔázraʔ ɣáamiʔ** *a dark blue suit*. **fáatiḥ** and **ɣáamiʔ** can only appear in the masculine singular form in this context but, in association with the invariable colour adjectives in **-i** and provided that the noun is feminine, they may optionally be used in the feminine forms **fátḥa** and **ɣámʔa**, e.g. **karafítta-rṣáaṣi fátḥa** (or **fáatiḥ**) *a light grey tie*, **bádla búnni ɣámʔa** (or **ɣáamiʔ**) *a dark brown suit*.

Plural patterns

Singular concord involved principally the distribution of corresponding adjectival forms with and without final **-a**, in association with a preceding noun of singular form; plural concord concerns the association of the plural form of nouns variously with the plural form of the adjective or with its form in **-a**. The latter form is identical with that of the feminine *singular*, so that if one gives to this form the designation *feminine* and if in the traditional way one considers gender to relate exclusively to the noun rather than to the total context, then it may be said of a noun like **ʔamíiṣ/ʔumṣáan** *shirt/s* that it is masculine in the singular (cf. **ʔamíiṣ wísix** *a dirty shirt*) but feminine in the plural (cf. **ʔumṣáan wísxa** *dirty shirts*).[1] The

[1] The words " feminine in the plural " conflict with the later statement (top p. 47) that there is no gender distinction in the plural. One might, therefore, amend the form of words to read, say, ". . . but in its plural form is associated with the feminine singular adjective."

plural form **wisxiin** is only used with the plural form of nouns of personal reference, so that once again it is necessary to know the class of noun with which one is concerned in order to get concords right. It is equally necessary again to know the category of adjective involved. Not only do adjectives of origin and invariable adjectives generally behave as in singular patterns, cf. **sagáayir ingiliizi** *English cigarettes*, **náas báladi** *low-class people*,[1] **ʃarabáat sáada** *plain socks*, but those adjectives of which the plural form is of "broken" pattern, e.g. **kibiir-kibiira/kubáar**, are variously in *either* the plural *or* the form in **-a** when the noun they accompany is not one of personal reference; cf. **biyúut kubáar** *or* **kibiira** *big houses*, **ganáayin kubáar** *or* **kibiira** *big gardens*. Where alternative possibilities exist, the form in **-a** is on the whole the more usual.

The following rules may be helpful:

(i) The adjective accompanying plural nouns, other than nouns of personal reference, almost always has the form of the feminine singular adjective. Those adjectives having a broken plural may be in either the plural or, more commonly, the feminine singular form;

(ii) the plural form of adjectives, whether broken or in **-iin**, is used with nouns of personal reference; some adjectives which never accompany such nouns, rarely occur in plural forms, e.g. **matiin** (m.s.)-**matiina** (f.s.)/**mutáan** (pl.) *strong, durable*.

Adjectives of nationality following nouns of personal reference do not always behave in the manner of other **i**-ending adjectives, cf. **náas ingiliiz** *English people*, **banáat ʕalmáan** *German girls*, but, as expected, **náas maʂriyyiin** *Egyptian people*, **banáat ʕasbaniyyiin** *Spanish girls*.

Differences of plural concord, therefore, do not parallel those of the singular. The difference between **ʈawiila** and **ʈuwáal** is relevant to plural concord but not to the difference between, say, **riggáala** *men* and **sittáat** *women* as the difference between **ʈawiil** and **ʈawiila** was relevant to the difference between **ráagil** *man* and **sitt** *woman*; cf. **riggáala-ʈwáal rufayyaɛiin** *tall, thin men* and **sittáat ʈuwáal rufayyaɛiin** *tall, thin women*, and

[1] **magáalis baladiyya** *local councils* is exceptional and may perhaps be regarded as a loan from the written language. Similarly, **ʕingiliziyya** is used with **baɖáayiɛ** *goods* but **ʕingiliizi** is also possible.

contrast the earlier singular examples. It may therefore be convenient for practical purposes to say that there is no gender distinction in the plural, but, as has been shown, concordial differences of a similar kind relate as much to plural as to singular associations of noun and adjective.

Other patterns

Dual.—The plural form of the adjective is essential with the dual form of the noun, e.g. **betéen kubɑ́ɑr** *two big houses*, **ʕamiṣéen wisxíin** *two dirty shirts*. Even rare plurals are necessary in this context, e.g. **ʕamiṣéen mutáan** *two strong shirts*.

Collectives.—The adjective accompanying the collective form of a collective noun is in the (masculine) singular, e.g. **wáraʕ kuwáyyis** *good paper*, **xóox ṣɑ́ɑbiħ** *fresh peaches*.[1] Plural adjectives usually accompany the "little plural" form of collectives, e.g. **tálat xoxáat ṣabħíin** 3 *fresh peaches*, **tálat ʃagɑrɑ́ɑt ṣuɣayyɑriin** 3 *little trees*, but the feminine singular form of those adjectives which are "broken" in the plural may optionally be used, e.g. **tálat xoxáat kibíira** (or **kubɑ́ɑr**). Contrast the compulsory use of the singular form of the adjective **ɛáali-ɛálya/ɛalyíin** in, say, **ʃahadáat ɛálya** *high qualifications*, where the ending **-aat** is not that of the "little plural"

Co-ordinate nouns.—The plural adjectival form is necessary in association with co-ordinate sequences of singular nouns, e.g. **sikkíina-w ʃóoka wisxíin** *a dirty knife and fork*, **fúrʃa-w miʃṭĭgdáad** *a new brush and comb*.

DEFINITION

Concord operates between noun and adjective in Arabic in respect not only of gender and number but also of what may be called "definition" or "definiteness". **béet kibíir** *a big house* is *indefinite*, **ʕilbéet ikkibíir** *the big house* (lit. *the house the big*) is definite. In the definite pattern the article **ʕil**[2] is prefixed to the adjective as well as to the noun.

[1] An exception is **bɑṭɑ́ɑṭiṣ maʕlíyya** *chip potatoes, crisps*.

[2] The *l* of the article is pronounced as the following consonant before **t, d, s, z, ṭ, ḍ, ṣ, ẓ, n, r, ʃ, k,** and **g,** and as **l** before all other consonants: e.g. **ʕi*l*rɑ́ɑgil** = **ʕirrɑ́ɑgil** *the man*, **ʕi*l*ṣúfrɑ** = **ʕiṣṣúfrɑ** *the dining-table*, but **ʕilmáktab** *the office, the desk*, **ʕilfilúus** *the money*, etc.

Nouns may be defined in a number of ways:

(i) By the prefixation of the article, e.g. **ʕigginéena** *the garden*;

(ii) by the addition of a pronominal suffix, e.g. **banáat** *daughters* + **u(h)** *his* = **banáatu(h)** *his daughters*;

(iii) by belonging to the category of proper noun, which is only associated with definite concord, e.g. **maṣr** *Cairo, Egypt*;

(iv) by close association with a following noun which is itself defined, e.g. **ḅáab ilbéet** *the door of the house*. Feminine nouns when so defined have the ending **-(i)t** in place of **-a** (see under *Dual* above), e.g. **ginént** (or **ginéenit**) **ilbéet** *the garden of the house*;

(v) by association with the vocative particle **ya**, e.g. **ya wálad !** *boy !*, **ya ʒúmar !** *Omar !*

Nouns defined in the manner of (i)–(iv) must be accompanied in the noun-adjective phrase by adjectives which are also defined by the prefixation of the article, e.g. **ʕigginéena-lwarraníyya** *the back garden*, **banáatu-lḥilwíin** *his pretty daughters*, **máṣr ilʕadíima** *Old Cairo*, **ginént ilbéet ilwarraníyya** *the back garden of the house*. Nouns defined in the manner of (v) are accompanied by adjectives with which **ya** is also associated, e.g. **ya wálad ya ṭawíil !** *I say, the tall young man !*, **ya ʒúmar ya-ṣɣáyyar !** *young Omar !*

It will be seen that a noun may not bear more than one defining characteristic; for example, the article is precluded from association with **banáatu(h)** by the presence of the pronominal suffix, from similar association with **ginént** by the fact of the following defined noun, and may not precede **ṣuɣáyyar** when **ṣuɣáyyar** is preceded by **ya** in **ya ʒúmar ya-ṣɣáyyar !** (cf. **ʒúmar iṣṣuɣáyyar** *young Omar*).[1] It is in this light that the inclusion of the particle **li** (elsewhere = *to, for*, etc.) is to be seen in, say, **ḍárbu l-ilwálad** *his hitting (of) the boy*; the verbal noun **ḍarb** may not be defined twice as in a hypothetical ***ḍarbu-lwalad**.

Other important facts concerning "definition" are given subsequently, notably with reference to the phrase-marker **ʕílli** (see below, pp. 101–5).

[1] **ya** does not, however, exclude other "definers", cf. **ya-mḥámmad y-axúuya !** *(O) my brother Mohamed !*

THE CONSTRUCT AND THE NOMINAL SENTENCE

The sequence of nouns illustrated in the preceding section by **báab ilbéet** and **ginént ilbéet** is traditionally referred to in Arabic grammar as *the construct.* The indefinite **báab béet** *a house door* and **ginéenit béet** *a house garden,* in which the article is not prefixed to the second noun and the first noun is therefore not defined, are also examples of the construct. Sequences of constructs, in which the final noun only may be associated with the article, are also possible, e.g. **báab béet ilmudiir** *the door of the manager's house,* **mawaɛiid fátḥi máktab taftiiʃ ilpaṣporṭáat** *the office hours of the passport department* (lit. *the hours of opening the office of inspecting the passports*). *'s, of,* or a compound is generally necessary in translation. Notice that, although most constructs exhibit a singular/plural difference only in their first component, e.g. **ʕáarib innagáah/ʕawáarib innagáah** *lifeboat/s,* there are nevertheless some in which two components vary, e.g. **ɣáṭa-lɛidda/ɣuṭyáan ilɛidad** *bonnet/s* (*car*), **náaẓir ilmaḥáṭṭa/nuẓẓáar ilmaḥaṭṭáat** *stationmaster/s.*

It may be noted that earlier examples such as **ʃánṭa gild** *a leather bag* are partly defined as noun-adjective phrases because of final **-a,** not **-(i)t,** in the noun (cf. the construct **ginéenit béet**). Moreover, as expected, and again in contrast with the construct, both components of the noun-adjective phrase are prefixed with the article when the context is definite, e.g. **ʕiʃʃánṭa-ggild** *the leather bag*; cf., too, **ʕálam ḥibr** *fountain-pen* and **ʕálamak ilḥibr** *your fountain-pen.*

Adjectives are not interposed between constituent nouns of the construct but are placed at the end of the total phrase, e.g. **sáaḥil xaliig issuwées ilɣárbi** *the west shore of the Gulf of Suez,* in which **ilɣárbi** is associated with **sáaḥil**; **mádnit gáamiɛ ɛálya** *the tall minaret of a mosque* is another example, cf. **mádnit gáamiɛ ɛáali** *the minaret of a tall mosque.* Other examples are **rubáaṭ** (masc. sing.) **gázma ʕáswar** *black shoe-laces* and **rubáaṭ gázma sámra** *black-shoe laces, i.e. laces of* or *for black shoes.*

An alternative form to, say, the **sáaḥil xaliig issuwées ilɣárbi** of the last paragraph involves the use of a particle (**min** or **li**) between the nominal elements **sáaḥil** and **xaliig issuwées** so that the construct relation no longer obtains between them; any adjective associated with **sáaḥil** will then follow it immediately and, moreover, the total noun-adjective phrase will be defined by the prefixation of the article, i.e. **ʕissáaħil ilɣárbi min xalíig issuwées.** In the example **ʕissáaħil ittáani m-ilbáħr** (or **l-ilbáħr**) **ilʕáħmar** *the other shore of the Red Sea* the particle separates two noun-adjective phrases. These particle constructions, however, have a distinctly literary flavour about them.

Considering two-component examples of the noun-adjective phrase as well as the construct in terms of the association of components with the definite article, we have so far seen the following possibilities:

(i) Both components without the article, e.g. **béet kibíir** *a big house*;

(ii) both components with the article, e.g. **ʕilbéet ikkibíir** *the big house*;

(iii) the first component without, the second with the article, e.g. **báab ilbéet** *the door of the house.*

The fourth possibility, i.e. the first component with and the second without the article, e.g. **ʕilbéet kibíir** *the house is* (*a*) *big* (*one*), is the pattern of the so-called nominal sentence. In translation, the appropriate form of the present tense of the verb *to be* is usually necessary. Constructs and noun-adjective phrases may, of course, constitute the first component of the nominal sentence, cf. **ʃibbáak ittazáakir maftúuħ** *the booking-office* (*ticket-window*) *is open,* **ɛubúur ilkanáal lingilíizi ɡáɛbi ɡíddan** (**ɡíddan** is adverbial) *the English Channel crossing is very unpleasant.*

bitáaɛ

ʕilbáab bitaɛ ilbéet is a very common alternative to **báab ilbéet** *the door of the house.* When **bitáaɛ** is used, then the article must be prefixed to the first noun. In the great majority of contexts, the construct and the construction with **bitáaɛ** may be used indifferently, but there are circumstances in which one is regularly employed rather than the other; thus, for example, if in response to a knock at the door an occupant of the house is mistakenly on his way to the front door, a second occupant may direct him to the back door whence the knock came by exclaiming **báab ilbéet ilwarráani!** (*it's at*) *the back door!*; the construction with **bitáaɛ**, i.e. **ʕilbáab ilwarráani-btaɛ ilbéet,** would be quite inappropriate to this context but may be used freely elsewhere. Notice that a further effect of the inclusion of **bitáaꜥ** is that an adjective relating to the first noun follows that noun and is thus interpolated between the two nouns of the construction; **ʕilbáab ilwarráani-btaꜥ ilbéet** is thus parallel to the earlier **ʕissáaḥil ilɣárbi min xaliig issuwées** and both of them different from **sáaḥil xaliig issuwées ilɣárbi.**

bitáaꜥ itself is always in construct with the following noun and thus "looks both ways" in the total construction, since at the same time it must agree with the preceding noun in terms of gender and number. **bitáaꜥ** is the masculine form of the total series **bitáaꜥ-bitáaꜥit/bitúuꜥ**; cf. **ʕigginéena-btaꜥt ilbéet** *the garden of the house*, which varies more or less freely with **ginént ilbéet,** and **ʕilbiyúut bituꜥ** (or **bitaꜥt**) **iʃʃirka** *the company's houses,* to which the construct **biyúut iʃʃirka** provides an alternative.

By virtue of this threefold differentiation of form, **bitáaꜥ** and its following noun are adjectival in function, parallel to, say, **ʕaliil ilʕádab-ʕalilt ilʕádab/ʕuláal ilʕádab** *ill-mannered, rude*; such adjectival constructs are, however, rare.

Since a noun cannot be defined twice, e.g. by construct relationship with a following defined noun and by a pronominal suffix, **bitáaꜥ** is essential in, say, **ꜥilbit ikkabriit bitáꜥti (bitaaꜥa** + pronominal suffix **-i)** *my box of matches.*

PARTICLES

In the nominal sentence **dá-btaꜥ issitt** *that belongs to the lady,* **bitáaꜥ** behaves in the manner of such prepositional particles as **fi** *in,* **li** *to, for,* **bi** *by, with,* **min** *from, of,* **ꜥand** *at, with,* **zayy** *like,* **ꜥála** *on, against,* **wáyya** *with, in company of,* etc., in, say, **ʕilʕamíiṣ f-iddúrg** *the shirt is in the drawer,* **húwwa min máṣr** *he's from Cairo.* Such particles have no independent status and occur only before a noun or a pronominal suffix (see below). The prepositional phrase illustrated in the examples functions very commonly as the final component of the nominal sentence.

Certain particles, as **fooʕ** *on, above,* **taḥt** *below, under,* **gúwwa** *inside,* **bárra** *outside,* **ʕuddáam** *facing, opposite, in front (of),* behave similarly to those of the preceding paragraph in, say, **ʕilhudúum fóoʕ idduláab** *the clothes are on top of the cupboard* or **ʕissandúuʕ táḥt issiriir** *the box is under the bed,* but may also occur independently. In reply to **ꜥúmar féen?** *where is Omar?*

we may say **fooʕ** *above, upstairs,* **taḫt** *below, downstairs,* **gúwwa** *inside,* **bárra** *outside,* **ʕuddáam** *in front.* These forms are also distinguished by the fact that adjectives may be formed from them by the addition of a suffix **-aani,** e.g. **taḫtáani** *lower,* **guwwáani** *inner,* **barráani** *outer.*

The forms of the last paragraph may be termed *adverbial particles.* They differ from *adverbs* in that certain of the latter, e.g. **gíddan** *very,* **xáaliṣ** *thoroughly, completely,* are regularly associated with adjectives, while others, as the " time-words " **dilwáʕti** *now,* **baɛdéen** *afterwards, later,* **ʕimbáariḫ** *yesterday,* **ʕinnahárda** *to-day,* **búkra** *to-morrow,* etc., like **gíddan** and **xáaliṣ,** never appear with a following noun or pronominal suffix.[1]

Note the " reciprocal " **baɛḍ,** which frequently follows a particle as in **fóoʕ báɛḍ** *on top of each other,* **záyyi báɛḍ** *like each other, the same,* **gámbi báɛḍ** *next to one another,* **wáyya báɛḍ** *in each other's company.*

A particle complex may sometimes occur, as, for example, **min ɛala** in **háat idduséeh min ɛa-lmáktab** *fetch the file from the desk!*

The particle **bi** occurs frequently in adverbial and adjectival phrases, e.g. **bi súrɛa** *fast, quickly* (lit. *with speed*), **b-iẓẓábṭ** *exactly, perfectly,* **ʕissáfar b-issíkka-lḫadíid** *rail travel* (lit. *the travel by the iron way*), **ṭayyáara-b muḫarrikéen** *a two-engined aircraft.*

PRONOUNS

Two classes of pronominal forms have to be distinguished: (i) independent pronouns, (ii) pronominal suffixes. The independent pronouns are as follows:

	Sing.	*Pl.*
1st person	**ʕána** *I*	**ʕíḫna** *we*
2nd person masc.	**ʕínta** *you*	**ʕíntu** *you*
2nd person fem.	**ʕínti** *you*	
3rd person masc.	**húwwa** *he, it*	**húmma** *they*
3rd person fem.	**híyya** *she, it*	

As with the adjective, gender distinctions (2nd and 3rd persons) relate to the singular only. This is true in general of Egyptian Arabic and will be found again elsewhere, notably in the verb and the demonstratives.

[1] Unlike **gíddan, xáaliṣ,** etc., the " time-words " are frequently associated with a preceding particle.

Pronominal suffixes, for their part, are added to nouns, verbs, and particles. Added to a verb, the 1st person singular suffix is **-ni,** not **-i** or **-ya** as with nouns and particles, but otherwise the suffixes are the same irrespective of the grammatical category with which they are associated. Singular suffixes except **-ni** and **-ha** differ in form according to whether the noun, verb, or particle ends in a consonant or a vowel. The suffixes are as follows:

	Singular *Post-consonantal*	*Post-vocalic*		*Plural*
1st person .	**-i** (**-ni** after verb)	**-ya**	*my, me*	**-na** *our, us*
2nd pers. m. .	**-ak**	**-k**	*your, you*	**-ku** or **-kum** *your, you*
2nd pers. f. .	**-ik**	**-ki**	*your, you*	
3rd pers. m. .	**-u(h)** [1]	**-h**	*his, its/him, it*	**-hum** *their, them*
3rd pers. f. .	**-ha**	**-ha**	*her, its/her, it*	

Final vowels are lengthened in accordance with the general rule when suffixes are added, e.g. **wáyya** *with,* **wayyáaki** *with you* (fem.), **wayyáah** *with him.* In the speech of many, final **-h** is not pronounced but the vowel is still long and prominent in **wayyáa** *with him.*

The "extra" vowel required to obviate a sequence of three consonants, which elsewhere is invariably **ĭ,** is more frequently **ă** or **ŭ** with the pronominal suffixes. With the exception of **-na,** which requires **ĭ,** the vowel is the same as that of the suffix, e.g. **ʕuxtăha** *her sister,* **ʕuxtŭku**(m) *your* (pl.) *sister,* but **ʕuxtĭna** *our sister.*

The suffixed forms of certain common particles are somewhat irregular and need special attention. The alternative forms in the following paradigms are given in the order corresponding to the estimated frequency of their occurrence in educated speech:

fi	**bi**	**li** [2]	**wáyya**
fíyya	**bíyya**	**líyya**	**wayyáaya**
fiik	**biik**	**liik, lak,** or **lik**	**wayyáak**

[1] Often pronounced with a weak final **h** before a pause. This has been shown by the use of brackets where appropriate.

[2] Suffixed to verbs, there is a different set of **li**-forms (see below).

fi	bi	li	wáyya
fiiki	bíiki	líiki or líki	wayyáaki
fiih	biih or bu(h)	lu(h) or liih	wayyáah
fiiha	bíiha	láha, líha, or líiha	wayyáaha
fiina	bíina	lína or líina	wayyáana
fiiku(m)	bíiku(m)	lúku(m) or líiku(m)	wayyáaku(m)
fiihum	bíihum	lúhum or líihum	wayyáahum

ɛála	ɛand	min
ɛaláyya	ɛándi	mínni
ɛaléek	ɛándak	mínnak
ɛaléeki	ɛándik	mínnik
ɛaléeh	ɛándu(h)	mínnu(h)
ɛaléeha	ɛandáha	mínha or minnáha
ɛaléena	ɛandína	mínna or minnína
ɛaléeku(m)	ɛandúku(m)	mínku(m) or minnúku(m)
ɛaléehum	ɛandúhum	mínhum or minnúhum

It should be remembered that whenever a noun in **-a** is defined, as for example by suffixation, then **-t-** appears, e.g. **gineena** + **u(h)** = **ginéntu(h)** *his garden*, **ɛarabiyya** + **na** = **ɛarabiyyítna** *our car.*

It should also be borne in mind that a noun cannot be defined twice and that, therefore, **bitáɛti** and not the pronominal suffix **-i** was associated with **ɛílbit** in the earlier example **ɛílbit ikkabriit bitáɛti** *my box of matches*, to which may be added the comparable example **gawazáat issáfar bitaɛítku(m)** *your* (pl.) *passports*. Duals also require the **bitaaɛ**-construction, e.g. **ʕilbetéen bitúuɛi** *my two houses.*

Independent and suffixed pronouns are sometimes used together for emphasis, as in **da-btáaɛu húwwa, múʃ bitaɛak ínta** *that's his, not yours.*

The use of the independent 3rd person pronominal forms at the head of certain interrogative sentences and in agreement with a following noun is also noteworthy, e.g. **hiyya-lfilúus ilmasmúuḥ bíiha mawgúuda-f gawáaz issáfar bitáaɛi?** *is the currency allowance* (lit. *the money the permitted with it*) *stated* (lit. *present*) *in my passport?*

rigléen *legs*, **ʕidéen** *hands*, **ɛenéen** *eyes* merit special notice when pronominally suffixed, since **-n** of the dual suffix is dropped, e.g. **ɛenéeh** *his eyes*, **ʕidéeki** *your* (fem.) *hands.* Notice particularly the forms of the 1st person singular, e.g. **rigláyya** *my legs*, not ***rigleeya.**

The nouns **ʕaxx** *brother* and **ʕabb** *father* also require particular attention. They are of the forms **ʕaxu** and **ʕabu** (*a*) before a pronominal suffix, (*b*) in construct; e.g. **ʕaxúuh** *his brother*, **ʕaxu-brahíim** *Abraham's brother*. Contrast **ʕáxxi múslim** *a Muslim brother*, **ʕaxxéen** *two brothers*, and compare, too, **ʕaxúuh ibrahíim** *his brother Abraham* and **ʕáxu ʕabúuh** *his father's brother*. In vocative constructions, the form **abu** followed by a proper noun is to be translated *son*, cf. **y-abu ɛáli yá-bni!** (*O*) *Son of Ali, my son!* In similarly "less sophisticated" Arabic, the form **aba** may also be heard in vocative contexts when a father, father-in-law, or an older male relative or close friend of the family is being addressed, e.g. **y-aba ɛáli!** *Uncle Ali!*

Not only adjectives but also pronouns, verbs, demonstratives, etc., of the 3rd person are commonly in the singular feminine form in agreement with a preceding plural noun, e.g. **ʕilbiyúut di** [1] **hiyya-lli** [2] **ʕultílak** [3] **ɛaléeha** *these are the houses I told you about* (*them*); notice, too, the extremely common use of the pronominal suffix referring back to an earlier noun or pronoun (see pp. 104–5).

The adverbial particles often occur with the pronominal suffixes, e.g. **waráah** *behind him*, **ʕuṣádha** *opposite her*. In most cases they may optionally be compounded with **min**, so that, for example, we may say **ʕidduláab taḥtu-tráab** or **ʕidduláab taḥti mínnu-tráab** *there's dust under the cupboard* (lit. *the cupboard under it dust*). In the case of **bárra** *outside*, **min** is essential; one cannot say ***barraaha** but must use **bárra mínha** *outside it* (fem.).

The particle **ɛand** + pronominal suffix is an especially common combination and is perhaps particularly noteworthy since it generally relates in translation to an appropriate form of the verb *to have*, e.g. **ɛándak sagáayir?** *have you any cigarettes?* **li**, **wáyya**, and **máɛa** are often used in a similar way to **ɛand**, **li** generally being used with reference to property and translatable by *to own, possess*, and **wáyya** and **máɛa** usually relating to small, portable objects carried on the person, e.g.

[1] Feminine singular demonstrative adjective.
[2] The relative particle **ʕilli** *the one that*.
[3] = **ʕult** *I said* + **lak** *to you*.

líyya ɛízba *I have, own a farm,* **maɛáak filúus?** *have you any money on you?*

Finally, notice the use of **li** and a following time-word in, say, **híyya f-issúuʕ láha sáaɛa** *she's been at the market for an hour.*

fiih

ʕilʕóoḍa fíiha náas kitíir *there are a lot of people in the room* is parallel to **ʕidduláab taḥtu-tráab** *there's dust under the cupboard* above, but both sentences have the alternative forms which introduce the special and extremely common use of **fi** + the 3rd person sing. masc. suffix **-h**, corresponding in translation either to *there is, there are,* or to the indefinite article *a, an.* The alternative forms are **fíih náas kitíir f-ilʕóoḍa** and **fíih turáab taḥt idduláab.**

The noun following **fiih** is always indefinite. **ráagil bárra** is incomplete and may be completed by **fiih** in **fíih ráagil bárra** *there's a man outside, a man is outside,* which may be fairly contrasted with **ʕirráagil bárra** *the man is outside*; cf., too, **fíih ráagil biyṣálli gúwwa** *there's a man* (or *a man is*) *praying inside* and **ʕirráagil biyṣálli gúwwa** *the man is praying inside.*

fiih may be used independently as, for example, in the answer (**ʕáywa**) **fíih** (*yes*) *there is* to the question **fih ḥáddi mawgúud?** *is* (*there*) *anyone there?*

DEMONSTRATIVES AND DEICTICS

Of two series of demonstratives, pronominal and adjectival—the latter when following the noun—**da** (m.s.)/**di** (f.s.)/**dool** (pl.) *this/that, these/those* is much commoner than **dúkha/díkha/dúkham.** The use of the latter series is usually pronominal and largely confined to cases of specific contrast, as **múʃ dá lakin dúkha** *not this but that* or **ʕiʃʃánṭa di ʕátʕal min díkha** *this bag is heavier than that.*

As with **bitáaɛ** of the adjectival phrase, the ordinal numeral following the noun (see below), and other contexts, a noun preceding **da** must take the article; if another adjective is present, then **da** may follow either noun or adjective, e.g. **ʕilḥáaga di-lkuwayyísa** or **ʕilḥáaga-lkuwayyísa di** *this nice thing.* **díyya** and **díyyat** are alternative forms of adjectival **di** but are comparatively rare and may be ignored for practical purposes.

da and **di** are often suffixed to the noun with attendant difference of accentuation; thus, both **ʕilʕálam dá** and **ʕilʕalámda** *this/that pencil*, **ʕissána dí** and **ʕissanáadi** *this year*, are possible forms. As a rule the first alternative is more emphatic but the difference may relate in some cases to the geographical origin of the speaker.

Remember that the feminine singular form of adjectives, demonstratives, pronouns, verbs, **bitáaʕ**, etc., will where appropriate accompany plural nouns of non-personal reference, e.g. **ʕikkútub di** (or **dool**) *these/those books*, **ʕilḥagátdi kulláha** *all these/those things*; plural forms are, of course, necessary in association with the dual noun, e.g. **ʕikkitabéen dóol** *these/those two books*.

The deictic forms, translated usually *here/there is/are . . .*, are **ʕaho** (m.s.)/**ʕahe** (f.s.)/**ʕahum** (pl.) and the invariable **ʕáadi**. Before pause, **ʕaho** and **ʕahe** are generally pronounced with final **h**.

The deictics are used with either a noun or a verb and, in the case of **ʕaho/ʕahe/ʕahum**, independently. They may either precede or follow the noun they accompany, e.g. either **ʕahúm** (or **ʕahé**) **ikkútub** or **ʕikkútub ahúm** (or **ahéh**) *there are the books!* Following the noun and in isolation, a variety of related forms occur as alternatives, thus

Q.		A.
(i)	**ʕirrágil féen?** *where is the man?*	**ʕahóh** or **ʕahúwwa** (or, rarely, **ʕahúwwat**)
(ii)	**ʕilʕóoḍa féen?** *where is the room?*	**ʕahéh** or **ʕahíyya** (or, rarely, **ʕahíyyat**)
(iii)	**ʕilwiláad féen?** *where are the boys?*	**ʕahúm** or **ʕahúmma** (or, rarely, **ʕahúmmat**)

With verbal forms, we find as expected **ʕaho géh!** *here he is!* (lit. *has come*), **ʕahe gát!** *here she is!*, **ʕahum gúm!** *here they are!* When verbal forms of other than the third person are involved, **ʕahó** is used as an invariable form in association with the appropriate independent pronoun, e.g. **ʕahó-na** (= **ʕana**) **géet!** *here I am!*, **ʕahó-nti géeti!** *here you* (fem.) *are!* **ʕahúwwa** is sometimes used for **ʕaho** in this context, e.g. **ʕahuww-ána géet!**, **ʕahuwwá-nti géeti!**

ʕáadi can be substituted for **ʕaho/ʕahe/ʕahum** but it must always precede the noun or verb, e.g. **ʕáadi maḥaṭṭitna!** *this* *is us !, this is our stop !* **ʕáadi** is compounded with the suffixed, as opposed to the independent pronoun in, say, **ʕadíiku** (= **ʕahó-ntu**) **géetu** ! *there you* (pl.) *are !* Noteworthy, too, is the fact that the verbal **-ni** is used as the first person singular suffix with **ʕáadi**, e.g. **ʕadíini géet** ! (= **ʕahó-na géet** !) *here I am !*

ʕáadi and **ʕaho**/**ʕahe**/**ʕahum** may combine, or **ʕaho**/**ʕahe**/**ʕahum** may be repeated, e.g. **ʕadi** (or **ʕaho**) **-ʃʃéex ꞓazíiz ahóh** ! *there's Sheikh Aziz !*

COMPARISON OF ADJECTIVES

The comparative adjective is invariable in form, i.e. exhibits no distinctions of gender and number, and is generally of the pattern ʕáCCaʕ, e.g. **kibíir** *big*-**ʕákbar** *bigger*, **ṣuɣáyyar** *small*-**ʕáṣɣar** *smaller*; when the second and third radicals are the same, the comparative pattern is ʕaCáCC, e.g. **xafíif** *light*—**ʕaxáff** *lighter*, **muhímm** (with prefix **mu-**) *important*—**ʕahámm** *more important*; of adjectives ending in **-w** and **-i**, the comparative pattern is ʕáCCa, e.g. **ḥilw** *sweet, nice, pretty*—**ʕáḥla** *sweeter, etc.*, **ɣáali** *dear*—**ʕáɣla** *dearer*.

The so-called comparative form (e.g. **ʕákbar**) is to be translated by the English comparative (*bigger*) or superlative (*biggest*) according to context. **ʕilwálad ilʕákbar** may correspond to either *the bigger boy* or *the biggest boy* but, without the article, an Egyptian comparative-superlative distinction may be marked by position: **wálad ákbar** may be properly translated *a bigger boy* but **ʕákbar wálad** can only be *the biggest boy*; **ʕilwálad ilʕákbar f-ilwiláad dóol** and **ʕákbar wálad f-ilwiláad dóol** *the biggest of those boys* are for some speakers variant possibilities. Similar alternatives in which pre-nominal position is associated with omission of the article and post-nominal position with its inclusion are also found with the ordinal numerals and with the interrogative **ʕánhu**/**ʕánhi**/**ʕánhum** *which ?* (see below).

The particle **min** precedes a second noun or pronoun with which comparison is made, e.g. **ʕilwálad ákbar m-ilbínt** *the boy is bigger than the girl.* It is possible but less usual to use the positive form of the adjective followed by the particle **ꞓan**, i.e. **ʕilwálad kibíir ꞓan ilbínt.** This latter construction is used regularly with adjectives of colour and physical defect, e.g. **ʕilḥaʃíiʃ da ʕáxḍar ꞓan dá** *this grass is greener than that.*

ʕáktar *more* and **ʕaʕáll** *less* are used with those forms, especially participles, which have no comparative, e.g. **húwwa mitɛállim ʕáktar mínha** *he is more educated than her*.

Pronominal suffixes may be added to the comparative form, e.g. **ʕaɣláahum** *the dearest of them*.

NUMERALS

CARDINALS

It will be seen from the following list than *1* and *3–10* have two forms (" masculine " and " feminine "), that " tens " are characterized by a suffix **-iin** and " teens " by **-ṭaaʃar**, that " hundreds " from *300* on have their own special pattern, and that **míyya** *100* and **ʕalf** *1,000* are like nouns in that they have dual and plural forms:

wáaḥid, wáḥda *1*, **ʕitnéen** *2*, **tálat, taláata** *3*, **ʕárbaɛ, ʕarbáɛa** *4*, **xámas, xámsa** *5*, **sitt, sítta** *6*, **sábaɛ, sábɛa** *7*, **táman, tamánya** *8*, **tísaɛ, tísɛa** *9*, **ɛáʃar, ɛáʃara** *10*, **ḥiḍáaʃar** *11*, **ʕiṭnáaʃar** *12*, **talaṭṭáaʃar** *13*, **ʕarbaɛṭáaʃar** *14*, **xamasṭáaʃar** *15*, **siṭṭáaʃar** *16*, **sabaɛṭáaʃar** *17*, **tamanṭáaʃar** *18*, **tisaɛṭáaʃar** *19*, **ɛiʃríin** *20*, **wáaḥid wi ɛiʃríin** *21*, **ʕitnéen wi ɛiʃríin** *22*, **taláata-w ɛiʃríin** *23*, **ʕarbáɛa-w ɛiʃríin** *24*, **xámsa-w ɛiʃríin** *25*, **sítta-w ɛiʃríin** *26*, **sábɛa-w ɛiʃríin** *27*, **tamánya-w ɛiʃríin** *28*, **tísɛa-w ɛiʃríin** *29*, **talatíin** *30*, **wáaḥid wi talatíin** *31*, **ʕitnéen wi talatíin** *32*, **taláata-w talatíin** *33*, **ʕarbiɛíin** *40*, **xamsíin** *50*, **sittíin** *60*, **sabɛíin** *70*, **tamaníin** *80*, **tisɛíin** *90*, **míyya** *100*, **míyya w-itnéen** *102*, **míyya-w tísɛa** *109*, **míyya taláata-w sittíin** *163*, **mitéen arbáɛa-w talatíin** *234*, **tultumíyya** *300*, **rubɛumíyya** *400*, **xumsumíyya wáaḥid wi xamsíin** *551*, **tusɛumíyya-tnéen wi sittíin** *962*, **ʕalf** *1,000*, **ʕálfi-w míyya** *1,100*, **ʕálfi tusɛumíyya tísɛa-w xamsíin** *1,959*, **ʕalféen míyya-tnéen wi tisɛíin** *2,192*, **xámast aláaf xumsumíyya-w sabɛíin** *5,570*, **ḥiḍáaʃar álf** *11,000*, **milyóon** *1,000,000*, **ʕitnéen milyóon** *2,000,000*, **xámsa milyóon** *5,000,000*.

It will be seen that " tens " from *20* on may be formed by adding **-iin** to the appropriate " masculine " unit, with vowel-elision in **ɛiʃríin** (*20*), **xamsíin** (*50*), **sabɛíin** (*70*), and **tisɛíin** (*90*); notice the vowel **i,** not **a,** in **ɛiʃríin** and **ʕarbiɛíin** (*40*). In the case of " teens ", add **-ṭaaʃar** to the " masculine " unit form;

note **-ṭṭ-** in **talaṭṭáaʃar** (*13*) and **siṭṭáaʃar** (*16*): **ḥiḍáaʃar** (*11*) and **ʕiṭnáaʃar** (*12*) should be learned separately but are clearly related to **wáaḥid** and **ʕitnéen.** From *300* to *900* there is a regular pattern; **tultumiyya** (*300*), **rubʕumíyya** (*400*), **xumsumíyya** (*500*), **suttumíyya** (*600*), **subʕumíyya** (*700*), **tumnumíyya** (*800*), **tusʕumíyya** (*900*). The relation between the two forms of *3–10* numerals is not always a simple one of the presence or absence of final **-a,** cf. **tálat, taláata** (*3*), **xámas, xámsa** (*5*), **sábaʕ, sábʕa** (*7*), **táman, tamánya** (*8*), **tísaʕ, tísʕa** (*9*). Like the *3–10* numerals, **wáaḥid, wáḥda** (*1*) has two forms but all other numerals including **ʕitnéen** (*2*) have one form only. **míyya** (*100*) and **ʕalf** (*1,000*) behave in some ways like nouns and exhibit dual forms **mitéen** *200* and **ʕalféen** *2,000.* **milyóon** *1,000,000* is also basically nominal but, as will be seen, behaves in the manner of a loan-word.

Syntactically, enumerations involving a numeral and a noun require the recognition of numeral categories "*1*", "*2*", "*3–10*", "*11* and above", as well as that of such nominal categories as noun of personal reference and noun of value and measurement as opposed to those nouns—the great majority—which belong to neither category. In addition, it is neçessary to consider the relative order of numeral and noun and the possibilities of association with the definite article.

wáaḥid, wáḥda is mostly used adjectivally, e.g. **kitáab wáaḥid** *one book*, **sítti wáḥda** *one woman*. The numeral does, however, occur preceding the noun, as in the fairy-tale formula **káan fiih wáaḥid ṣulṭáan** *there was once a* (*certain*) *sultan*. Noteworthy, too, is the use of **wáaḥid** with the article as in **ʕilwáaḥid ma-byiʕdárʃ** *one can't, it can't be done.*

The use of the numeral **ʕitnéen** is to be compared with that of the dual form of the noun. It has already been seen that nouns referring to human beings—other than kinship terms—do not occur in a dual form but are regularly associated with the numeral; e.g. **ʕitnéen muʕallimíin** *two teachers*, **ʕitnéen ʕasáakir** *two soldiers*. In this context, nouns of the category stated appear in their plural form but certain common loan-words of value and measurement, which do not usually occur in a dual form, appear in the singular, e.g. **ʕitnéen ginéeh** *£2*, **ʕitnéen mítr** (sometimes, but rarely, **mitréen**) *two metres*, **ʕitnéen kíilu** (or **kéelu**) *two kilograms* or *kilometres.*

"*3–10*" numerals occur in two patterns of enumeration, the first of which is the commoner: (i) "masculine" numeral + plural noun, (ii) "feminine" numeral + singular noun of value or measurement. Examples: **xámas riggáala/ʕurúuʃ/banáat/daʕáayiʕ** *5 men/piastres/girls/minutes* but **xámsa ginéeh/taɛríifa/mallíim/kíilu** *5 £/half-piastres* [1]*/millemes/kilograms* or *kilometres*.

"*11* and above," in contrast with "*3–10*", require the singular form of a following noun of whatever category; with **xámas riggáala**/etc. of the preceding paragraph, compare **ḥiḍáaʃar/talatíin/ʕálf ráagil/ʕirʃ/bínt/daʕíiʕa** *11/30/1,000 men/piastres/girls/minutes*.

With the exception of **wáaḥid, wáḥda,** numerals may not follow the noun unless the article is present. Without the article, only **tálat riggáala** *3 men* and **xamasṭáaʃar ráagil** *15 men* are possible, but with the article, both **ʕittálat riggáala** and **ʕirriggáala-ttaláata** *the 3 men* and, again, both **ʕilxamasṭáaʃar ráagil** and **ʕirriggáala-lxamasṭáaʃar** *the 15 men*, are found. The "feminine" form of "*3–10*" numerals is regularly used when the numeral follows the noun and, moreover, given the order noun-numeral, the noun is always plural in form, whatever the category of numeral involved. It will be seen, therefore, that when the numeral follows the noun, it behaves in respect of definition in the manner of the adjective, e.g. **ʕiddíini-lkitabéen litnéen** *give me both* (or *the two*) *books* (lit. *the books the two*), **banáatu-ttaláata** *his three daughters* (lit. *his daughters the three*).

In contexts in which the numeral does not enumerate a following noun, for example in isolation, following the noun, and in compound numerals, the "masculine" form of "*1*" and the "feminine" form of "*3–10*" numerals are used, e.g. **wáaḥid wi ɛiʃríin** *21*, **míyya xámsa-w sittíin** *165*.

The order of compound numerals corresponds to the English order with the important exception that units precede tens; the particle **wi** *and* always precedes the final numeral, e.g. **ʕalféen míyya sítta-w tisɛíin** *2,196*, **ʕálfi-w míyya** *1.100*. Not only are "*3–10*" numerals in compounds always in the "feminine" form but a following noun is always in the singular, e.g. **míyya-w ɛáʃara ʕirʃ** *110 piastres*.

[1] **taɛríifa** is only used with reference to the numbers 1, 3, and 5.

míit ʕírʃ i-w ʒáʃara is a commoner alternative form of the last example and illustrates in another way the nominal nature of **míyya**; **-t** in **miit** is the **-t** of the feminine noun in construct, cf., too, **tultumíit sána** *300 years*. The plural form of **míyya** is **miyyáat**, as in **ʒándu miyyáat** *he has hundreds*. **milyóon** *1,000,000* behaves as a loan-word of value and measurement, cf. **ʕitnéen milyóon** *2,000,000* (cf. **ʕitnéen ginéeh** *£2* above), **xámsa milyóon** *5,000,000* (not ***xamas malayiin**); cf., too, **ʒándu malayíin** *he has millions*. **ʕalf** *1,000* also behaves in the manner of a noun, cf. the dual form **ʕalféen** *2,000*, the singular form in **ḫiḏáaʃar álf** *11,000*, the plural form in **tísaʒt aláaf** *9,000*. The last example illustrates the interesting occurrence of a linking **-t-**, not to be identified with **-t** of the construct, between " *3–10* " numerals and nouns which elsewhere begin with **ʕ**.

It is not with every **ʕ**-beginning noun that this linking **-t-** appears. Contrast with **tálat-t-aláaf** *3,000*, for example, **tálat ʕuzúun baríid** *3 postal orders*, or **tálat ʕaráanib** *3 rabbits*. **-t-** commonly occurs with nouns of the pattern ʕaCCaaC, e.g. **ʕayyáam** *days*, **ʕafráan** *ovens*; moreover, such nouns, though often with **a** in the first syllable when initial or in isolation, appear with **i** when in close grammatical relation with a preceding noun or particle; thus, **ʕayyáam ilʕusbúuʒ** *the days of the week* but **liyyáam** *the days*. **ʕilʕayyáam**, however, is a possible form in place of **liyyáam** and, indeed, is on the whole commoner among educated speakers. As far as the forms with **-t-** are concerned, comparison should be made between **xámas-t-iyyáam** *5 days* and **xámas ʕurúuʃ** *5 piastres*, **sábaʒ-t-iṣnáaf** *7 kinds* and **sábaʒ banáat** *7 girls*, **tálat-t-úʃhur** and **tálat ʕáʃhur** (or, more commonly, **tálat ʃuhúur**) *3 months*. Once more, **xámas ʕayyáam** or **xámsit ʕayyáam** (possibly due to the identification of **-t-** with **-t** of the construct) tend to be commoner among educated speakers; what a man says, however, depends on the situation in which he says it—the educated man may tend in general to use **xámas ʕasdáas** or **xámsit ʕasdáas** *five-sixths* but he will use **xámas-t-isdáas** when talking to a fitter, for example.

FRACTIONS

The linking **-t-** is common with fractions, of which **ʕasdáas** in the preceding paragraph was an example and which exhibit their own special pattern for fractions from *one-half* to *one-tenth*; **nuṣṣ/ʕanṣáaṣ** $^{1}/_{2}$, **tilt/ʕatláat** $^{1}/_{3}$, **rubɛ/ʕarbáaɛ** $^{1}/_{4}$, **xums/ʕaxmáas** $^{1}/_{5}$, **suds/ʕasdáas** $^{1}/_{6}$, **subɛ/ʕasbáaɛ** $^{1}/_{7}$, **tumn/ʕatmáan** $^{1}/_{8}$, **tusɛ/ʕatsáaɛ** $^{1}/_{9}$, **ɛuʃr/ʕaɛʃáar** $^{1}/_{10}$. The vowel of the singular pattern is **u** with the exception of **tilt.** With the exceptions of **nuṣṣ** and **suds,** the fractions are directly relatable to the other numeral forms. The dual is used quite regularly, e.g. **tiltéen** $^{2}/_{3}$. In junctions of " *3–10* " numerals and fractions, the exceptional form **irbaɛ** is especially noteworthy, e.g. **tálat-t-írbaɛ** (not ***irbaaɛ**) $^{3}/_{4}$. For fractions in which the denominator exceeds *10*, the cardinal numeral is used preceded by **ɛála,** e.g. **wáahid ɛala-ḥdáaʃar** $^{1}/_{11}$, **taláata ɛala ɛiʃríin** $^{3}/_{20}$,**taláata-w xámsa ɛala-ṭnáaʃar** $3\ ^{5}/_{12}$.

Fractions are particularly relevant to telling the time, cf. **ʕissáaɛa taláata-w ɛáʃara/rúbɛ/tílt/núṣṣ/núṣṣ illa xámsa** *it's ten/a quarter/twenty/half/twenty-five past three* and **ʕíssáaɛa taláata-(ʕi)lla rúbɛ/tílt** *it's a quarter/twenty to three.* Notice particularly **ʕissáaɛa taláata-w núṣṣĭ-w xámsa** *it's twenty-five to four* (lit. *a half and five past three*).

It may be observed in passing, and still on the subject of time-reference, that the names of the first five days of the week are clearly related to other numeral forms; thus, **yóom ilḥádd** *Sunday,* **yóom litnéen** *Monday,* **yóom ittaláat** *Tuesday,* **yóom lárbaɛ** *Wednesday,* **yóom ilxamíis** *Thursday* (**yóom iggúmɛa** *Friday,* **yóom issábt** *Saturday*). The article is omitted after **kull** *every,* e.g. **kúllĭ yóom gúmɛa** *every Friday.* The manner of specifying dates is illustrated by **yóom ilxamíis, xámsa-w ɛiʃríin ʕaγúṣṭuṣ, sanat ʕálfĭ tusɛumíyya-w sittíin** *Thursday, 25th August, 1960.*

ORDINALS

There is a special " *3–10* " ordinal pattern. The pattern is shared by **wáaḥid, wáḥda,** among the cardinals above. The ordinal is essentially adjectival in function, with masculine and feminine forms but, of course, no plural form. " *3–10* " ordinals are as follows: **táalit, tálta** *third,* **ráabiɛ, rábɛa** *fourth,* **xáamis, xámsa** *fifth,* **sáatit, sátta** [1] *sixth,* **sáabiɛ, sábɛa** *seventh,* **táamin, támna** *eighth,* **táasiɛ, tásɛa** *ninth,* **ɛáaʃir, ɛáʃra** *tenth.*

[1] **sáadis** occurs as a learned form for **sáatit**; cf. the fraction **suds.**

A noun accompanying the ordinal is, of course, always singular, but the numeral may precede or follow. When it follows, then there is the customary agreement in respect of gender and definition; e.g. **ráagil táalit** *a third man*, **ʕirráagil ittáalit** *the third man*, **ʕissitt ittálta** *the third woman*. When the ordinal precedes, it is invariable in the masculine form and the reference of the whole phrase is definite; thus, **táalit ráagil** (or **ʕirráagil ittáalit**) *the third man*, **táalit sitt** (or **ʕissitt ittálta**) *the third woman*. It has already been stated that this relation between pre-nominal position and definite reference in the absence of the article is also found with the comparative form of the adjective and with the "particularizing" interrogative particle **ʕánhu/ʕánhi/ʕánhum** *which?* To take one example, however, **táalit sitt** and **ʕissitt ittálta** are not freely interchangeable in all contexts. Use of the definite article is generally more "particularizing" and would, in this instance, relate to contexts in which more than three women are directly concerned; thus, cf. **ʕissitt ittálta túdxul**[1] *let the third woman* (of a known queue of women) *come in* and **ʕáadi táalit sitti túdxul** *that's the third woman to come in* (there may or may not be any more). Another example of the latter type is **ʕahó da táalit riɣiif yáklu**[1] (or **wáklu**[1]) **dilwaʕti** *that's the third loaf he's eaten*.

Ordinals from *eleventh* on have the same shape as cardinals but are distinguished as ordinals by the facts that (*a*) they always follow the noun and (*b*) the noun is always in the singular. Contrast **ʕirráagil ilḥiḍáaʃar** *the eleventh man* with the cardinal in **ḥiḍáaʃar ráagil** *eleven men* and **ʕilḥiḍáaʃar ráagil** or **ʕirriggáala-lḥiḍáaʃar** *the eleven men*.

Like **wáaḥid, wáḥda,** and **ʕitnéen** among the cardinals, so *first* and *second* need special attention. **ʕáwwil** *first* may precede or follow the noun and is invariable in the former case, e.g. **ʕáwwil fáṣl** or **ʕilfáṣl ilʕáwwil** *the first chapter*. More common, however, at least following the noun, are the adjectival forms **ʕawwaláani-ʕawwalaníyya/ʕawwalaniyyíin,** for the first two of which **ʕáwwal** and **ʕúula** are often heard from educated speakers, e.g. **ʕiṣṣáfḥa-lʕawwalaníyya** or **ʕiṣṣáfḥa-lʕúula** *the first page*, **dáraga ʕúula** *first class*. **táani, tánya** *second* are often used

[1] Verbal and participial forms are explained below.

together with the plural form **tanyiin,** in the sense of *other,* e.g. **wáaḥid táani** *another one, someone else,* **ʕittanyiin féen?** *where are the others?* As with **ʕáwwal** and **ʕúula,** so **ʕáaxar** (masc.) and **ʕúxra** (fem.) are sometimes heard from educated speakers for **táani** and **tánya** in the sense of *other,* e.g. **ʕikkitáab ilʕáaxar** *the other book*; cf. **dáraga tánya** (or **sukúndu**) *second class.*

ʕáaxar should not be confused with **ʕáaxir** *last,* which is an ordinal behaving in a completely parallel manner to **ʕáwwil** above, cf. **ʕáaxir fáṣl** or **ʕilfáṣl ilʕáaxir** *the last chapter.* Again in parallel with **ʕáwwil,** there are adjectival forms which, following the noun, are commoner than **ʕáaxir,** viz. **ʕaxráani-ʕaxraníyya/ʕaxraniyyiin,** and yet again, there are "learned" forms, **ʕaxiir** (masc.) and **ʕaxiira** (fem.), which are heard from educated speakers for the commoner **ʕaxráani** and **ʕaxraníyya.**

VERBS

TYPES OR CONJUGATIONS

The Arabic verb is divisible into four types or conjugations corresponding to differences in the pattern of the radicals. Thus, **kátab** *he wrote* has the favourite three-radical pattern but **ʕaal** *he said* has **aa** in place of a second radical, **ráma** *he threw* has **a** and **míʃi** *he went* has **i** in place of a third radical, and **ḥabb** *he liked, wanted,* has the same consonant as second and third radicals and no vowel between them. These conjugational types are termed (i) regular (**kátab**), (ii) hollow (**ʕaal**), (iii) weak (**ráma, míʃi**), (iv) doubled (**ḥabb**). Differences between the conjugations will be formulated subsequently; similarly, it will later become apparent why for the time being verbs are quoted in the form of the 3rd person singular masculine perfect tense.

"FORMS" OR ASPECTS

A number of "forms" or aspects are applicable to all conjugational types. These forms may be divided for convenience into one *simple* form (as **kátab, ʕaal, ráma, míʃi,** and **ḥabb** above) and a number of others variously *derived* from the simple form. Ignoring for the present differences in the pattern of short vowels between simple and derived forms, two processes of derivation may be distinguished: (i) internal modification (ii) prefixation. Some forms combine both.

Three internally derived forms are characterized by:

(1) The doubling or gemination of the second radical, e.g. **fáhhim** *he explained*, **sállim** *he delivered*; this is by far the commonest of the derived forms.
(2) A long open vowel infixed after the first radical, e.g. **ʕáabil** *he met.*
(3) **t** infixed after the first radical, e.g. **ʕiftákar** *he thought, believed*; **ʕi-** is prefixed, as in the forms derived by prefix below, in order to obviate the inadmissible pattern of two initial consonants.

The prefixes of forms derived in the second manner are:

(4) (ʕi)**t-**, e.g. **ʕitwágad** *it was found.*
(5) (ʕi)**n-**, e.g. **ʕinbáṣaṭ** *he was happy.*
(6) (ʕi)**sta-**, e.g. **ʕistáfham** *he inquired*; notice the lack of vowel between the second and third radicals.

In the above prefixed forms, the prefixes are associated with the pattern of the simple form, but the prefix (ʕi)**t-** also appears in " doubly derived " forms in association with forms (1) and (2) above, thus:

(7) = (4) + (1), e.g. **ʕitkállim** *he spoke.*
(8) = (4) + (2), e.g. **ʕitnáaʕiʃ** *he discussed.*

The foregoing forms of the verb may be tabulated as follows; the simple form is considered in the table to exemplify both zero-infix and zero-prefix. Only the regular verb-type has so far been exemplified but in the table (p. 67) all verb-types, regular (R), hollow (H), weak (W), and doubled (D), are illustrated.

It cannot be assumed for a given verb that the simple form corresponding to a derived form necessarily occurs, or vice versa. The " simple form " is simply one of a total range of " forms ". Moreover, there is no foolproof correspondence of meaning between the simple and a derived form or between two derived forms. The geminate form is often causative, e.g. **fáhhim** *he explained, made to understand* (cf. **fihim** *he understood*), **náḍḍaf** *he cleaned, made clean* (cf. **niḍiif** *clean*), or intensive, e.g. **kássar** *he smashed* (cf. **kásar** *he broke*), but these are by no means the only possibilities and, with other derived forms, such

Infix ↓ / Prefix →	Zero	(ʕi)t-	(ʕi)n-	(ʕi)sta-
Zero	(R) **kátab**[1] (H) **ʕaal** (W) **ráma, miʃi** (D) **ḩabb**	(R) **ʕitwágad** (H) **ʕitbáaɛ** *it was sold* (W) **ʕitnása** *it was forgotten* (D) **ʕitɛádd** *it was counted*	(R) **ʕinbáʂaṭ** (H) **ʕinbáaɛ** *it was sold* (W) **ʕinḩáka** *it was told* (D) **ʕinbáll** *it was wetted*	(R) **ʕistáfham** (H) **ʕistaʕáal** *he resigned* (W) **ʕistákfa** *he had enough* (D) **ʕistaḩáʕʕ** *he deserved*
Gemination of C2	(R) **fáhhim** (H) **ḩáwwil** *he transferred,* **ɛáyyin** *he appointed* (W) **fáḍḍa** *he emptied* (D) **ḩáddid** *he fixed, limited*	(R) **ʕitkállim** (H) **ʕitḩáwwil** *he was transferred,* **ʕitɛáyyin** *he was appointed* (W) **ʕitʕáwwa** *he improved* (D) **ʕitḩáddid** *it was fixed, limited*		
(C1)aa-	(R) **ʕáabil** (H) **gáawib** *he answered* (W) **náada** *he called* (D) no ex. available	(R) **ʕitnáaʕiʃ** (H) **ʕitgáawib** *it was answered* (W) **ʕitráaḍa** *he agreed* (D) no ex. available		
(ʕiC1)t-	(R) **ʕiftákar** (H) **ʕixtáar** *he chose* (W) **ʕiʃtára** *he bought* (D) no ex. available			

[1] Where no translation is given, the form has been quoted above.

relations are even more difficult to establish in a general way. In making his own word-list the student should learn the meaning of each existing form separately; this is best done, moreover, by collecting words and forms in useful sentences rather than in isolation.

The prefix **(ʕi)t-** is generally a passive, intransitive, or reflexive sign. **(ʕi)n-** and **(ʕi)t-** are theoretically interchangeable; thus, both **ʕitwágad** and **ʕinwágad, ʕitbáaɛ** and **ʕinbáaɛ** are possible. In practice, however, the prefixes tend to become specialized, e.g. **ʕinkásar** *it was broken* rather than **ʕitkásar, ʕitɛámal** *it was done* rather than **ʕinɛámal**; in general, it would seem that **(ʕi)t-** is commoner than **(ʕi)n-** in Cairo. **(ʕi)t-** forms associated with gemination and especially with **-aa-** frequently require an accompanying particle, e.g. **huwwa-tnáaʕiʃ wayyáah f-ilmawḍúuɛ** *he discussed the matter with him, they had a discussion about it*; there is little difference of meaning between **huwwa kallímu(h)** and **huwwa-tkállim wayyáah** *he spoke to him*. As with *l* of the article, so the junction of certain consonants with preceding *t* of the derived prefix has special implications as to pronunciation. These are as follows:

(ʕi)*t* + **d** = **(ʕi)dd-**, e.g. **ʕiddálaʕ** *it was spilt*
(ʕi)*t* + **ṭ** = **(ʕi)ṭṭ-**, e.g. **ʕiṭṭállaɛ** *he peered through* (e.g. *window*)
(ʕi)*t* + **ḍ** = **(ʕi)ḍḍ-**, e.g. **ʕiḍḍáffar** *it was plaited*
(ʕi)*t* + **ṣ** = **(ʕi)ṣṣ-**, e.g. **ʕiṣṣáwwar** *he was photographed*
(ʕi)*t* + **ẓ** = **(ʕi)ẓẓ-**, e.g. **ʕiẓẓábaṭ** *he was caught out (in wrong-doing)*

(ʕi)*t* + **s** = **(ʕi)ts-** or **(ʕi)ss-**, e.g. **ʕitsálax** or **ʕissálax** *it was skinned*
(ʕi)*t* + **k** = **(ʕi)tk-** or **(ʕi)kk-**, e.g. **ʕitkállim** or **ʕikkállim** *he spoke*
(ʕi)*t* + **ʃ** = **(ʕi)tʃ-** or **(ʕi)ʃʃ-**, e.g. **ʕitʃáɛlil** or **ʕiʃʃáɛlil** *it flared up (fire)* (a quadriliteral verb—see below)

(ʕi)*t* + **z** = **(ʕi)dz-** or **(ʕi)zz-**, e.g. **ʕidzáyyit** or **ʕizzáyyit** *it was oiled*
(ʕi)*t* + **g** = **(ʕi)dg-** or **(ʕi)gg-**, e.g. **ʕidgáraḥ** or **ʕiggáraḥ** *he was wounded*

(ʕi)*t* + **ɣ** = **(ʕi)dɣ-**, e.g. **ʕidɣálab** *he was defeated*

Notice from the table of derived forms that in forms exhibiting gemination or the infixation of **aa**, with or without the prefix (**ʕi**)**t-**, hollow and doubled verbs, when they occur, are treated exactly as regular verbs. In the case of hollow verbs, **w** or **y** appears as the second radical. Etymologically, hollow and weak verbs are those with **w** or **y** as second and third radical respectively. Verbs with **y** as first radical do not occur and those with **w** are not irregular save that in the derived form containing the infixed **t**, **ʕi*w*t-** = **ʕitt-** in pronunciation, e.g. **ʕittáfaʕ** *he agreed*, **ʕittákal** (**ɛala**) *he relied* (*on*).

The prefix (**ʕi**)**sta-** appears in a pattern exhibiting gemination elsewhere in the common (hollow) verb **ʕistaráyyaḥ** *he rested*, but the example is unique of its kind and the pattern has not, therefore, been included in the table above.

Also omitted from the table are a few "learned" derived forms characterized by a prefix **ʕa-**, e.g. **ʕársal** *he sent*, corresponding to the more usual and typically colloquial **báɛat**. **ʕafáad** (hollow) *he informed, it was useful* and **ʕárḍɑ** (weak) *it pleased, satisfied* are other examples of this derived form which occur in the speech of the educated, but the form is nevertheless rare and need never be used.

Colour verbs

Also excluded so far is a form of the verb which, unlike the others, relates regularly and almost exclusively to adjectives of colour. This form is characterized by gemination of the third radical, e.g. **ʕiḥmárr** *he went red, blushed*, **ʕibyáḍḍ** *he turned white*, etc. **ʕiḥláww** *it became sweet* (cf. **ḥilw** *sweet*) also belongs to this class.

Quadriliteral verbs

A large number of verbs contain four radicals; four different ones, e.g. **xárbiʃ** *he scratched*, **láxbaṭ** *he confused*; the first and third, or third and fourth, the same, e.g. **kárkib** *he muddled*, **ẓáʕṭaṭ** *he was overjoyed*; the same two in the same order in both syllables, e.g. **wáʃwiʃ** *he whispered*, **báṣbaṣ** *he ogled*.

The only derived form of quadriliteral verbs is with the prefix (**ʕi**)**t-**, e.g. **ʕitláxbaṭ** *he was confused*, **ʕitʃáɛlil** *it flared up* (*fire*).

TENSES

For each form, two tenses, perfect and imperfect, must be distinguished. Distinctions of person, gender, and number within each tense parallel those of the independent and suffixed pronouns. The perfect tense is characterized by suffixes, the imperfect by prefixes (in three persons, by a combination of prefix and suffix). The tense affixes are the same for all forms and basically the same for all conjugational types, though some qualification in respect of doubled and weak verbs, and also of verbs of colour, will be made subsequently. It is because it is possible in the case of the perfect tense to derive all other persons from the unaffixed shape of the 3rd person singular masculine that verbs have been quoted primarily in relation to this " basic " shape.

In the overwhelming majority of cases the affixes are:

		Perfect	**Imperfect**	
		Suffix	*Prefix*	*Suffix*
Sing.	3rd person masculine	**-**	**y(i)-**	
	3rd person feminine	**-it**	**t(i)-**	
	2nd person masculine	**-t**	**t(i)-**	
	2nd person feminine	**-ti**	**t(i)-**	**-i**
	1st person	**-t**	**ʕa-**	
Pl.	3rd person	**-u**	**y(i)-**	**-u**
	2nd person	**-tu**	**t(i)-**	**-u**
	1st person	**-na**	**n(i)-**	

Note

The bracketed vowel of the imperfect prefixes (variously **i** or **u**—see below) is required by the phonological pattern and is not really part of the prefix.

With reference at first to the simple form only, the bases to which the above affixes apply are as follows:

	Perfect	**Imperfect**	*Examples*[1]
Regular	CaCaC CiCiC	-CCiC	**kátab, yíktib** *to write*
		-CCuC	**ṭálab, yúṭlub**[2] *to ask*
		-CCaC	**fíhim, yífham** *to understand*

[1] Verbs are quoted in the corresponding perfect and imperfect 3rd pers. masc. sing. forms and translated by the English infinitive.
[2] See Note (*a*) below.

	Perfect	Imperfect	Examples
Hollow	CaaC	-CiiC	**ʃaal, yiʃíil** *to carry*
		-CuuC	**ʕaal, yiʕúul** *to say*
		-CaaC	**naam, yináam** *to sleep*
Weak	CaCa	-CCi	**ráma, yírmi** *to throw*
	CiCi	-CCa	**nísi, yínsa** *to forget*
Doubled	CaCC	-CiCC	**ħabb, yiħíbb** *to like, want*
		-CuCC	**ħaṭṭ, yiħúṭṭ** *to put*

Notes

(*a*) If, in the imperfect tense, the vowel between the second and third radicals of the regular type is **i** or **a**, then the vowel of the first syllable is **i**; if the vowel is **u**, then the vowel of the first syllable is usually **u** also. It is, however, fairly common to hear **i** for **u** in the first syllable, i.e. **yídxul** for **yúdxul** *he enters*, **yíṭlub** for **yúṭlub** *he asks*.

(*b*) **a** in the above formulation does duty for both open vowels; there is no doubt that much of the difference between the close vowels **i** and **u** could also be accounted for by reference to the consonant context. In Arabic writing short vowels are rarely written and when they are differentiation is threefold, corresponding to **i/u/a**; if Egyptian ever comes to be written as a language in the Arabic script, some modification of present conventions will be desirable.

The vowel-sequences **a-a** and **i-i** in the perfect tense of the regular verb correspond to a rough division of transitive and intransitive verbs, but there are numerous exceptions, e.g. **símiɛ** *he heard*, **mísik** *he grasped*. The sequence **u-u** occurs for **i-i** with some speakers, e.g. **xúruṣ** *he was struck dumb*; **i-i,** however, is much more frequent and may always be used. It will be remembered that the **i-i** pattern exhibits elision of the second **i** when the perfect suffix begins with a vowel, e.g. **fihim** + **it** = **fíhmit** *she understood*, **fihim** + **u** = **fíhmu** *they understood*.

As far as hollow verbs are concerned, when the *imperfect* vowel is **ii** or **uu,** the same vowel (**i** or **u**) appears in place of **a** in those five forms of the *perfect* in which the suffix begins with a consonant, e.g. **ʃilt** *I carried* (cf. **yiʃíil**), **ruħt** *I went* (cf. **yirúuħ**). When the imperfect vowel is **aa,** the perfect vowel in these five persons may be either **i** or **u** and there is no certain means of predicting which, e.g. **nimt** *I went to sleep* (cf. **yináam**), **xuft** *I was afraid* (cf. **yixáaf**).

Two sub-types of weak verb must be recognized in the perfect, those ending in **-i** and those ending in **-a**. Final **-i** is lengthened when the suffix begins with a consonant (**miʃi** + **t** = **miʃiit** *you* (m.s.) *went*) and **y** appears when the suffix is vowel-beginning (**miʃi** + **it** = **míʃyit** *she went*). It is feasible to regard **míʃi** as **miʃiy**, **-iy** being pronounced as **-i**, whence **miʃiy** + **t** = **miʃiyt**, **miʃiy** + **it** = **miʃyit**. Final **-a** of the perfect, e.g. **ráma** *he threw*, is dropped in the formation of other persons from the 3rd person sing. masc., e.g. **rama** + **it** = **rámit** *she threw*.

The perfect suffixes for the **ráma**-subtype of weak verb and for the doubled verb are special in that for those five persons in which elsewhere the suffix is consonant-beginning the vowel **ee** precedes the suffix consonant; this is also a characteristic of colour verbs. Examples: **laʕéet/laʕéeti/laʕéet/laʕéetu/laʕéena** *you* (m.s.)/*you* (f.s.)/*I*/*you* (pl.)/*we found* (cf. **láʕa** *he found*), **ḩabbéet/ḩabbéeti/ḩabbéet/ḩabbéetu/ḩabbéena** *you* (m.s.)/*you* (f.s.)/*I*/*you* (pl.)/ *we liked*, **ʕiḩmarréet/ʕiḩmarréeti/ʕiḩmarréet/ʕiḩmarréetu/ʕiḩmarréena** *you* (m.s.)/*you* (f.s.)/*I*/*you* (pl.)/*we blushed, went red.*

The complete paradigms of the simple form of the four conjugational types is as follows:

Regular verb: kátab, yíktib *to write*, **ṭálab, yúṭlub** *to ask*, **fihim, yífham** *to understand*

		Perfect		
Sing.	3rd pers. masc.	**kátab**	**ṭálab**	**fihim**
	3rd pers. fem.	**kátabit**	**ṭálabit**	**fihmit**
	2nd pers. masc.	**katábt**	**ṭalábt**	**fihímt**
	2nd pers. fem.	**katábti**	**ṭalábti**	**fihímti**
	1st pers.	**katábt**	**ṭalábt**	**fihímt**
Pl.	3rd pers.	**kátabu**	**ṭálabu**	**fihmu**
	2nd pers.	**katábtu**	**ṭalábtu**	**fihímtu**
	1st pers.	**katábna**	**ṭalábna**	**fihímna**

		Imperfect		
Sing.	3rd pers. masc.	yíktib	yúʈlub	yifham
	3rd pers. fem.	tíktib	túʈlub	tífham
	2nd pers. masc.	tíktib	túʈlub	tífham
	2nd pers. fem.	tiktíbi	tuʈlúbi	tifhámi
	1st pers.	ʕáktib	ʕáʈlub	ʕáfham
Pl.	3rd pers.	yiktíbu	yuʈlúbu	yifhámu
	2nd pers.	tiktíbu	tuʈlúbu	tifhámu
	1st pers.	níktib	núʈlub	nífham

Hollow verb : ʃaal, yiʃiil *to carry, take away,* **raaḥ, yirúuḥ** *to go,* **naam, yináam** *to sleep,* **xaaf, yixáaf** *to fear, be afraid*

		Perfect			
Sing.	3rd pers. masc.	ʃaal	raaḥ	naam	xaaf
	3rd pers. fem.	ʃáalit	ráaḥit	náamit	xáafit
	2nd pers. masc.	ʃilt	ruḥt	nimt	xuft
	2nd pers. fem.	ʃílti	rúḥti	nímti	xúfti
	1st pers.	ʃilt	ruḥt	nimt	xuft
Pl.	3rd pers.	ʃáalu	ráaḥu	náamu	xáafu
	2nd pers.	ʃíltu	rúḥtu	nímtu	xúftu
	1st pers.	ʃílna	rúḥna	nímna	xúfna

		Imperfect			
Sing.	3rd pers. masc.	yiʃiil	yirúuḥ	yináam	yixáaf
	3rd pers. fem.	tiʃiil	tirúuḥ	tináam	tixáaf
	2nd pers. masc.	tiʃiil	tirúuḥ	tináam	tixáaf
	2nd pers. fem.	tiʃiili	tirúuḥi	tináami	tixáafi
	1st pers.	ʕaʃiil	ʕarúuh	ʕanáam	ʕaxáaf
Pl.	3rd pers.	yiʃiilu	yirúuḥu	yináamu	yixáafu
	2nd pers.	tiʃiilu	tirúuḥu	tináamu	tixáafu
	1st pers.	niʃiil	nirúuḥ	nináam	nixáaf

Weak verb : miʃi, yimʃi *to walk, go,* **ráma, yirmi** *to throw,* **nísi, yínsa** *to forget,* **láʕa, yilʕa** *to find*

		Perfect			
Sing.	3rd pers. masc.	**míʃi**	**ráma**	**nísi**	**láʕa**
	3rd pers. fem.	**míʃyit**	**rámit**	**nísyit**	**láʕit**
	2nd pers. masc.	**miʃíit**	**raméet**	**nisíit**	**laʕéet**
	2nd pers. fem.	**miʃíiti**	**raméeti**	**nisíiti**	**laʕéeti**
	1st pers.	**miʃíit**	**raméet**	**nisíit**	**laʕéet**
Pl.	3rd pers.	**míʃyu**	**rámu**	**nísyu**	**láʕu**
	2nd pers.	**miʃíitu**	**raméetu**	**nisíitu**	**laʕéetu**
	1st pers.	**miʃíina**	**raméena**	**nisíina**	**laʕéena**

		Imperfect			
Sing.	3rd pers. masc.	**yimʃi**	**yirmi**	**yínsa**	**yilʕa**
	3rd pers. fem.	**timʃi**	**tirmi**	**tínsa**	**tilʕa**
	2nd pers. masc.	**timʃi**	**tirmi**	**tínsa**	**tilʕa**
	2nd pers. fem.	**timʃi**	**tirmi**	**tínsi**	**tilʕi**
	1st pers.	**ʕámʃi**	**ʕármi**	**ʕánsa**	**ʕálʕa**
Pl.	3rd pers.	**yimʃu**	**yirmu**	**yínsu**	**yilʕu**
	2nd pers.	**timʃu**	**tirmu**	**tínsu**	**tilʕu**
	1st pers.	**nimʃi**	**nirmi**	**nínsa**	**nilʕa**

Doubled verb : ħabb, yiħíbb *to like, want,* **ħaṭṭ, yiħúṭṭ** *to put*

		Perfect		*Imperfect*	
Sing.	3rd pers. masc.	**ħabb**	**ħaṭṭ**	**yiħíbb**	**yiħúṭṭ**
	3rd pers. fem.	**ħábbit**	**ħáṭṭit**	**tiħíbb**	**tiħúṭṭ**
	2nd pers. masc.	**ħabbéet**	**ħaṭṭéet**	**tiħíbb**	**tiħúṭṭ**
	2nd pers. fem.	**ħabbéeti**	**ħaṭṭéeti**	**tiħíbbi**	**tiħúṭṭi**
	1st pers.	**ħabbéet**	**ħaṭṭéet**	**ʕaħíbb**	**ʕaħúṭṭ**
Pl.	3rd pers.	**ħábbu**	**ħáṭṭu**	**yiħíbbu**	**yiħúṭṭu**
	2nd pers.	**ħabbéetu**	**ħaṭṭéetu**	**tiħíbbu**	**tiħúṭṭu**
	1st pers.	**ħabbéena**	**ħaṭṭéena**	**niħíbb**	**niħúṭṭ**

The perfect and imperfect affixes are applied to all derived forms in the same way as to the simple form; in contrast with the simple form of the regular and weak verb, however, the structure of the " base ", i.e. the remainder of the form when the affixes have been subtracted, remains the same in both the perfect and imperfect tenses of the derived forms, cf. **fáhhim, yifáhhim** *to explain*, **gáawib, yigáawib** *to answer*, **ʕiftákar, yiftíkir** *to think*, **ʕitwágad, yitwígid** *to be found*, **ʕinkásar, yinkísir** *to be broken*, **ʕistáɛmil, yistáɛmil** *to use*, **ʕitɛáyyin, yitɛáyyin** *to be appointed*, **ʕitnáaʕiʃ, yitnáaʕiʃ** *to discuss*. The facts of vowelling in the tenses and of vowel-correspondences between the tenses remain to be stated and are set out in the following table:

(Table follows on pp. 76–80.)

Regular	Hollow	Weak	Doubled
Simple form The second vowel of the imperfect may be **a** (or **ɑ**), **i**, or **u**. As a general rule, when the second vowel of the perfect is **a**, the corresponding imperfect vowel is **i** or **u**, while **i** in the perfect corresponds to **a** in the imperfect. Certain consonants, however, occurring as second or third radical, "prefer" **a** in the imperfect even when the corresponding perfect vowel is also **a**; these consonants are **x, ɣ, ḥ, ɛ, h, ṣ, ṭ, ẓ, ḍ, ṛ**, and sometimes **ʕ** (cf. **fátaḥ, yíftaḥ** *to open*, **ḍárab, yíḍrab** *to hit*). These remarks should only be taken as a general guide and the imperfect of any verb should be learnt in conjunction with the perfect as it is met.	When the imperfect vowel is **ii** or **uu**, the same vowel (**i** or **u**) appears in those five persons of the perfect which contain a consonant-beginning suffix, e.g. **ʃilt** (cf. **yiʃiil**), **ruḥt** (cf. **yirúuḥ**). In the less frequent case of imperfect vowel **aa**, the perfect vowel in these five persons may be either **i** or **u** and there is no way of predicting which.	As a general rule, if the perfect ends in **-i**, the imperfect ends in **-a**, and vice versa, e.g. **nísi, yínsa**, but **ráma, yírmi**. There are exceptions, however, e.g. **míʃi, yímʃi**, and **láʕa, yílʕa**, so that once again it is necessary to learn the vowels associated with each verb as it is met.	The vowel of the perfect is always **a**, that of the imperfect variously **i** (**yiḥíbb**) and **u** (**yiḥúṭṭ**). If the imperfect vowel is **u**, one of the radicals is almost certain to belong to the list of consonants given opposite under the regular verb.
Form with C2 geminated There is no vowel-differentiation between the	Treated exactly as the regular verb, e.g.	The perfect always ends in **-a**, the imper-	Treated exactly as the regular verb, e.g.

tenses. The first vowel is always **a**, e.g. **lábbis, yilábbis** *to dress, clothe*. The second vowel is either **i** or **a**, generally **a** if preceded or followed by one of the consonants listed under the simple form above, e.g. **náḍḍaf, yináḍḍaf** *to clean*.	**ḥáwwil, yiḥáwwil** *to transfer*, **ṣáwwar, yiṣáwwar** *to photograph*.	fect in **-i**, e.g. **wádda, yiwáddi** *to move, take away*. The 3rd pers. sing. masc. perfect of *all* derived forms of weak verbs ends in **-a**. *N.B.*—In all derived forms of the weak verb, the 3rd pers. sing. fem. suffix is **-at**, not **-it**, e.g. **wárrat** *she showed*, **ʕiʃtárat** *she bought*.	**ḥáddid, yiḥáddid** *to fix, limit*.
Form with aa infixed after C1 Again no vowel difference between perfect and imperfect. The second vowel is always **i**, e.g. **ʕáabil, yiʕáabil** *to meet*.	Again treated as the regular verb, e.g. **gáawib, yigáawib** *to answer*.	Again the perfect ends in **-a**, the imperfect in **-i**, e.g. **náada, yináadi** *to call*.	No example available.
Form with t infixed after C1 The vowel sequence **a-a** occurs without exception in the perfect and usually corresponds to **i-i** in the imperfect, e.g. **ʕiftákar, yiftíkir** *to think, believe*; **ʕiʃtáɣal, yiʃtáɣal** *to work* is exceptional.	There is no vowel difference between perfect and imperfect, e.g. **ʕixtáar, yixtáar** *to choose, elect*. In contrast with the simple form the vowel **a** remains throughout both tenses, e.g. **ʕixtárna** *we chose*.	**a-a** always occurs in the perfect, invariably corresponding to **i-i** in the imperfect, e.g. **ʕiʃtára, yiʃtíri** *to buy*, **ʕibtáda, yibtídi** *to begin*.	No example available.

Regular	Hollow	Weak	Doubled
Form with (ʕi)t prefixed to simple form			
The perfect vowel pattern is always **a-a,** and that of the imperfect **i-i,** e.g. **ʕitságan, yitsígin** *to be imprisoned.*	The vowel **a(a)** remains throughout perfect and imperfect, e.g. **ʕitḫáal, yitḫáal** *to retire.*	As in the regular verb, perfect vowelling is invariably **a-a,** with imperfect **i-i,** e.g. **ʕitnása, yitnísi** *to be forgotten.*	As in the hollow verb, the vowel **a** remains throughout, e.g. **ʕitʒádd, yitʒádd** *to be counted.*
Form with (ʕi)t prefixed and C2 geminated			
Vowelling is as for the corresponding form without **(ʕi)t,** e.g. **ʕitʒállim, yitʒállim** *to learn,* **ʕitkássar, yitkássar** *to be smashed.*	As for the regular verb, e.g. **ʕidgáwwiz, yidgáwwiz** *to be, get married.*	In contrast with the corresponding form without **(ʕi)t,** and in agreement with the other conjugational types, there is no vowel difference between perfect and imperfect, e.g. **ʕitʕáwwa, yitʕáwwa** *to become strong* (contrast **ʕáwwa, yiʕáwwi** *to strengthen*).	As for the regular verb, e.g. **ʕidgánnin, yidgánnin** *to go mad.*

Form with (ʕi)t prefixed and aa infixed after C1			
Vowelling is again as for the form without (ʕi)**t**, e.g. **ʕitnáaʕiʃ, yitnáaʕiʃ** *to discuss.*	As for the regular verb, e.g. **ʕiggáawib, yiggáawib** *to be answered.*	Again in contrast with the corresponding form without (**ʕi)t** and in agreement with the other conjugational types, there is no vowel difference between perfect and imperfect, e.g. **ʕiddáawa, yiddáawa** *to be treated, cured* (contrast **dáawa, yidáawi** *to treat, cure*).	No example available.
Form with (ʕi)n prefixed to simple form			
As for (ʕi)**t**- + simple form above e.g. **ʕinkásar, yinkísir** *to be broken.*	As for (ʕi)**t**- + simple form above, e.g. **ʕinbáaɛ, yinbáaɛ** *to be sold.*	As for (ʕi)**t**- + simple form above, e.g. **ʕinɧáka, yinɧíki** *to be told, narrated.*	As for (ʕi)**t**- + simple form above, e.g. **ʕinbáll, yinbáll** *to be wetted, get wet.*

Regular	Hollow	Weak	Doubled
Form with (ʕi)sta prefixed to simple form (with elision of first vowel) As in the case of forms with C2 geminated (with and without (ʕi)t-), the vowel between C2 and C3 is either **a** or **i** depending on the consonants of the syllable, e.g. **ʕistáɛmil, yistáɛmil** *to use,* but **ʕistáɣrab, yistáɣrab** *to be surprised.* There is no vowel difference between perfect and imperfect tenses. *Note.*—A distinction is commonly made in educated colloquial between **yistáhlik** *consumes* and **yustáhlak** *is consumed*; the latter form is borrowed from the written language.	**aa** in the perfect corresponds to **ii** in the imperfect, e.g. **ʕistaʕáal, yistaʕíil** *to resign.* In contrast with the simple form, (**a**)**a** remains throughout the perfect, e.g. **ʕistaʕált** *you* (m.s.)/*I resigned.*	There is no vowel difference between perfect and imperfect, e.g. **ʕistákfa, yistákfa** *to have enough.*	**a** in the perfect usually corresponds to **i** in the imperfect, e.g. **ʕistamárr, yistamírr** *to continue,* but cf. **ʕistaḥáʕʕ, yistaḥáʕʕ** *to deserve.*

Addenda

(i) There is no vowel difference between perfect and imperfect tenses of verbs of colour, e.g. **ʕiḫmárr, yiḫmárr** *to redden, blush.*

(ii) Quadriliteral verbs behave in respect of vowelling in the manner of the forms in which C2 is geminated, cf. **wáʃwiʃ, yiwáʃwiʃ** *to whisper* but **báɣbaɣ, yibáɣbaɣ** *to ogle.*

THE IMPERATIVE

The imperative is derivable in all cases from the 2nd person forms (masc. sing., fem. sing., and plural) of the imperfect, with the prefix omitted but the suffixes (of the fem. sing. and plural forms) retained. Since no form may begin with two consonants, **ʕi-** is required in the imperative forms of

(i) the simple form of regular and weak conjugational types, e.g. **ʕíktib/ʕiktíbi/ʕiktíbu** *write !*, **ʕírmi/ʕírmi/ʕírmu** *throw !*, **ʕílʕa/ʕílʕi/ʕílʕu** *find !*;

(ii) the (C1)**t-** form, all conjugations, e.g. **ʕiʃtáɣal/ʕiʃtáɣali/ʕiʃtáɣalu** *work !*, **ʕixtáar/ʕixtáari/ʕixtáaru** *choose !*, **ʕiʃtíri/ʕiʃtíri/ʕiʃtíru** *buy !*;

(iii) all derived forms containing a prefix, all conjugations, e.g. **ʕitḫáal/ʕitḫáali/ʕitḫáalu** *retire !*, **ʕitkállim/ʕitkallími/ʕitkallímu** *speak !*, **ʕistáɛlim/ʕistaɛlími/ʕistaɛlímu** *inquire !*

Conversely, **ʕi-** is not necessary in the imperative forms of

(i) the simple form, hollow and doubled conjugations, e.g. **ʃiil/ʃíili/ʃíilu** *carry, take away !*, **ruuḫ/rúuḫi/rúuḫu** *go !*, **ḫuṭṭ/ḫúṭṭi/ḫúṭṭu** *put !*;

(ii) the derived form (unprefixed) in which C2 is geminated, e.g. **fáhhim/fahhími/fahhímu** *explain !*;

(iii) the (C1)**aa-** derived form (unprefixed), e.g. **ʕáabil/ʕábli/ʕáblu** *meet !*; notice the feature of elision, expected with vowel-beginning suffixes in such a context.

THE PREFIXES bi- AND ḫa-

Contrast must be made between the use of the imperfect tense (*a*) without prefix and (*b*) with one of two (aspectival) prefixes, **bi-** and **ḫa-**. Compare, for example,

huwwa yíktib iggawáab dilwáʕti *he shall* (or *he is to*) *write the letter now*
huwwa-byíktib iggawáab dilwáʕti *he is writing the letter now*
huwwa ḥayíktib iggawáab dilwáʕti *he is going to write the letter now*

bi- is used when reference is to continuative or habitual action, e.g. **bitiɛmil éeh?** *what are you doing?*, **biyúxrug min ʃúɣlu bádri-f ramaḍáan** *he leaves work early during Ramadan*, **ʕana baɛráfu min múdda ṭawíila ʕáwi** *I've known him for a very long time*, **biyikkállim ɛárabi-kwáyyis** *he speaks Arabic well*.

ḥa- is a future prefix and usually relates to impending action and to the firm intention of doing something; thus, **ḥa-** is used in, say, **ḥaktíblak baɛdi yoméen taláata** *I'll write to you in two or three days' time*, **ḥatínzil fi lukánda?** *are you going to stay in a hotel?* but not in questions which seek instructions as to future action, as **ʕaktíblu walla ʕéeh?** *shall I write to him or what?* or **níḍrab lúhum tilifóon?** *shall we phone them?* Other examples of **ḥa-** are **ʕaẓúnni múʃ min ilmuḥtámal innu ḥayíigi hína ʕabli búkra** *I think it's unlikely he'll be here before to-morrow*, **fih ṭayyáara ḥatʕúum issáaɛa tamánya** *there's a plane taking off at eight o'clock*. The use of the prefix is also to be compared with that of the auxiliary **yíbʕa** (see below under **Other means of time reference**).

In place of **ḥa-**, the invariable **raḥ** or the inflected **ráayiḥ** (m.s.)/**ráyḥa** (f.s.)/**rayḥíin** (pl.) may sometimes be used; **ḥayilɛábu, raḥyilɛábu, rayḥíin yilɛábu** *they are going to play* all occur but the reader is advised to adopt only **ḥa-** for his own use.

Notice the elision of ʕ of the 1st person singular when **bi-** and **ḥa-** are prefixed, e.g. **bálɛab** (**bi** + **ʕalɛab**) *I play, am playing*, **ḥálɛab** (**ḥa** + **ʕalɛab**) *I shall play, am going to play*.

THE IMPERFECT WITHOUT PREFIX

The commonest contexts in which the imperfect tense is used without the particles **bi-** and **ḥa-** are the following:

(1) in association with a series of forms which are themselves largely specialized by use with a following imperfect tense and may be called " auxiliaries ". Auxiliaries may

(i) be of the pattern of the active participle (q.v. *infra*) and regularly inflected for gender and number;

particularly common is **ɛáawiz** (*or* **ɛáayiz**)/**ɛáwza**/**ɛawzíin** *wanting to*, and also noteworthy is **náawi**/**náwya**/**nawyíin** *intending to*; cf. **ɛáawiz táakul?** *do you want to eat?*, **húmma nawyíin yirúuḥu l-issúuʕ** *they intend to go to the market.* Notice, too, **ɛammáal**/**ɛammáala**/**ɛammalíin** as in **ɛammáal aʕúll-úskut** *I'm forever telling him to be quiet*;

(ii) belong to one of three sets of related verbal (including participial) forms, **láazim**/**malzúum**, **múmkin**/**yímkin**, and **gáayiz**/**yigúuz**. All these forms are invariable with the exception of **malzúum**, which is inflected for gender and number.

To consider each set in turn, **láazim** may or may not be associated with pronominal suffixes, usually with some difference of meaning. Examples are: **láazim arúuḥ** *I must, ought to go*, **lazímni-arúuḥ** *it is necessary for me to go, I need to go*, **ʕana malzúum arúuḥ** *I must, am bound to go.* **ɛala** + pronominal suffix is often used in the same way as **láazim**, i.e. **ɛaléek tirúuḥ** *you ought to go*, and **labúdd** is likewise used substantially in the manner of **malzúum**, e.g. **labúddi-trúuḥ** *you must go, are bound to go.* In passing may be noted the related impersonal form **yílzam**, invariable in the form of the 3rd pers. sing. masc. imperfect tense, which is used with and without a pronominal suffix before a following noun, as in **yílzam káam ginéeh?** *how much* (lit. *how many pounds*) *is wanted?*, **yilzámni-flúus** *I need money.*

múmkin and **yímkin** occur both with and without pronominal suffixes, e.g. **múmkin tiddíini kitáabak ʃuwayya?** *could you let me have your book a minute?*, **yímkin tiʃúfhum hináak** (*perhaps*) *you may see them there*, **yimkínn-addíilak xámsa-gnéeh báss** *I can only give you £5.*

gáayiz and **yigúuz** are both necessarily associated with the particle **li** + pronominal suffix, e.g. **gayízl-arúuḥ** *I can* (*am allowed to*) *go*, **yigúzlak tirúuḥ?** *are you able* (sc. *allowed*) *to go?* The use of one form rather than the other seems to involve little or no difference of meaning.

(iii) be one of a set of specialized nominal forms which ar always used with a pronominal suffix agreeing with the following verbal form; these forms are **nifs, bidd ʕaṣd,** and **ɣáraḍ,** the last two of which are frequently interchangeable. Examples are **ʕana nífs-arúuḥ** (= **nifsi** + **ʕaruuḥ**) *I very much want to go,* **ʕúmar bíddu-yráwwaḥ** *Omar would like to go home,* **ʕaṣdúhum** (or **ɣaráḍhum**) **yikkallímu-mʕáah** *they are determined to talk to him.* **nifs** should not be confused with (**bi**) **nafs** in, say, **ʕana-b náfsi ḥarúuḥ** *I'll go myself.*

(2) as an independent form with an imperative sense, e.g. **ma ḥáddiʃ yistáʕmil maktábi w-ana ɣáayib** *nobody is to use my office while I'm away,* **níxlaṣ m-ilkaláam ilfáariɣ** *let's stop talking nonsense*; similar use is observable in conjunction with **ʕáḥsan** or **ʕilʕáḥsan** *better,* as in **núʕʕud hín-áḥsan** *we had better stay here* (lit. *let us stay here, it is better*), **ʕáʃrab máyy-áḥsan** *I would rather drink water,* **ʕilʕáḥsan tirúuḥ f-ilmáɣrib** *you'd better go in the evening*; the 1st pers. pl. form is used with a similar sense following **yálla** and **yálla bíina** as in **yalla-nrúuḥ nitɣádda** *let's go and have lunch,* **yalla bíina nitmáʃʃa** *let's go for a walk.* It may be noted in passing that elsewhere **yálla** is particularly common with a following imperative, as **yálla ráwwaḥ** *go home!,* **yálla áʃrab** *drink up!*

(3) as one, other than the first, of a series of imperfect forms linked by the particle **wi** *and,* **wálla** *or,* or **wála** *nor,* e.g. **la ḥatʃúuf wala tísmaʕ** *you're neither going to see nor hear,* **la-byíʕra wala yíktib** *he neither reads nor writes*; the omission of the prefixes is, however, optional.

(4) in association with and following a number of common verbs including **ʕídir, yíʕdar** *to be able to,* **ʕírif, yíʕraf** *to know how to,* **ḥabb, yiḥíbb** *to like to,* **xálla, yixálli** *to let, allow to,* **fíḍil, yífḍal,** or **ʕáʕad, yúʕʕud** *to continue to,* **fáḍḍal, yifáḍḍal** *to prefer to,* **ʕibtáda, yibtídi** *to start, begin to,* **ḥáawil, yiḥáawil** *to try to,* **nísi, yínsa** *to forget to.* Examples are: **níʕdar nikkállim w-íḥna maʃyíin** *we can talk as we go along,* **yíʕraf yiʕúum** *he can swim,* **nisíit agíibu(h)** *I forgot to bring it,* **ʕan-afáḍḍal asáafir b-iṭṭayyáara** *I prefer going by air,* **ḥaḥáawil abaṭṭálu(h)** *I'm going to try to give it up.* As will have appeared, these verbs are themselves

frequently used without prefix; both **yiɛraf yiɛúum** and **biyiɛraf yiɛúum** are possible. Also very commonly used without prefix to introduce a sentence is **ʕiftákar, yiftikir** *to think*, e.g. **tiftikir issáfar b-ilʕáṭr áḥsan?** *do you think it's better to go by train?* The active participles (see below) of the verbs in the above list are, of course, similarly used where appropriate with a following unprefixed imperfect, cf. **miʃ ʕáadir asmaɛ ḥáaga** *I can't hear a thing*, **miʃ ɛáarif aɛmil éeh** *I don't know what to do*. Notice in passing the invariable form **tann**, which, pronominally suffixed, is often used for **fiḍil, yifḍal**, or **ʕáɛad, yúʕɛud**, e.g. **tannűhum** (or **fiḍlu** or **ʕáɛadu**) **yiʃtáɣalu liḥaddi núṣṣ illéel** *they went on working till midnight.*

(5) following and in agreement with a noun or pronominal suffix when both belong to an object clause as in **xalliihum yistarayyáḥu** *let them rest*, **hiyya ɛawzáak tiɛmillih zayyi kida** *she wants you to do it like this*. The clause may be introduced by the particle **ʕinn** as in **ʕizzáay tintiẓir innűhum yiʃtáɣalu?** *how do you expect them to work?* Conveniently included at this point is the context in which the clause contains two objects, as is commonly the case following **ʕidda, yiddi** *to give*, e.g. **ʕiddiini-taṣriiḥ amḍiih** *give me the permit to sign* (lit. *I sign it*), **miin illi middiik ʕizni timʃi?** *who's given you permission to go?*, in which **middiik** = participle + pronominal suffix.

(6) with a purposive or continuative sense following verbs of motion, as in **xáraɡ yigri** *he came out running*, **ráaḥ yiʃúuf ilmudiir** *he went to see the manager*, **rúuḥ indah innaggáar yiigi-yṣálláḥ ilbáab** *go and tell* (lit. *call*) *the carpenter to come and mend the door.*

(7) in many "greetings" formulae, e.g. **ʕalláah yibáarik fiik** in reply to **mabrúuk** *congratulations!*, **ʕalláah yisallimak** in response to **maɛa-ssaláama** *good-bye!*

(8) in the alternative **ya ... ya ...** *either ... or ...* construction, often with an imperative sense, e.g. **ya-trúuḥ ya tistánna** *either go or stay*, **ya taxúdha, ya ɛáli yaxúdha y-ána-axúdha** *one of us takes her, either you, Ali or me* (lit. *either you take her or . . .*).

(9) after **báɛdi ma** *after*, **ʕábli ma** *before*, **lámma** *when*, **wáʕti ma** *at the time that*, **ɛándi ma** *while*, **bádal ma** *instead of*,

min yéer ma *without*, **ɛalaʃáan** or **ɛaʃáan** *in order to, so that*, and similar particles introducing an adverbial clause, e.g. **báɛdi ma nitɛáʃʃa, ḥanrúuḥ issínima** *we're going to the cinema after dinner* (lit. *after we dine*), **ʕábli ma yíwṣal, ḥayiddílhum xábar** *he'll let them know before he arrives*, **bitrúuḥ ilmadrása ɛa(la)ʃáan titɛállim** *you go to school to learn.*

(10) in the 2nd pers. sing. and pl. only

(i) in the negative imperative, e.g. **ma tidxúlʃ** (or **tud-**) *don't go in !* (**ma -ʃ** is the sign of negation);

(ii) following the "exhortative" particles **ʕiyyáak/-ki/-ku(m)**, **ʕíwɛa/ʕíwɛi/ʕíwɛu** (an imperative series) and **ma** (not to be confused with **ma** of the negative), e.g. **ʕiyyáak tígi wáxri !** *mind you* (masc. sing.) *don't come late !*, **ʕíwɛi-trúuḥi-hnáak !** *mind you* (fem. sing.) *don't go there !*, **ma-trúuḥu-hnáak !** *why don't you go there, then !* Beware of the translation pitfall: **ʕíwɛa ma-tgíiʃ !** = *mind you come*, not **mind you don't come.* **ʕiyyáak** is also used like **ʕinʃálla** in the sense of *I hope*, e.g. **ʕiyyáak tilʕáah hináak** *I hope you'll find him there.*

THE VERB kaan, yikúun

The hollow verb **kaan, yikúun** *to be*, as a means of ringing the changes on the time-reference of sentences, has both independent status and also that of an auxiliary verb used with a following tense (or participle).

Examples of **kaan, yikúun** used as a main verb are **ʕissandúuʕ kan malyáan** *the box was full* (cf. the so-called nominal sentence **ʕissandúuʕ malyáan** *the box is full*), **kúnti** (or **kútti**) **ɛayyáan imbáariḥ** *I was ill yesterday*, **ʕilʕákli ḥaykun gáahiz baɛdi-ʃwáyya** *the meal will soon be ready.* In **fiih**-type sentences and other particle-sentences of a kind noted above (see p. 51 ff.), the verb **kaan, yikúun** is invariable in the 3rd pers. sing. masc. forms, e.g. **kan fiih ḥádsa f-iʃʃáariɛ dilwáʕti** *there was an accident in the street just now*, **ʕana ḥaʕsímha bénku ɛaʃan ma-ykúnʃi fih dáwʃa** *I'm going to divide it between you so that there won't be any quarrelling*, **kan ɛandína waʕti-ktíir** *we had plenty of time*, **ḥaykúun ɛandína-ḍyúuf búkra l-ilyáda** *we shall have guests for lunch to-morrow.* The imperative forms **kuun/-i/-u** are rare; cf. **xallíik ráagil !** *be a man !*

The use of **kaan, yikúun** as an auxiliary in association with the two tenses gives the following range of possibilities: **ʒamal** *he did, has done*/**kaan ʒamal** *he had done*/**yikuun ʒamal** *he will have done*; **biyiʒmil** *he does, is doing*/**kaan biyiʒmil** *he used to do, was doing*/**yikuun biyiʒmil** *he will be doing*; **ḥayiʒmil** *he will do, is going to do*/**kaan ḥayiʒmil** *he was going to do.* Examples are: **kan ʒámal iʃʃúɣlî lamma daxált** *he had done the job when I went in,* **kan biyíʒmil iʃʃúɣlî lamma daxált** *he was doing the job when I went in,* **f-ilwáʕtî dá-ykunu-byiʒmílu-ʃʃúɣl** *they will be doing the job then,* **kuntî ḥáʒmil iʃʃúɣlî-w baʒdéen nisíit** *I was going to do the job but then forgot.* Notice the fact that ***yikuun ḥa-** does not occur and compare the use of **ʕúrrab** + imperfect in, say, **yikun** (or **ḥaykun**) **ʕúrrab yúxrug f-ilwaʕtída** *he'll be about to come out then.*

kaan, yikúun may precede any of the so-called " auxiliaries " (see above), e.g. **kuntî ʒáawiz arúuḥ** *I wanted to go,* **kan bídd-arúuḥ** *I would have liked to go,* **ʕana ʕáasif ma kanʃî mumkínn-agi-mbáariḥ liʕannî kan lazímn-aẓúur axúuya f-ilmustáʃfa** *I'm sorry I couldn't come yesterday but I had to visit my brother in hospital.* In this context, notice the use of the perfect (**ruḥt**) as opposed to the imperfect in, say, **kan láazim rúḥt** *I ought to have gone.*

PARTICIPLES

The simple form of the verb has both an active and passive participle; to memorize the active pattern, notice that it is also that of the masculine ordinal numeral, e.g. **ʒáarif** *knowing, having known,* **ʃáayif** *seeing, having seen* (hollow verb), **máaʃi** *walking* (weak verb), **ḥáaṭiṭ** *putting, having put* (doubled verb): the passive participle is characterized by a prefix **ma-** and, except in the case of the weak verb, by the vowel **-uu-** infixed between the 2nd and 3rd consonants, e.g. **maftúuḥ** *open,* **maʃdúud** *pulled* (doubled verb). The pattern of the weak passive participle is illustrated by **mánsi** *forgotten.* There is no passive participle of the simple form of the hollow verb, cf. **minbáaʒ** or **mitbáaʒ** *sold,* which are the participles of the derived **ʕin-** or **ʕitbáaʒ/yin-** or **yitbáaʒ** *to be sold* (cf. **baaʒ/yibíiʒ** *to sell*). Both participles are inflected for gender and number, i.e. **ʒáarif-ʒárfa/ʒarfíin, ʃáayif-ʃáyfa/ʃayfíin, máaʃi-máʃya/maʃyíin, ḥáaṭiṭ-ḥáṭṭa/ḥaṭṭíin, maftúuḥ-maftúuḥa/maftuḥíin, mánsi-mansíyya/mansiyyíin.**

Derived forms have one participle only; generally speaking, it may be formed by substituting **m-** for **y-** of the 3rd pers. sing. masc. imperfect, e.g. **mitrími** (*having been*) *thrown* (**ʕitráma/yitrími**), **minάḍḍaf** *cleaning, having cleaned* (**náḍḍaf/yináḍḍaf**), **mixálli** *allowing, having allowed* (**xálla/yixálli**), **mitnáḍḍaf** (*having been*) *cleaned* (**ʕitnáḍḍaf/yitnáḍḍaf**), **migáawib** *answering, having answered* (**gáawib/yigáawib**), **mitgáawib** (*having been*) *answered* (**ʕitgáawib/yitgáawib**), **mixtílif** *differing, different* (**ʕixtálaf/yixtílif**), **mixtáar** *choosing,* (*having*) *chosen* (**ʕixtáar/yixtáar**), **minkább** or **mitkább** (*having been*) *poured* (**ʕin-** or **ʕitkább/yin-** or **yitkább**), **minbáaɛ** or **mitbáaɛ** (*having been*) *sold* (**ʕin-** or **ʕitbáaɛ/yin-** or **yitbáaɛ**). Notice those forms of the weak verb in which the participle, in contrast with the imperfect tense, ends in **-i**, e.g. **mitxálli** (*having been*) *left, withdrawn* (**ʕitxálla/yitxálla**), **mitráaḍi** (*having been*) *placated, having agreed* (**ʕitráaḍa/yitráaḍa**), **mistákfi** (*having been*) *satisfied, having had enough* (**ʕistákfa/yistákfa**).

The participle of verbs of colour is characterized by the vowel **-i-** in the second syllable, e.g. **miḥmírr** (*having*) *turned red, blushing* (**ʕiḥmárr/yiḥmárr**).

The prefix **musta-** is often preferred to **mista-** by educated speakers; thus, **musta-** or **mistáɛlim** *inquiring, having inquired* (**ʕistáɛlim/yistáɛlim**), **musta-** or **mistábʃar** *having good news, being optimistic* (**ʕistábʃar/yistábʃar**), **musta-** or **mistaɛídd** *ready* (**ʕistaɛádd/yistaɛídd**). In Classical and Modern Literary Arabic, derived forms of the verb have both an active participle (**-i-** in the final syllable) and a passive participle (**-a-** in the final syllable). In the Egyptian colloquial, this distinction is maintained by educated speakers for certain **musta-** (not **mista-**) participles; **mustáɛmir** *colonist* and **mustáɛmar** *colonized* are " learned " forms but both are in current use. Compare, too, **da-ktáab mustáɛmil** (or **mistáɛmil**) *this is a second-hand book* and **ʕilkitáab dá mustáɛmal** (not **mista-**) **kitíir** *this book is used a lot.* Usage, however, is not always fixed and individual variation is encountered. The " Classical " form is used by educated speakers for some participles of other than the **ʕista-** derived form, e.g. **muxtálif** *different* for **mixtílif**, **munfáɛil** *angry* for **minfíɛil**, **mutaʃákkir** *thank you* for **mitʃákkir**, **mutawáṣṣiṭ** *average* for **mitwáṣṣaṭ**. The use of " learned " participial forms is one of the most characteristic signs of *educated* colloquial. Notice, too, in colloquial usage such contrasts as **miʕállim** *teaching, having taught* (**ʕállim/yiʕállim**) and **muʕállim** *teacher*, **mifáttiʃ** *inspecting, having inspected* (**fáttiʃ/yifáttiʃ**) and **mufáttiʃ** *inspector*.

The participles with suffixes

Final **-a** of feminine forms is lengthened in accordance with the general rule (q.v. *supra*) when a consonant-beginning suffix is added, e.g. **híyya maskáah** *she is holding him/it*, **dí maʕṣuláali-b sítta-gnéeh** *this was sold to me (after bargaining) for £6*.

Although the participle is nominal (adjectival) in form and, unlike the tenses, exhibits no distinction of person, its partly verbal character is revealed by a number of features including its association with the 1st pers. sing. pronominal suffix **-ni** (not **-i**), e.g. **híyya maskáani** *she is holding me*.

Use of the participles

It has just been said that the participle is nominal in form with no distinction of person. It is, therefore, possible to consider, say, **káatib iggawáab** in the sentence **húwwa káatib iggawáab** as a sequence of two nouns in construct and to translate *he is the writer of the letter*. But the participle of many verbs, of which **kátab/yíktib** *to write* is one, may be said to refer to the state of having performed the verbal action, and in the appropriate context the translation of **húwwa káatib iggawáab** is *he has written the letter*. Other verbs, notably verbs of motion, behave differently and it is not surprising that translation in English will often take different forms. Here are some examples:

hiyya-mnaḍḍáfa-lʕóoḍa *she has cleaned the room* (contrast **bitnáḍḍaf ilʕóoḍa** *she is cleaning the room*); **huwwa ráakib ilḥuṣáan** *he is riding (i.e. has mounted) the horse* (contrast **biyírkab ilḥuṣáan** *he is mounting the horse*); **ʕana wáakil** *I have eaten, am full*; **ʕana mistaʕmílha min zamáan** *I have used* (or *been using*) *it for a long time*; **ʕana-mráttib ilhudúum** *I've arranged the clothes*; **humma sakníin fi béet mitráttib kuwáyyis** *they live (i.e. have settled) in a well-appointed house*; **ʕana laʕéetu-mgáawib ʕaléeh** *I found he'd answered it*; **ʕana laʕéetu mitgáawib ʕaléeh** *I found it had been answered*; **ʕana mistanníik baʕáali saʕtéen** *I've been waiting two hours for you*;

huwwa middíini kilma-nnu gáay *he's promised me he'll be coming.*

There is no past-time sense with verbs of motion in the following examples:

huwwa ṭáaliʕ baʕdi-ʃwáyya *he'll be coming out soon* (**ḥa-**, i.e. **ḥayíṭlaʕ**, is possible here and in the following examples); **ʕana-msáafir búkra** *I'm leaving to-morrow*; **ḥásan misáafir máṣr** *Hasan is going to Cairo*; **huwwa náazil dúyri** *he'll be (coming) down right away.*

Past-time reference is similarly often absent when the participle is associated with negation, e.g. **ʕana miʃ wáakil** *I'm not going to eat* (or *I have not eaten*); **hiyya miʃ minaḍḍáfa-lʕóoḍa** *she's not going to clean the room* (or *she hasn't cleaned the room*); **mantaʃ ʕáamil zayyi ma baʕúllak!** *aren't you going to do as I tell you!*

In the common sentence-pattern illustrated by **laʕéetu káatib iggawáab** *I found he had written the letter*, the perfect tense may be used as an alternative to the participle, i.e. **laʕéetu kátab iggawáab**; in the case of verbs of motion, however, a difference of meaning is involved between the use of participle or perfect tense, e.g. **ʃúftu xáarig m-ilbéet** *I saw him coming out of the house* and **ʃúftu xárag m-ilbéet** *I saw him come out of the house.* More striking, however, is the difference of meaning between the two sentences containing the participles **káatib** and **xáarig**; use of the participle **xáarig** in the case of the verb of motion corresponds to that of the imperfect tense with the prefix **bi-** in the case of the non-motive verb, thus compare **ʃúftu xáarig m-ilbéet** *I saw him coming out of the house* with **laʕéetu-byíktib iggawáab** *I found him writing the letter.* With the verb of motion, the imperfect with **bi-** has the sense of habitual action, e.g. **ʃúftu-byúxrug m-ilbéet kúlli yóom** *I saw him come* (or *coming*) *out of the house every day.* Another example of the similar function of the motive participle and the non-motive imperfect tense with **bi-** is provided by **ʕabílna ṣáaliḥ f-issíkka w-iḥna-mrawwaḥíin** *we met Ṣāliḥ in the street as* (= **wi**) *we were going home* and **ʕabílna** (= **ʕaabil** + pronominal suffix **-na**) **ṣáaliḥ f-issíkka w-iḥna-bnitkállim wayya báʕḍ** *Ṣāliḥ met us in the street as we were talking together.* With the prefix **ḥa-**, there is little or no observable difference of use between motive and non-motive verbs, thus **ʃúftu ḥayúxrug m-ilbéet** *I saw him about to leave the house* and **laʕéetu ḥayíktib iggawáab** *I found him about to write the letter.*

Like the tenses, the participle may be preceded by **kaan/yikúun** with corresponding differences in the time-reference of the whole; thus, **lamma daxált kan káatib** (or **kan kátab**) **iggawáab** *he'd written the letter when I went in* and **ʕissítti kanit minaḍḍáfa** (or **kanit naḍḍáfit**) **ilbéet** *the woman had cleaned the house.* There is again difference of behaviour between motive and non-motive verbs, compare **kan káatib iggawáab** *he'd written the letter* with **kan máaʃi f-iʃʃáariʕ** *he was walking in the street*; one says **kan náazil dúɣri lakin ma-nizilʃ** *he was coming down straight away but hasn't done so* but one cannot say ***kan kaatib iggawaab lakin ma katabuuʃ**, cf. **kan ḥayíktib iggawáab lakin ma katabúuʃ** *he was going to write the letter but hasn't done so.* Similarly with **yikúun**, compare and contrast **f-ilwáʕti dá-ykunu xargíin** *they'll be leaving then* and **f-ilwáʕti dá-tkun minaḍḍáfa** (or **naḍḍáfit**) **ilʕóoḍa** *she'll have cleaned the room by then*, **f-ilwáʕti dá-ykunu xárugu** *they'll have left by then*, with **f-ilwáʕti da-tkun bitnaḍḍaf ilʕóoḍa** *she'll be cleaning the room then.* In the pattern exemplified by **laʕéetu ɛáamil ʃúɣlu(h)** *I found he'd done his work*, **kaan** may be included or not before **ɛáamil** with little or no difference in meaning; frequently, however, when **kaan** is included, its inclusion will relate to the presence of a perfect tense form elsewhere in the context, thus **káan ɛáamil** relates to **miʃi** in such an exchange as **A. ʕilwálad miʃi bádri léeh? B. laʕeetu kan ɛáamil ʃúɣlu-w ʕultílu rúwwaḥ.** *A. Why has the boy gone early? B. I found he'd done his work and told him to go home.*

It will be seen from the foregoing that *the greengrocer has closed* is a more literal translation of **ʕilbaʕʕáal ʕáafil** than *the greengrocer('s) is closed*; the corresponding passive participle **maʕfúul** cannot be used with a noun of personal reference but cf. **ʕiddukkáan maʕfúul** *the shop is closed.* As a rule the passive participle of this pattern is purely adjectival in function. In some contexts there is little or no difference between the use of this passive participle and the perfect tense of the derived forms in which the prefixes **ʕit-** and **ʕin-** are associated with the simple form of the verb, thus **ʕana ʕabilt innaggáar wi ʕálli maktábak maɛmúul** (or **itɛámal**) *I met the carpenter and he told me your* *desk is* (or *has been*) *made*; contrast the case of difference between **ʃúft iʃʃibbáak maftúuḥ** *I saw the window* (*was*) *open* and **ʃúft iʃʃibbáak infátaḥ** *I saw the window open* (sc. *of its own accord*). In the majority of contexts the passive participle of the simple form of the verb tends to be preferred to the participles of the derived forms with the passive and intransitive prefixes **ʕit-** and **ʕin-**, thus **mármi** *thrown* rather than **mitrími**, **makbúub** *poured* (*out*) rather than **mitkább** or **minkább**; it should nevertheless be remembered that grammatical statements are generally statements of tendencies rather than watertight rules, and accordingly we cannot use, say, **mábni** for **mitbíni** in **mitbíni gáahiz** *ready-built*: in some contexts, moreover, and notably in association with **líssa**, the two participles are clearly differentiated, thus compare **ʕiddóoraʕ líssa malyáan** *the jug is still full* with **ʕiddóoraʕ líssa mitmíli** *the jug has just been filled*, **ʕiddukkáan líssa maftúuḥ** *the shop is still open* with **ʕiddukkáan líssa mitfítiḥ** *the shop has just been opened*, and **ʕilfustáan líssa mablúul** *the dress is still wet* with **ʕilfustáan líssa mitbáll** *the dress has just been wetted* (or *got wet*). Since **ʕit-** is usually a passive prefix, corresponding derived forms with and without the prefix may be considered passive and active respectively, i.e. **minádḍaf** (active)-**mitnáḍḍaf** (passive) *cleaned*, **migáawib** (active)-**mitgáawib** (passive) *answered*; this also applies to quadriliteral verbs, e.g. **miláxbaṭ** (active)-**mitláxbaṭ** (passive) *confused*.

The fact of two nouns following a participle or tense-form in a transitive construction, as in, say, **ɛáli-mkáttib fáṭmaggawáab** *Ali has made Fatima write the letter*, is readily assimilated by native speakers of English; the similarly constructed **ɛáli ḍáarib ilḥéeṭa búhya** *Ali has painted the wall* (lit. *has struck the wall paint*) or **huwwa ʕáaṭiɛ ilḥábli nuṣṣéen** *he's cut the rope in two* (lit. *has cut the rope two halves*) tend to offer rather more difficulty, but more difficulty still is encountered with corresponding passive forms: cf. **ʕilḥéeṭa maḍrúuba búhya** *the wall is* (or *has been*) *painted*, **ʕiggázma maḍrúuba warniiʃ** *the shoes are* (or *have been*) *polished*, **ʕilɛáṣa mitkassára ḥítat** *the stick has been broken into pieces*, **ʕilxáṭṭi mitʕássim iṭnáaʃar ʕísm** *the line is divided into twelfths*. Cf., too, **ʕilʕóoḍa malyáana náas** *the room is full of people*.

The passive participle of what may be called " prepositional verbs", i.e. those compounded of verb and particle, is invariable in such patterns as **ʕana laʕéetu mitgáawib ɛaléeh** *I found it* (m.) *had been answered*, **maḥkúum ɛaléeha b-issígnī tálat ʃuhúur** *she's been sentenced to three months' imprisonment*, **ʕilfilúus ilmasmúuḥ bíiha** *the permitted currency*. Compare the similar structure of **maksúur li ɛáli ɛáṣa** *one of Ali's sticks is broken*, which is paralleled by the (active) participle of the intransitive verb **ḍaaɛ/yiḍiiɛ** *to be lost* in **ḍáayiɛ li ɛáli-ktabéen** *Ali has lost a couple of his books, two of Ali's books have been lost.*

OTHER MEANS OF TIME-REFERENCE

There are, of course, numerous means of time-reference outside and in association with the system of tenses and participles, with and without **kaan, yikúun.** Particularly noteworthy are

(i) **zamáan** (unsuffixed) in, say, **zaman kanu-byiḥráʕu-lfáḥmi-f ʕafránhum** (*formerly*) *they used to burn charcoal in their ovens*, and **zamáan** + pronominal suffix in, for example, **zamánhum miʃyu** *they came some time ago*, **law kúnna-mʃiina sáaɛit maʕultílak, kan zamánna-hnáak dilwaʕti** (a conditional sentence, q.v. *infra*) *if we'd gone when I said* (*to you*), *we'd have been there some time ago* (or *by now*).

(ii) the verbal form **báʕa** and the prepositional particle **li,** both pronominally suffixed, and the prepositional particle **min,** all three preceding a specific time-word; e.g. **ʕana mistanníik baʕáali núṣṣi sáaɛa** *I've been waiting half an hour for you*, **baʕáali sitt úʃhur ma ʃuftúuʃ** *I haven't seen him for six months*, **híyya f-ilbéet laha saɛtéen** *she's been in the house* (*for*) *two hours*, **ʕáhlan, ma ʃuftákʃī min zamáan hullo,** *I haven't seen you for a long time*..

(iii) the auxiliary **ʕíbʕa/-i/-u** (imperative) and **yíbʕa,** etc. (imperfect), followed by the imperative and imperfect tense respectively, are used to mark future time; e.g. **ṣaḥḥíini-ssaɛa sítta w-ibʕa hátli mayya súxna ɛaʃan ilḥiláaʕa** [1] *call me at 6 o'clock and bring me hot water for shaving* (note that without **ʕíbʕa,** the order would be for the water to be brought at once), **xúd, ʕadi-gnéeh ! w-ibʕa**

[1] **ʕíbʕa** may be placed before the first imperative, i.e. **ʕíbʕa ṣaḥḥíini-ssaɛa sítta-w hátli máyya,** etc.

raggaꜥúuli (or **wi tibʕa-traggaꜥúuli**) **baꜥdéen** *here's a pound! you can return it to me later*, **ʕilʕáḥsan innak tibʕa tisʕal ikkumsáari lamma yiigi yúṭlub ittazáakir** *you'd better ask the ticket-collector when he comes around asking for the tickets*. The use of the auxiliary is to be compared both with that of the prefix **ḥa-** and with that of the imperfect tense alone: **ʕádfaꜥ káam?** and **ʕabʕ-ádfaꜥ káam?** *how much shall I pay?* are both requests for instructions, e.g. from a business superior, as to action which, in the first case, is to be immediate and, in the second, not. Both contrast with **ḥádfaꜥ káam?** *how much am I going to (have to) pay?*, the most likely context for which is a bargaining-match in the market. **ḥa-** may be used with **yibʕa** but, as might be expected, **ḥabʕ-azúrku baꜥdéen** *I'll call on you later* is a less definite, more remote undertaking than **ḥazúrku baꜥdéen.**

CONDITIONAL SENTENCES

ʕiza (or **ʕin** or **law**) **kúnti-trúuḥ búkra, ḥaddíilak ilfilúus**
ʕiza (or **ʕin** or **law**) **rúḥti búkra, ḥaddíilak ilfilúus**
law tirúuḥ búkra, ḥaddíilak ilfilúus

All (seven) of the above possibilities relate to the translation *If you go to-morrow, I'll give you the money*. Of the three conditional particles **ʕiza**, **ʕin**, and **law**, **ʕiza** is the commonest. The main difference between the Arabic patterns above concerns the presence or absence of **kaan** (inflected for person, gender, and number) following the particle; moreover, if **kaan** is included, the following verb is in the imperfect but if **kaan** is omitted, the verb is in the perfect except after **law**, in which case either perfect or imperfect is permissible. Notice that the imperfect **yikúun** is never used after the conditional particles.

The second type of conditional sentence, involving difference of time-reference from the above, exhibits less variety of possible form: **ʕiza** (or **ʕin** or **law**) **kúnti rúḥt imbáariḥ, kúnt iddétlak ilfilúus** *if you had gone yesterday, I would have given you the money*. Egyptians brought up in the schools of traditional grammar may say that only **law** is possible in this context but in fact all three particles are currently used. In this type

kaan is best included after the particle and is invariably followed by the perfect tense, but an even more marked difference from the earlier type is the essential presence of **kaan** in the *second* clause. In the example given, since the context relates to money which was not actually handed over, **ḫaddiilak** is possible for **ʕiddétiak** in the second clause, i.e. **ʕana kúntí ḫaddiilak ilfilúus** *I was going to give you the money*, but in the great majority of cases the perfect tense is necessary after the second **kaan,** as in **ʕiza kúntí géet imbáariḫ, kuntí ʃúftí ɛáli** *if you'd come yesterday, you'd have seen Ali.* **law,** especially followed by the particle **ʕinn,** is sometimes used for greater emphasis, e.g. **law ʕínnak kuntí géet imbáariḫ, kuntí ʃúftí ɛáli** *if* ONLY *you'd come yesterday, etc.* Other practice examples are: **law kunna-mʃiina sáaɛit ma ʕultiilak, kunna-wṣilna-hnáak dilwáʕti** *if we'd left when I told you, we'd have been there now,* **law kúntí ṭalabtáha mínni, kunt iddethàalak** *if you'd asked me for it, I'd have given it to you* and, of the first type, **ʕiza nazzilt ittáman ʃuwáyya, yímkin aʃtíri** *if you brought the price down a bit, I might buy.*

A conditional particle may introduce a nominal clause in the manner of English *if, whether,* e.g. **ʕisʕálu-za kan miggáwwiz** *ask him if he's married*; this, of course, is not an example of the two types of conditional sentence that have been considered above, and the occurrence of the participle (**miggáwwiz**) should be noted and also the fact that **kaan** is essential. With a following tense form, **ʕiza** as well as **kaan** may be omitted, cf. **ma-yhímmiʃ (iza) gúm walla ma gúuʃ** *it doesn't matter whether they come or not.*

The use of **kaan** following the " optative " particle **yaréet** in, say, **yaréet kunt áɛraf innúhum ḫayiigu walla láʕ** *I wish I knew whether they are coming or not* is reminiscent of that in the conditional sentences above.

VERB-SEQUENCES

Verbal forms often immediately succeed each other where in English a linking " and " or a device of rhythm or intonation corresponds; the total verbal complex in Arabic is frequently unitary in the manner of, say, " try and do " or " go and tell " in, for example, " he's gone and told him." Arabic imperative examples are: **xúd iʃrɑb** ! *take and drink !*, **taɛáalu-ʕɛúdu** ! *come* (pl.) *and sit down !*, **rúuḩ ráwwɑḩ** ! *go on home !*, **rúuḩ ʕáblu dilwáʕti** ! *go and see him now !*, **xúdu-ʃrábu(h)** ! *take it and drink it !*, **xúd ikkitáab waddíih l-axúuk** ! *take the book* (*and take it*) *to your brother !*, **rúuḩ índah innaggáɑr yíigi-yṣállɑḩ ilbáab** ! *go and tell* (lit. *call*) *the carpenter to come and mend the door !*

The maximum number of such forms is five, as in the imperfect example **tiḩíbbi tíigi tiʕúum nirúuḩ niẓúur ɛáli ?** *do you want to come and* (lit. *come and get up and go*) *visit Ali ?*, in which it will be seen that a change of person is involved between the first and second parts of the sequence; a partial sequence without change of person is probably limited to a maximum of three forms as in the example. In long sequences of this kind a verb of motion is almost certain to appear. Examples involving the perfect tense are (**ʕiḩna ʕáwwil ma-btadéena niʃtáɣal**) **gum ɛɑṭṭɑlúuna** (*as soon as we started working*) *they came and interrupted us*, **ɛáli ʕáam ṭiliɛ gáab ikkitáab** *Ali went off to fetch the book.*

The verb **ʕaam, yiʕúum** (elsewhere *to stand up*) frequently occurs in these sequences of verbal forms and has already been illustrated. **ʕáam ḍɑrábni** *he hit me* is reminiscent of the jocular English *he upped and hit me*, but that **ʕaam** forms one piece with the following verb and that the meaning of the verb elsewhere is irrelevant to the total piece is shown by the fact that, say, **ʕúmti nimt** = not only *I went off to bed* but also in the appropriate context *I fell asleep*. **ʕaam** serves to punctuate or mark off incidents as they are related as in, say, **miʃiit ʕam ḩáʃni** *I started off but he stopped me* and is especially common in this narrative function in association with **ʕaal** *he said*, e.g. **géh wi ʕálli . . . ʕúmt ana ʕultílu(h) . . . ʕam irrágil ʕálli . . .** *he came up and said to me . . . whereupon I said to him . . . then the man said to me. . . .*

SOME IRREGULAR VERBS

The perfect and imperfect tenses and the imperative of four commonly occurring verbs which do not conform to the standard pattern are as follows:

kal, yáakul *to eat*

	Perfect	*Imperfect*	*Imperative*
Sing.	**kal** (*he*)	**yáakul**	
	kálit (*she*)	**táakul**	
	kalt (*you* (m.s.))	**táakul**	**kul**
	kálti (*you* (f.s.))	**tákli**	**kúli**
	kalt (*I*)	**ʕáakul**	
Pl.	**kálu** (*they*)	**yáklu**	
	káltu (*you*)	**táklu**	**kúlu**
	kálna (*we*)	**náakul**	

xad, yáaxud *to take*

	Perfect	*Imperfect*	*Imperative*
Sing.	**xad**	**yáaxud**	
	xadt	**táaxud**	
	xadt	**táaxud**	**xud**
	xádti	**táxdi**	**xúdi**
	xadt	**ʕáaxud**	
Pl.	**xádu**	**yáxdu**	
	xádtu	**táxdu**	**xúdu**
	xádna	**náaxud**	

Note

dt in **xadt, xádti,** and **xádtu** is pronounced **tt**, i.e. **xatt, xátti,** and **xáttu.** Initial *t* of the perfect suffixes often has special implications as to pronunciation; cf. **ʕaɛád*t*** (pronounced **ʕaɛátt**) *I/you sat down,* **ʕinbaşáṭ*t*** (pronounced **ʕimbaşáṭṭ**) *I was/you were pleased.*

ʕídda, yíddi *to give*

	Perfect	*Imperfect*	*Imperative*
Sing.	**ʕídda** (*he*)	**yíddi**	
	ʕíddit (*she*)	**tíddi**	
	ʕiddéet (*you* (m.s.))	**tíddi**	**ʕíddi**
	ʕiddéeti (*you* (f.s.))	**tíddi**	**ʕíddi**
	ʕiddéet (*I*)	**ʕáddi**	
Pl.	**ʕíddu** (*they*)	**yíddu**	
	ʕiddéetu (*you*)	**tíddu**	**ʕíddu**
	ʕiddéena (*we*)	**níddi**	

geh,[1] **yíigi** *to give*

	Perfect	*Imperfect*
Sing.	**geh**	**yíigi**
	gat	**tíigi**
	geet	**tíigi**
	géeti	**tíigi**
	geet	**ʕáagi**
Pl.	**gum**	**yíigu**
	géetu	**tíigu**
	géena	**níigi**

Note

There is no imperative of **geh, yíigi**; cf. **taɛáala/ taɛáali/ taɛáalu** *come (here)!* **gaa-** and **guu-**, not **geh** and **gum**, are used when a suffix follows, e.g. **gáani** (or **gáali**) *he came to me,* **ma gúuʃ** *they didn't come.*

[1] Or **gih.**

Etymologically, hollow and weak verbs are those with **y** or **w** as 2nd and 3rd radical respectively. Verbs with **y** as 1st radical do not occur and those with **w**, e.g. **wíṣil, yíwṣal** *to arrive*, are regular with two exceptions, viz. **wíʕif, yúʕaf** *to stop* and **wíʕiɛ, yúʕaɛ** *to fall*, in the imperfect tense of which **w** is dropped and the vowel of the first syllable is **u**; thus

	Imperfect	*Imperative*
Sing.	**yúʕaf** (*he*)	
	túʕaf (*she*)	
	túʕaf (*you* (m.s.))	**ʕúʕaf**
	túʕafi (*you* (f.s.))	**ʕúʕafi**
	ʕáʕaf (*I*)	
Pl.	**yúʕafu** (*they*)	
	túʕafu (*you*)	**ʕúʕafu**
	núʕaf	

Note

i is sometimes heard for **u** in the first syllable of these verbs.

VERB + PRONOMINAL SUFFIX

The addition of pronominal suffixes to verbs involves differences of pronunciation, especially in the matters of vowel-length and accentuation, between the suffixed and unsuffixed forms. As has already been remarked above, final vowels are lengthened when a suffix is added, e.g. **fihmu-fihmúuh** *they understood it/him*, **fihmúuha** *they understood it/her*, **fihimti-fihimtíina** *you* (f.s.) *understood us*. Final **-h** of the 3rd pers. sing. masc. suffix is not always pronounced but the final accented long vowel is retained, i.e. **fihmúu**. Again as with nouns, the "extra" vowel will vary with the suffix, e.g. **fihimtína** *you* (m.s.) *understood us*, **fihimtåha** *I/you* (m.s.) *understood her*, **fihimtůhum** *I/you* (m.s.) *understood them*.

Do not confuse the verbal tense suffix **-u** (2nd and 3rd pers. pl.) and the pronominal suffix **-u**(**h**) (3rd pers. sing. masc.); cf. **kátabu** either *they wrote* or *he wrote it*, **bitiɛráfu** either *you* (pl.) *know* or *you* (m.s.) *know him* or *she knows him*.

The particle **li** + pronominal suffix is often added to verbs and has similar implications as to the placing of the accent in comparison with corresponding unsuffixed forms; cf. **ʕísmaḥ** *excuse, forgive !*, **ʕismáḥli** *excuse me !*, **ʕismaḥíili** *excuse* (f.s.) *me !*

The following series of **li**-forms suffixed to verbs will be seen to differ from that given above under **Particles**: **li, lak, lik, lu(h), líha, lína, lúku(m), lúhum.** If the "l-piece" consists of two syllables, i.e. **líha, lína, lúku(m), lúhum,** and if the verbal form ends in a consonant, then **líha, lína,** etc., are treated as separate words from the point of view of accentuation, e.g. **ʕísmaḥ lína** *excuse us!* If, on the other hand, the verb ends in a vowel, then the vowel following **l** is elided and the whole complex of verb + **l**-piece treated as one word, e.g. **ʕismaḥúlna** *excuse* (pl.) *us!*, **ʕismaḥílha** *excuse* (f.s.) *her!*

Double suffixation

It is quite common for both a pronominal suffix and an **l**-piece to be added in that order to a verb, in which case the same rules of accentuation as those given in the preceding paragraph obtain. This feature is especially frequent with **ʕídda, yíddi** *to give*, e.g. **ʕiddiháali** *give it* (f.) *to me!*, **ʕiddíhli** *give it* (m.) *to me!*, **ʕiddetúlha** either *I/you* (m.s.) *gave it* (m.) *to her* or *you* (pl.) *gave to her*, **ʕiddetháalu(h)** *I/you* (m.s.) *gave it* (f.) *to him*, **ʕiddéthum lúhum** *I/you* (m.s.) *gave them to them*. Other examples are **hathálha** *bring it* (f.) *to her!*, **ʕimlahúmlu(h)** *fill them for him!*, **ʕimlahálhum** *fill it* (f.) *for them!*, **ʕimláahum lúhum** *fill them for them!*

THE VERBAL NOUN

Verbal nouns of the simple form of the verb are of more than one pattern; **ḍɑrb** *striking*, **ʃurb** *drinking*, **ʕámal** *doing*, **duxúul** *entering*, are examples, among which **ḍɑrb** illustrates the commonest pattern. Patterns of derived forms are fixed; where plural forms of the verbal noun occur, these are regularly in **-aat**, e.g. **taʕlimáat** *instructions*, **miʕaksáat** *quarrels*. Derived patterns, illustrated by regular verbs, are as follows:

Verb (Perfect)	*Verbal Noun*
ʕállim (*he taught*)	**taʕlíim** (pl. **taʕlimáat**) *teaching, instruction*
ʕáakis (*he quarrelled*)	**miʕáksa** (pl. **miʕaksáat**) [1] *quarrelling, quarrel*

[1] There is a tendency among educated speakers to use **mu-** for **mi-** as the prefix in verbal nouns of this form, cf., too, **muʃáwra** *consultation*. The loan-word **munáwra** *manoeuvre* exhibits the same pattern.

Verb (Perfect)	*Verbal Noun*
ʔiɛtáraf (*he confessed*)	**ʔiɛtiráaf** (pl. **ʔiɛtirafáat**) *confessing, confession*
ʔinfágar (*it exploded*)	**ʔinfigáar** (pl. **ʔinfigaráat**) *exploding, explosion*
ʔistáɛlim (*he inquired*)	**ʔistiɛláam** (pl. **ʔistiɛlamáat**) *inquiring, inquiry*
ʔikkábbar (*he was self-satisfied*)	**takábbur** *self-satisfaction*
ʔitfáahim (*he came to an understanding* (*with*))	**tafáahum** *understanding*

Note

There is no **ʔit-** form corresponding to **ʔinfigáar.**

In the derived forms characterized by gemination of the second radical, by the infixation of long **aa,** and by the infixation of **t,** the verbal nouns of weak verbs end in **-iya, -ya,** and **-a** respectively, e.g. **tasníya** *seconding, supporting* (**sánna, yisánni** *to second, support*), **minádya** *calling* (**náada, yináadi** to call), **ʔibtída** (**ʔibtáda, yibtídi** *to begin*). The verbal noun of weak verbs is only common in these forms. The consonant **y** appears in the verbal noun of hollow verbs when in the form derived by the infixation of **t,** e.g. **ʔixtiyáar** *electing, election* (**ʔixtáar, yixtáar** to elect).

The verbal nouns of the "colour" verbs and quadriliteral verbs are of the patterns illustrated by **ʔiḥmiráar** *turning red, blushing* (**ʔiḥmárr, yiḥmárr** *to redden, blush*) and **laxbáṭa** *muddling, muddle, confusion* (**láxbaṭ, yiláxbaṭ** *to muddle, confuse*).

In accordance with the rule that a noun may not be defined more than once, when the verbal noun governs either two nouns or a pronominal suffix and a noun then the particle **li** must be included between the two; e.g. **ḍárbu l-ilɛiyáal b-iʃʃaklída muʃ kuwáyyis** *his beating the children like that isn't right,* **kitábt** (< **kitáaba**) **ilwálad l-iggawáab yámda giddan** *the boy's writing of the letter is completely illegible.*

Certain verbal nouns of the simple form are similar to collective nouns in that they may be suffixed with **-a** and **-aat** when reference is to the number of times an action is performed, e.g. **ḍarábtu ḍárba gámda ʔáwi** *I gave him a really terrific blow,* **ḍarábtu tálat ḍarbáat ɛala wiʃʃu(h)** *I hit him three* *times on his face.* In this intensive use the verbal noun usually follows a given tense-form of the same root.

Further examples of the verbal noun are as follows:

xad wáʕtĭ ṭawiil fi ʕamálha laṭiifa b-iʃʃaklída (verbal noun **ʕámal**) *he took a long time to make it* (f.) *as nice as that,* **fih máaniʕ min ʕuʕáadi hína ?** (**ʕuʕáad**) *is there any objection to* (or *do you mind*) *my sitting here ?,* **ʕana-smíʕtĭ ʕan muʕablítku maʕa báʕḍ** (**muʕábla**) *I heard of your meeting* (or *that you had met*) *each other,* **ma baḥíbbĭʃ migíyyu hína-ktiir** (**migíyy**) *I don't like him* (or *his*) *coming here a lot,* **ʕilmáʃyi-f wúsṭ iʃʃáariʕ xáṭar ʕaléek** (**maʃy**) *it's dangerous* (*for you*) *to walk in the middle of the road,* **huwwa miʕtimid ʕala-msaʕdíthum lú(h)** (**musáʕda**) *he's counting on them* (or *their*) *helping him,* **ma fiʃ fáyda m-ilgidáal** (**gidáal**) *it's no use arguing.*

THE PHRASE- AND CLAUSE-MARKERS ʕilli AND ʕinn

ʕilli usually introduces an adjectival (relative) phrase, less commonly a nominal one; **ʕinn** introduces a subordinate nominal clause only.

ʕilli

ʕilli is to be seen within the total context of " definition " (see above). By joining either of the sentences **biyízʕal bisúrʕa** *he loses his temper quickly* or **yistaḥáʕʕ ittarʕíya** *he deserves promotion* to **huwwa ráagil** *he is a man* we obtain the new sentences **huwwa ráagil biyízʕal bisúrʕa** *he is a man who loses his temper quickly* and **huwwa ráagil yistaḥáʕʕ ittarʕíya** *he is a man who deserves promotion,* in the English translation of which the relative *who* is required to introduce the qualifying phrase. Now, if the same original sentences are joined to **huwwa-rráagil** *he is* THE *man,* then **ʕilli** is necessary in Arabic, i.e. **huwwa-rráagil illi-byízʕal bisúrʕa** *he is the man who loses his temper quickly* and **huwwa-rráagil illi yistaḥáʕʕ ittarʕíya** *he is the man who deserves promotion.* **ʕilli** is necessary if the preceding noun is defined. This is reminiscent of noun-adjective agreement with and without the article as in **ráagil ṭawiil** *a tall man,* on the one hand, and **ʕirráagil iṭṭawiil** *the tall man,* on the other; compare similarly **ṣaḥíbna-lmáṣri** *our Egyptian friend* and **ṣaḥíbna-lli tiʕrafúuh** *our friend whom you know* (*him*).

In fact, **ʕilli**, the definite article **ʕil**, and other such " definers ", occur in different, that is mutually exclusive, grammatical contexts. **ʕilli** introduces an adjectival (relative) *phrase*, which, in the corresponding indefinite context, either (i) begins with a verb or (ii) consists variously of a prepositional phrase or an adverb. The verbal form **biyṣálli**, for example, behaves adjectivally in, say, **ráagil biyṣálli** *a man saying his prayers*, which should be compared with **fiih ráagil biyṣálli** *a man is saying his prayers* (or *there is a man saying his prayers*) and, more particularly for the present purpose, with the definite **ʕirráagil illi biyṣálli** *the man* (*who is*) *saying his prayers*. Parallel to the difference between **ráagil biyṣálli** (indefinite) and **ʕirráagil illi biyṣálli** (definite) is that between, say, **ráagil ʕa-lbáab ʕáyzak** (indefinite) *a man at the door wants you* and **ʕirráagil illi ʕa-lbáab ʕáyzak** (definite) *the man at the door wants you*, in which **ʕa-lbáab** is a prepositional phrase qualifying **ráagil.**

In certain contexts not only the presence or absence of the article with the noun but also a difference of prepositional particle in the prepositional phrase relates to the indefinite-definite distinction. It is possible for **ʕirráagil illi min máṣr** (definite) *the man from Cairo* to correspond to **ráagil min máṣr** (indefinite) *a man from Cairo* but the more usual definite form is **ʕirráagil bitaʕ máṣr,** in which **bitáaʕ** marks the definite nature of the adjectival phrase in the same way as **min** characterizes the indefinite **min máṣr.** A similar distinction to that between **min** and **bitáaʕ** holds between **bi** and **ʕábu/ʕumm** in, say, **wálad bi bálṭu** (indefinite) *a boy in a coat* and **ʕilwálad abu bálṭu** (definite) *the boy in a coat*; **ʕábu** is used when the antecedent is masculine, as in the example given, while **ʕumm** relates to a feminine context, e.g. **ʕissáaʕa-lfáḍḍa ʕummi ʕástik gild** *the silver watch with a leather strap.*

The vocative context, marked by the vocative particle **ya,** should be specially noticed. It has been said that a noun may not be defined more than once and this is borne out in the vocative example **ya wálad ya ṭawiil** *I say, the tall young man there !*, wherein the occurrence of **ya** excludes the definite article, cf. **ʕilwálad iṭṭawiil** *the tall young man.* In the case of noun + adjectival phrase, however, not only is **ya** repeated before each element in the manner required by the definite concord pattern but also **ʕilli, bitaaʕ,** or **ʕabu** remain to mark the phrasal nature of the second element, e.g. **ya ráagil ya-lli**

bitṣálli[1] *I say, the man there saying his prayers !*, **ya wálad ya ṭawíil ya-lli-hnáak** *I say, the tall young man over there !*, **ya ráagil ya-btaɛ máṣr** *I say, you from Cairo !*, **ya wálad y-abu bálṭu** *I say, the boy in the coat !*

To sum up, attention should be paid particularly to difference of grammatical types as follows:

Indefinite	*Definite*	*Definite-Vocative*
ráagil ṭawíil	**ʕirráagil iṭṭawíil**	**ya ráagil ya ṭawíil**
ráagil biyṣálli	**ʕirráagil illi biyṣálli**	**ya ráagil ya-lli bitṣálli**
ráagil min máṣr	**ʕirráagil bitaɛ / illi min } máṣr**	**ya ráagil ya-btaɛ / ya-lli min } máṣr**
ráagil bi bálṭu	**ʕirráagil abu bálṭu**	**ya ráagil y-abu bálṭu**

The above patterns are to be distinguished from that of the nominal sentence and of the sentence pattern comprising definite noun + verb:

ʕirráagil ṭawíil *the man is tall*
ʕirráagil biyṣálli *the man is saying his prayers*
ʕirráagil min máṣr *the man is from Cairo*
ʕirráagil bi bálṭu *the man is in a coat*

In **fiih**-type sentences it is the indefinite noun-adjective phrase which follows **fiih**:

fih ráagil ṭawíil gúwwa *a tall man is inside*
fih ráagil biyṣálli gúwwa *a man is saying his prayers inside*
fih ráagil min máṣrĭ gúwwa *a man from Cairo is inside*
fih ráagil bi bálṭu gúwwa *a man in a coat is inside*

ʕilli is also used without a preceding noun and in the manner of English *he who, those who, that which* to introduce a nominal phrase or clause, e.g. **ʕilli ɛandúhum filúus ɛandúhum nufúuz** *those with money have influence*, **háat illi fiih, ma ɛaléhʃ** *never mind* (= **ma ɛaléhʃ**), *fetch what there is*, **háat wáaḥid m-illi** (= **min** + **ʕilli**) **fóoʕ iṭṭarabéeẓa** *bring one of those (which are) on the table*, **xúd ill-ínta ɛáyzu(h)** *take what you want.* It is similarly used following the interrogative particles **miin** and **ʕeeh**, as in **míin illi wáaʕif hináak ?** *who is that standing over there ?*, **ʕéeh illi ɛáawiz tiɛráfu(h) ?** *what is it (that) you want to know ?* and, following the demonstrative pronoun, as in **dá-ll-ana ɛáwzu(h)** *that's what I want.*

With a definite antecedent, including demonstratives, the use of the 3rd person pronominal forms **húwwa/híyya/húmma**

[1] Notice the *2nd* person verbal form.

in association with following **ʕilli** characterizes a type of nominal sentence which is to be contrasted with the adjectival phrase. Compare **ʕilʕálam húwwa-lli ḍáaɛ** *it's the pen which has been lost* and **ʕilʕálam illi ḍáaɛ** *the lost pen*, also **ɛiyáal ḥásan húmma-lli bárra** *it's Hasan's children* (*who are*) *outside* and **ɛiyáal ḥásan illi bárra** (*those of*) *Hasan's children* (*who are*) *outside*. Contrast should also be made between sentence types with and without (**húwwa**/etc. + **ʕilli**), for example between the above **ʕilʕálam húwwa-lli ḍáaɛ** and **ʕilʕálam ḍáaɛ** *the pen has been lost*. The two patterns are used in somewhat different circumstances; **ʕilʕálam ḍáaɛ** would as a rule open a conversation, while its counterpart containing **huwwa-lli** would tend to be contrastive and to constitute a reply to another speaker. Other examples illustrating (**húwwa**/etc. + **ʕilli**) in association with a preceding demonstrative, pronominal and adjectival, are **da húwwa-lli ḍarábni** *he's* (or *that's*) *the one who hit me*, **ʕilbéet da húwwa-lli kúnna sakníin fiih** (or **da-lbéet illi kúnna sakníin fiih**) *that's the house we used to live in*.

A number of examples in the preceding paragraphs have contained an important feature already illustrated without comment elsewhere but particularly common in association with adjectival phrases, both definite and indefinite. A " conjoint " relationship between the noun and its qualifying phrase is indicated by the presence in the phrase of a pronominal suffix agreeing with the noun; the same device may also serve to link sentence-clauses. The presence or absence of the pronominal suffix often corresponds to such an English difference as that between, on the one hand, *whom* and *whose* and, on the other, *who*. " Conjoint " relationship covers the case of, say, **ʃahr** and **ismu** in **biyḥíggu-f ʃáhr ismu-lḥúgga** *they go on pilgrimage in a month called* (lit. *its name is*) *Al-Hugga*, as well as those of **ɛarabíyya** and **ṭalabtáha** in **ʕilɛarabíyya-lli ṭalabtáha mawgúuda**? *is the car I asked for ready?*, and of **waʕt** and **fiih** in **ʕéeh ʕánsab wáʕti ʕáʕdar aʃúufu fiih**? *what's the best time* (*at which*) *I could see him?* Further examples are:

Indefinite

zuhriyyáat ɛaléeha náʕʃ *engraved flower-vases* (lit. *flower-vases on them* or *on which engraving*), **fiih wáaḥid bárra ɛándu ʃákwa** *there's someone outside with a complaint*, **ʕúlli ɛala táman**

kúllī ḥáaga-ʃtarétha *tell me the price of everything you bought,* **ɛandína ʃúɣlī-ktiir lazim niɛmílu(h)** *we've a lot of work to do,* **ḥaʃtíri-ʃwáyyit ḥagáat abɛátha hadáaya-l ʕaṣḥáabi** *I'm going to buy a few things to send as presents to my friends,* **fiih sanadiiʕ búṣṭa maxṣúuṣa maktúub ɛaléeha " mustáɛgil "** *there are special post-boxes marked " Express "* (or *with " Express " written on them*).

Definite

ṣáḥbi-lli béetu f-ilḥáyy iggidíid *my friend whose house is in the new quarter,* **ʕahó-rráagil illi ʕultílak ɛaléeh** *there goes the man I told you about,* **ʕáadi-rragil ill-ínta ɛáwzu(h)** *there's the man you want,* **ɛágabak ikkitáab illi warretúulak imbáariḥ ?** *did you like the book I showed you yesterday ?*

ʕinn

The nominal clause introduced by **ʕinn** *that* occurs most frequently as a subordinate object-clause following one of a series of verbs including **símiɛ, yísmaɛ** *to hear,* **ʕiftákar, yiftíkir** or **ẓann, yiẓúnn** *to think, believe,* **ʃaaf, yiʃúuf** *to see,* **ɛírif, yíɛraf** *to know,* **ʕaal, yiʕúul** *to say,* **xaaf, yixáaf** *to fear,* e.g. **simíɛt inni ɛáli (ḥa)yíwṣal búkra** *I hear(d) (that) Ali is arriving to-morrow,* **ʕaftíkir inn ilwálad ráaḥ ilbéet** *I think the boy went home,* **ʕaẓúnn inni ɛandúhum filúus kitíir** *I think they've got a lot of money,* **nífriḍ inni ma ɛátʃi fiih** *let's suppose there isn't any more.* **ʕinn** is followed, where appropriate, by the pronominal suffixes, not by the independent pronouns; e.g. **ʕaftíkir innu raḥ ilbéet** *I think he went home,* **ʕaftíkir innak ɛáarif ill-ána ḥaʕulúulak** *I think you know what I am going to say to you,* **huwwa biyʕúul innu-tnáʕal lakin aftíkir innu-tráfad** *he says he's been transferred but I think he's been dismissed,* **huwwa ɛayyáan b-ilḥáṣba w-ana xáayif innu yíɛd-axúuh iṣṣuɣáyyar** *he's got measles and I'm afraid he'll give it to* (lit. *infect*) *his young(er) brother.* The demonstrative pronoun may be similarly suffixed to **ʕinn** as in **ʕana ma kúntiʃ ɛáarif innída kan ittartíib** *I didn't know that was the arrangement.*

ʕinn also occurs after a few impersonal verbs such as **yíẓhar** in, say, **yíẓhar inni fih fáyda mínnu(h)** *it seems there's some point in it,* but, although post-verbal occurrence of **ʕinn** is by far the most frequent circumstance, it is nevertheless possible for the particle to occur without a preceding verbal form[1]; e.g. **ʕana mabṣúuṭ innak géet** *I'm pleased you came*, **ʕínta mutaʕákkid innak muʃ ɛáwzu(h)?** *are you sure you don't want it?*, **múʃ min ilmuḥtámal innu ḥayíigi hína búkra** *it's unlikely he'll come here to-morrow*, **ʕilʕáḥsan innína-nrúuḥ bádri** *it's best for us to go early*, **ʕilʕimáan maɛnáah inn ilwáaḥid yiʕáamin bi-lláah** *the meaning of faith is that one believes in God*, **muhímmi ʕáwi-nní kúlli wáaḥid yitbaɛ niẓáam ilmurúur** *it is very important that everyone should* (or *for everyone to*) *follow the rule of the road*, **ʕilɣaráaba-nni ma fiiʃ ʃákk innak bitʕúul ilḥáʕʕ** *the extraordinary thing is that there's no doubt you're telling the truth.*

NEGATION

The means of negation are:

(1) a negative particle variously pronounced **muʃ** or **miʃ** *not* which precedes the word, phrase, or clause negated;

(2) a "split" negative (of the French *ne . . . pas* type) in which a particle **ma** precedes and **ʃ** is suffixed to the word negated;

(3) **la . . . wala . . .** *neither . . . nor . . .*

These particles are distributed as follows:

(1) is used

(i) with nouns, adjectives, participles, adverbs, prepositional phrases, clauses, etc., and especially within the framework of the nominal sentence; e.g. **múʃ ilwálad** *not the boy*, **múʃ bi súrɛa kida** *not so fast*, **múʃ min ixtiṣáaṣi** *it's not (of) my responsibility*, **ʕana miʃ fáahim da b-iẓẓábṭ** *I haven't understood that properly*, **ʕiḥna fúʕara, miʃ aɣníya** *we're poor, not rich*, **múʃ bassi kida** *that's not all* or *not only that*, **ʕiggazmáadi miʃ ɛala ʕáddi** *these shoes don't fit me*, **ʕilḥukúuma w-iggéeʃ múʃ ḍiddi báɛḍ** *the government and the army are not opposed to one another*, **ʕilʕúuṭa di lissa xáḍra-ʃwayya, miʃ mistiwíyya** *this tomato is still a bit green, it's not ripe*, **dí muʃ ill-ana ɛáwzu b-iẓẓábṭ** *this isn't exactly what I want*, **dí miʃ ʕáwwil márra-tʕúlli ɛaláada** *this isn't the first time you've told me about it.*

(ii) with the verbal auxiliaries of participial form, e.g. **ɛáawiz, láazim, múmkin**; e.g. **muʃ ɛáawiz táakul?**

[1] *sc.* tense-form.

don't you want to eat?, **muʃ láazim tiʃtiri** *you don't have to buy*, **muʃ múmkin óṭlaʕ dilwaʔti** *I can't come out now.*

(iii) with a following imperfect prefixed with **ḥa-**, e.g. **miʃ ḥáʔdar aʃúufak búkra** *I'm not going to be able to see you to-morrow*, **ʔin ma-ʃribtiʃ iddáwa, miʃ ḥatxiff** *if you don't take the medicine, you won't get better*, **ʔinnáas ilmadʕuyyiin miʃ ḥayáklu-w yiʃrábu-w húmma waʔfiin** *the guests aren't going to eat and drink standing up.*

(2) is used

(i) with verbal forms other than the imperfect prefixed with **ḥa-**, e.g. **ma-tsúʔʔiʃ ʔáktar min arbiʕiin kiilu f-issáaʕa** *don't drive at more than 40 kilometres an hour*, **ma-txáfʃ! ma yiʔdárʃi yidḥak ʕaláyya** *don't worry, he can't get the better of me*, **ma-ftikirʃ innak ḥatilʔáaha ṣáʕba** *I don't think you'll find it difficult*, **ma-ʔdírtiʃ áagi f-ilmaʕáad** *I couldn't arrive on time*, **da suʔáal ana m-aʔdárʃ agáawib ʕaléeh** *that's a question I can't answer*, **ma gatlúuʃ ʕiláawa ʕaʃan ma-byiʃtaɣálʃi-kwáyyis** *he hasn't had a rise* (lit. *a rise has not come to him*) *because he doesn't work well*, **ʔúllu ma-ygiiʃ táani** *tell him not to come again.*

Notes

(*a*) There is no special imperative form in the negative context; the appropriate imperfect forms are used.

(*b*) **ʃ** is always last in a group of suffixes added to a verbal form. As in the case of other suffixes, the addition of **ʃ** implies the lengthening of a preceding vowel, e.g. **ma katabúuʃ** either *they didn't write* or *he didn't write it*; contrast **ma katabúuʃ** with **ma katabúhʃ** *they didn't write it*. The "extra" vowel will frequently appear before **ʃ** in order to obviate a sequence of three consonants, e.g. **ma ruḥtiʃ** *I didn't go.*

(*c*) A maximum of three suffixes—excluding those of the tenses—may be added *en bloc* to a given form. Such a block consists of (pronominal suffix + (**li** + pron. suff.) + **ʃ**) and is illustrated by **ma baʕathaalíiʃ** *he didn't send it* (fem.) *to me*, of which **ma baʕatháaʃ líyya** is an alternative form. The second alternative containing the independent (**li** + suffix) form is essential in some contexts, probably for rhythmic reasons, e.g. **ma raggaɛháaʃ líyya** *he didn't return it to me* (not ***ma raggaɛhaaliiʃ**).

(*d*) **ʃi** is sometimes heard for **ʃ** before pause, e.g. **ma waʕʕaɛháaʃi** or **ma waʕʕaɛháaʃ** *he didn't drop it* (fem.). Further research may establish a connection between **ʃi** and feminine contexts but for practical purposes **ʃ** may always be used.

(*e*) The forms **gaa** and **guu** for **geh** and **gum** are used with **ʃ** as with other suffixes, e.g. **ma gáaʃ** *he didn't come, hasn't come,* **ma gúuʃ** *they didn't come, haven't come.*

(*f*) In the perfect tense of doubled and weak verbs, **-at-** not **-et-** appears in negative forms containing pronominal suffixes, e.g. **ʕana/ʕinta ma ḥabbatúuʃ** *I/you* (m.s.) *didn't like it,* **ʕinta ma kawatúuʃ** *you haven't ironed it.*

(ii) with verbal auxiliaries other than those at (1) (ii), i.e. both those of verbal form, as **yímkin, yigúuz,** and also **bidd-, nifs-, ʕaṣd,** and **ɣáraḍ,** e.g. **ma yimkínʃi ḥáddi yúdxul min ɣéer tazkára** *no one can go in without a ticket,* **ma-yguzlákʃ** *you may not,* **ma biddúuʃ yiráwwaḥ** *he would rather not go home.*

(iii) with the pronominally suffixed particles **ɛand, maɛa, li,** and **fi,** e.g. **ma ɛandináaʃ wáʕti-ktiir** *we haven't much time,* **ma-mɛáhʃi-flúus yídfaɛ táman ilʕákl** *he hasn't any money to pay for* (*the price of*) *the meal,* **da ma lúuʃ máɛna xáalis** *it doesn't make* (lit. *it hasn't any*) *sense at all,* **ʕilʕóoḍa ma fiháaʃ ʃabablik kifáaya ɛaʃan ittahwíya** *there aren't enough windows in the room for ventilation.*

Notes

(*a*) Of the particles which, pronominally suffixed, so frequently translate English *to have,* **ɛand, maɛa,** and **li** are associated with **ma -ʃ,** and so contrast with **wayya,** which is negated with **muʃ** (or **miʃ**), i.e. **míʃ wayyáaya** *I haven't* (*got it*), not ***ma wayyayaaʃ.**

(*b*) With **maɛa** and **li, ii** is used in the first pers. sing. negative, i.e. **ma-mɛiiʃ, ma liiʃ** (contrast **maɛáaya** and **líyya**); **maliyyáaʃ** occurs, but rarely.

(*c*) The vowel of the particle is elided in **ma l(a)háaʃ, ma l(i)kiiʃ, ma l(u)húmʃ, ma l(u)kúmʃ, ma l(i)náaʃ, ma m(a)ɛiiʃ, ma m(a)ɛákʃ, ma m(a)ɛakiiʃ,** etc.

(*d*) **ma ɛaléhʃ** *never mind, it doesn't matter* is an example of a form which occurs only in the negative; other examples are the impersonal verbals **ma-yhímmiʃ** *it doesn't matter, it's unimportant,* **ma-yṣáḥḥiʃ** *it's impossible.* Notice, too, the use of **ma ɛadʃ** (pronounced **ɛatʃ**) and **ma ɛadítʃ** in, say, **ma ɛátʃi fiih** *there isn't any more,* **ʕikkóora ma ɛadítʃi bitnúṭṭi-kwáyyis** *the ball doesn't bounce properly any longer.*

(iv) as the negative form of **fiih** *there is/are,* e.g. **ma fiiʃ máɛna-l lintiẓáar** *there's no point in waiting,* **ma fiiʃ luzúum l-izzáɛal** *there's no need to be angry* (lit. *for anger*), **ma fiiʃ** *there isn't any,* **ma fiiʃ ɛandína** (or **ma ɛandínáaʃ**) **béeḍ l-ilfuṭúur** *we haven't any eggs for breakfast.*

Note

No **h** is pronounced in the negative form **ma fiiʃ** corresponding to the affirmative **fiih. ma fiiʃ ḥáddi f-ilbéet** and **ʕilbéet ma fihʃi ḥádd** *there's nobody in the house* mean the same but are not equivalent grammatically; in the second example **h** is necessary in agreement with **beet** in the same way as **haa** was required in the earlier example of **ʕilʕóoḍa ma fiháaʃ ʃababíik kifáaya ɛaʃan ittahwíya** *there aren't enough windows in the room for ventilation.*

(v) with examples of all the above four categories, when compounded with **kaan, yikúun**; it is **kaan, yikúun** that takes **ma -ʃ,** e.g. **ma kánʃi-byiʃtáɣal ɛandína?** *didn't he used to work for us?,* **ma kúntiʃ áɛraf innúhum ʃuṭṭáar zayyi kída** *I didn't know they were as clever as that,* **ma kúntiʃ ɛáawiz arúuḥ** *I didn't want to go,* **ʕana ʕáasif ma kanʃi mumkinn-agi-mbáariḥ** *I'm sorry I couldn't come yesterday,* **ma kánʃi-mɛáaya wála wáḥda** *I didn't have a single one on me,* **ʕaḥyáanan ma biykúnʃi fiih** *as a rule there isn't any.*

Note

In conditional sentences (see above), either **kaan** or the following verb may take **ma -ʃ,** e.g. **ʕiza ma kúntiʃ tiigi búkra, ḥaddíilu-lfilúus,** or **ʕiza kúnti ma-tgiiʃ,** etc., *if you don't come to-morrow, I'll give him the money.*

(vi) as an alternative to **muʃ** (or **miʃ**), with the independent pronouns. These negative pronouns, written as single forms, are as follows; notice particularly the use of **ii** in the 1st pers. sing. form and the existence of alternative forms for the 3rd pers. sing. masc. and fem.:

	Singular		*Plural*
3rd pers. masc.	**mahuwwáaʃ** (or **mahúuʃ**)	3rd pers.	**mahummáaʃ**
3rd pers. fem.	**mahiyyáaʃ** (or **mahíiʃ**)		
2nd pers. masc.	**mantáaʃ**	2nd pers.	**mantúuʃ**
2nd pers. fem.	**mantíiʃ**		
1st pers.	**maníiʃ**	1st pers.	**maḥnáaʃ**

Examples are **mantíiʃ gáyya-** (or **gáaya-**) **mɛáana?** *aren't you* (fem.) *coming with us?*, **mántaʃ ɛáamil záyyi ma baʕúllak?** *aren't you going to do as I tell you?*, but alternative forms **muʃ ínti,** etc., and **muʃ ínta,** etc., are possible and, indeed, **muʃ** + pronoun is far more generally used than the "split" negative forms above.

(3) contains a negative particle **la** in the negative alternative construction corresponding to English *neither . . . nor . . . .* **wa** is prefixed to every **la** after the first and the number of words, phrases, or clauses which may be preceded by the particle is not limited to two. Examples are **láada** (= **la** + **da**) **waláada lakin dúkha** *neither this nor this but that,* **la-ṣɣáyyar wala-kbiir ʕáwi lakin mutawáṣṣiṭ** *neither too* (lit. *very*) *small nor too big but average,* **la ḥatʃúuf wala tismaɛ** *you'll neither see nor hear,* **la binzáwwid wala binnáʕʕaṣ, kaláinna wáaḥid** *we don't put our prices up or down, we have fixed prices* (lit. *our speech is one*), **ma káanʃi yiɛraf yiʕra wala yiktib** *he could neither read nor write,* **la géh ɛandína f-ilmáktab wala ʕáabil ilmudiir wala ḥáddi ʃáafu xáuliṣ** *he's neither been to us* (*here*) *in the office nor met the manager, nor has anyone seen him at all.*

It is possible for **ʃ** to be suffixed to a verbal form after the first as in **la katábti f-iggaráayid wala ɛamáltiʃ xúṭab** *I've neither written for* (lit. *in*) *the press* (lit. *papers*) *nor made speeches*; it is also possible for the first negative to be of the **ma -ʃ** type, i.e. **ma katábtiʃ f-iggaráayid wala ɛamáltiʃ xúṭab.**

Notes

(*a*) The particle **la** occurs sporadically elsewhere, as in **láa ʃéeʕ** *nothing*, **la ʃákk innak bitʕúul ilḩáʕʕ** *no doubt you're telling the truth*, and is conceivably identifiable (together with **ʃ**) as part of the unitary form **baláaʃ** as in **baláaʃ ḩíyal** *no tricks !*, **baláaʃ kaláam** *no* (or *stop*) *talking !*

(*b*) **la** may be compared with **laʕ** *no* ; cf. **ḩatíigi walla láʕ ?** *are you going to come or not ?*, **miʃ ʢáarif leh láʕ** *I don't know why not.* **laʕ,** when used for emphatic disagreement, often has the form **laa,** e.g. **láa, láa, ʕábadan** *no, no, never !*

(*c*) Do not confuse **wala** with **walla** *or* nor **la** with the comparatively rare emphatic particle **la** in **ʕúskut, l-aɖrábak !** *be quiet or I'll hit you !* Note the use of **wala** in, say, **ma-mʢíiʃ wala wáḩda** *I haven't a single one on me.*

Words commonly associated with negation

(i) **ḩadd** *anyone* and **ʢumr** *life* (+ pronominal suffix) occur in negative contexts either unaffixed or themselves affixed with **ma -ʃ** ; unaffixed **ḩadd** is generally associated with **ma fiiʃ** : e.g. **ʢúmri ma ʃúftiʃ wáaḩid záyyu(h)** or **ma ʢumríiʃ ʃúfti wáaḩid záyyu(h)** *I've never seen anyone like him*, **ma fiiʃ ḩáddi yiʢraf yiʢmílu(h)** or **ma ḩáddiʃ yiʢraf yiʢmílu(h)** *nobody knows how to do it.*

(ii) **ʕílla** (less commonly **ɣeer**) *except* and **líssa** (*not*) *yet, still* are never themselves negated but frequently occur in negative contexts, e.g. **liḩáddi dilwáʕti ma-tkallimnáaʃ ílla ʢa-ssiyáasa** *up to now we haven't talked* (*about anything*) *except politics* (or *we've only talked about politics*), **ma ḩáddiʃ yiʢraf yiʕra xáʈʈi ɣéeri ʕána** *nobody can read my writing but me*, **líssa ma gáaʃ** *he hasn't come yet*, **géh walla líssa ?** *has he come yet or not ?*

(iii) Also common in negative contexts is **ḩáaga** (*any*)*thing* and its more emphatic counterparts **wála ḩáaga** and **ʕáyyi ḩáaga,** e.g. **ma-fhímʃi ḩáaga** *he didn't understand anything*, **ma-fhímʃi wála ḩáaga** *he didn't understand anything at all*, **ma gablíiʃ ʕáyyi** (or **wála**) **ḩáaga** *he didn't bring me a thing.* **wála ḩáaga** *nothing* may be used independently as in **A. zaʢláan léeh ? B. wála ḩáaga.** *A. What are you cross about ? B. Nothing.*

Emphatic negation

The term "emphatic negation" is reserved for the use of **ma** without **ʃ**. **ʃ** is omitted in emphatic exclamatory contexts such as **yaréetu ma ráaḩ** *I wish he hadn't gone*, **ɛúmri ma ʃúftĭ wáaḩid záyyu(h)**, which is a more emphatic form of the earlier **ɛúmri ma ʃúftiʃ wáaḩid záyyu(h)** *I've never seen anyone like him*, but omission occurs most frequently in association with the "oaths" (**ḩulfáan**); the commonly occurring "oaths" are **walláahi** (lit. *and my God*), **w-innábi** (*and the Prophet*), **wi rabbína** (*and our Lord*), to which may be added for the present purpose **ʕinʃálla** (derived from **ʕin ʃáaʕ alláah** *if God wishes*) in the specialized use with a following perfect tense illustrated hereafter: thus, **láa walláahi m-áʕdar** or **láa w-innábi m-áʕdar** or **láa wi rabbína m-áʕdar** *no, by heaven, I can't*, **ʕinʃálla ma ḩáddĭ kál** *may nobody ever eat, then !*, **ʕinʃálla ma rúḩt** *go or not, as you please !*

Notes

(*a*) The "oaths" have greater variety, power, and binding force outside the towns and among less sophisticated townsmen. From sophisticated speakers, the above examples with **walláahi**, etc., mean little more than *I really can't*. The above use of **ʕinʃálla** is always associated with considerable displeasure and is more frequent in the speech of women.

(*b*) **la wálla** is a very common alternative to **láa walláahi.**

(*c*) Negative **ma** is not to be confused with a rather rare particle **ma** used with an imperative sense as in **ma titkállim** *speak up ! say something !*

INTERROGATION

It is often assumed that interrogation relates exclusively to the seeking of information but it should be remembered that the term is a grammatical one and that in general usage interrogative sentences may not only serve to elicit information but also be in the nature of suggestions (*what about having something to eat ?*, *wouldn't it be better if . . . ?*), exclamations (*really ?*, *what did I tell you !*, *is it as late as all that !*), threats (*are you going to do as I tell you ?*), gestures of politeness (*can*

I help you ? (shop assistant), *may I give you some water ?*), requests for instructions (*shall I phone them or what ?*) or for advice and help (*do you think . . . ?, could you possibly . . . ?*), and so on. It may be that between Arabic and English such linguistic functions do not correspond; thus, **ʕitfáḍḍal ʃáay** may be reasonably translated *may I give you some tea ?* but is not interrogative in Arabic, and **wálla** *really ?* is much more of an exclamation (*you don't say so !*) than a question: in general, however, correspondence of function may be established between the two languages. Thus, for example, suggestions and requests for instructions tend to be associated not only with 1st person verbal forms in the imperfect without **-ḥa** (**ʕarmiihum walla ʕéeh ?** *shall I throw them away or what ?*) but also with introductory 2nd person forms **tiḥíbb** and **tiigi**, as in **tiḥíbbi nitʕáabil yom lárbaɛ iṣṣúbḥ ?** *shall we meet on Wednesday morning ?* (lit. *do you want . . .*), **tiigi nistaḥámma ?** *shall we go for a swim ?* (lit. *will you come . . .*). Similarly, an introductory **tismaḥ/tismáḥi/tismáḥu** meets the requirements of politeness in, say, **tismaḥ tiwalláɛli** *can I trouble you for a light ?*, **tismaḥ áʕfil ilbáab** *do you mind if I close the door ?*, while **tiftikir** at the head of the sentence marks what follows as a question seeking advice or information, e.g. **tiftikir aʕúllu ʕéeh ?** *what ought I to say to him, do you think ?*, **tiftikir fiih fárʕi ben láhgit máṣr w-iskindiriyya ?** *is there any difference, do you think, between the speech of Cairo and Alexandria ?*

An Arabic sentence, affirmative or negative, may also be used as a question by varying the intonation. Compare the way in which the English sentences *he is the man I saw yesterday* and *is he the man I saw yesterday ?* differ. A questioning rise of the voice on *yesterday* corresponds to a similar feature at the end of Arabic interrogative sentences but in Arabic there is no difference of word-order as that between *he is* and *is he*. Get an Egyptian to say to you, both as statements and as questions, **biyikkállim ɛárabi-kwáyyis** *he speaks Arabic well* and *does he speak Arabic well ?* and the corresponding negatives **ma-byikkallímʃi ɛárabi-kwáyyis** *he doesn't, etc.*, and *doesn't he, etc.*, and notice particularly what happens intonationally to **-kwáyyis**; then, as always, mimic the informant. Get him, too, to utter the sentence on a tone of surprise or indignation, (*do you mean to tell me*) *he speaks/doesn't speak Arabic well ! ?* Here are some more examples to try out: **ʕiʃtaréet irrádyu-btáaɛak b-iṭṭaʕsiiṭ** ? *did you buy your wireless on hire-purchase ?*, **múmkin ḥágzi tazáakir muʕaddáman** ? *can tickets be booked in advance ?*, **tiɛraf ṭabiib ɛiyúun kuwáyyis** ? *do you know a good oculist ?*, **ɛandúku ṣabúun wiʃʃ** ? *have you (got) any toilet soap ?*, **ḥaykúun fih zawbáɛa** ? *is there going to be a storm ?*, **tiʕdar tifukkíli-gnéeh, min faḍlak** ? *could you (please) change me a pound ?*, **ma ɛandákʃ iggaríída-ṣṣabaḥíyya** ? *haven't you got the morning paper ?*

We can put the earlier English question another way and say *he's the man I saw yesterday, isn't he ?*, in which the first part as far as *yesterday* is typically said as a statement, the rise of the voice taking place on *isn't he*. Egyptian Arabic does much the same thing with the very common **muʃ kída** (lit. *not so ?*) and says **biyikkállim ɛárabi-kwáyyis, muʃ kída** ? *he speaks Arabic well, doesn't he ?* The formula is reminiscent of others in European languages, cf. French " n'est-ce pas ", German " nicht wahr ", Spanish " (no es) verdad ". In English the device varies with the form of the verb in the first part of the sentence, e.g. *doesn't he, aren't you, haven't they, etc.* There is generally little difference of meaning between this use of **muʃ kída** and the less common device of prefixing **muʃ** to the sentence (cf. French " n'est-ce pas que . . ."), e.g. **muʃ húwwa ragil ṭáyyib** ? *isn't he a good man ?*, **muʃ áḥsan inta tiɛmílu-b náfsak** ? *wouldn't it be better if you did it yourself ?*

Another very common interrogative construction is with **wálla** *or* used to introduce an alternative and most frequently in the fixed formula **walla láʕ** *or not.* The sentence up to **wálla** has the interrogative (rising) intonation while from **wálla** on it has the typically declarative (falling) pattern. This is again paralleled in English. For example, **húwwa-lli ʃúftu-mbáariḥ walla láʕ** ? *is he the one you/I saw yesterday or not ?*, **húwwa-lli ʃúftu-mbáariḥ walla káan fih wáaḥid táani** ? *is he the one you/I saw yesterday or was it someone else ?*, **ʕinta fáaḍi walla maʃɣúul dilwaʕti** ? *are you free or busy now ?*, **ɛáayiz ʕáhwa sáada walla-b súkkar** ? *do you want coffee with or without sugar* (lit. *unsweetened or with sugar*) ?, **géh walla líssa** ? *has he come yet or not ?*

The range of possibilities represented in English by (i) *he comes from Cairo, does he ?* (response on first being informed, *sc. so he comes from Cairo)*, (ii) *he comes from Cairo, doesn't he ?* (seeking confirmation), and (iii) *he doesn't come from Cairo, does he ?* (incredulous) corresponds to Arabic (i) **baʕa húwwa min mágr** (non-interrogative), (ii) either **miʃ húwwa min mágr ?** or **húwwa min mágr, miʃ kída ?**, and (iii) **huwwa míʃ min mágr, walla ʕéeh ? walla ʕéeh** in (iii) is frequently pronounced on a low level pitch of the voice.

The prefixation of sentences with the independent pronouns of the third person is a common interrogative device, the pronoun being followed by a noun with which it agrees, e.g. **huwwaxúuk gáyy innahárda ?** *is your brother coming to-day ?*, **hiyyalfilúus ilmasmúuḫ bíiha mawgúuda-f gawáaz issáfar bitáaɛi ?** *is the currency allowance stated in my passport ?*, **hummalʕagáanib biyiḫtáagu víiza ɛaʃan yidxúlu mágr ?** *do foreigners need a visa to enter Egypt ?* Before a pronoun of persons other than the third, **húwwa** is used as a neutral form, e.g. **matzaɛɛáʕʃi kída ! huww-an-átraʃ ?** *don't shout so ! I'm not deaf* (lit. *am I deaf ?*).

Sometimes, but not often, an interrogative sentence is characterized by the suffixation of **ʃ** (not to be confused with negative **ʃ**) to verbs, **fiih, ɛand** + pronominal suffix and similarly suffixed particles, e.g. **ʃúftiʃ duséeh ɛa-lmáktab ?** *did you see a file on the desk ?*, **ɛándakʃi sagáayir ?** *have you any cigarettes ?*, **ɛúmrakʃi ʃúfti liɛbit kóora ?** *have you ever seen a game of football ?*

In answer to negative questions, **ʕáywa** *yes* and **laʕ** *no* are often used in a way misleading to English speakers, affirming or denying the form of the question rather than the facts. For example, in reply to **ma rúḫtiʃ ?** *didn't you go ?* may be heard **ʕáywa, ma rúḫtiʃ** *no, I didn't* or **láʕ, rúḫt** *yes, I did.* **laʕ** for **ʕáywa** and vice versa is, however, possible.

Specific interrogative particles

Interrogative sentences are also marked as such by the presence of one of a series of specific interrogative particles which are as follows: **ʕeeh** *what*, **leeh** *why*, **feen** *where*, **minéen** *whence*, **ʕímta** *when*, **ʕayy** (also **ʕánhu/ʕánhi/ʕánhum**) [1] *which*,

[1] Elsewhere **ʕayy** and **ʕánhu**/etc. = *any*, but **ʕánhu** is comparatively rare; cf. **xúd ʕáyyi** (or **ʕánhu**) **-ktáab ɛáyzu(h)** *take any book you want.*

ʔizzáay *how,* **kaam** *how much, many,* **ʔáddi ʔéeh** (or **ʔaddéeh**) *how far, how much, to what extent,* **miin** *who.*

The typical unemphatic order of the following sentences containing these particles is an inverted one in relation to English: **bitiɛmil éeh ?** *what are you doing ?,* **ʔikkilmáadi maɛnáaha ʔéeh ?** *what does that word mean ?,* **ʔinta ɛayyáan bi ʔéeh ?** *what's the matter with you ?* (*sc. what are you suffering from ?*), **ma-byiʃtaɣalúuʃ léeh ?** *why aren't they working ?,* (**ʔinta**) **ráayiḥ féen ?** *where are you going ?,* **ʔagíib rúxṣa l-irrádyu-mnéen ?** *where do I get a wireless licence ?,* **ḥatúxrug ímta ?** *when are you going out ?,* **ɛiyátt** (or **ɛiyáadit**) **idduktúur bitíftaḥ ímta ?** *when does the doctor's surgery open ?,* **ʔinta ɛáwzu-b ʔáyyi lóon ?** *what colour do you want it ?,* **ḥatiɛmil iʃʃúrba-zzáay min ɣéer láḥma walla-xḍáar ?** *how are you going to make soup without meat or vegetables ?,* **ʔiʃtaréetu-b káam ?** *how much did you buy it for ?,* **ʔilɛárḍ ittáani ḥayibtidi-ssáaɛa káam ?** *what time* (lit. *the hour how many*) *does the next performance start ?,* **ʔilḥisáab ɛala míin ?** *who's going to pay* (lit. *the bill on whom*) *?*

Prepositional (adverbial) phrases, however, tend to follow the interrogative particle, e.g. **naʔálti ʔímta min ʃaʔʔítak ilʔadíima ?** *when did you move out of your old flat ?,* **fíkrak éeh f-innáas dóol ?** *what do you think of those people ?,* **ʔáalu ʔéeh f-innáʃra-ggawwíyya ?** *what was the weather forecast* (lit. *what did they say about, etc.*) *?,* **ʔinnahárda káam f-iʃʃáhr ?** *what's the date to-day ?,* **ʔixtáaru káam wáaḥid li mubaráat ilbuṭúula ?** *how many have they seeded for the* (*tennis*) *championship ?* Dependent clauses similarly follow the interrogative particle in, say, **gaṛálku ʔéeh bitzaɛɛáʔu** [1] **wayya báɛḍ ?** *what's the matter with you shouting at one another* (*like that*) *?,* **xátti** (> **xadt**) **ʔaddi ʔéeh ɛaʃan titɛállim iʃʃuɣláadi ?** *how long did you take to learn the job ?*

The placing of the interrogative particle at the head, e.g. **féen huwwa ?** *where is he ?,* **léeh baṭṭáltu-ʃʃúɣl ?** *why have you* (pl.) *stopped work ?,* often gives an emphatic turn to the sentence. This is not, however, the whole story. There would seem, for example, to be a tendency to place, say, **feen** before the definite phrase in **féen ʃibbáak ittazáakir ?** *where is the booking-office ?* or **féen báab málɛab issábaʔ** *where is the entrance to the race-course ?* or, again, **féen litnáaʃar ginéeh salliftúhúmlak**

[1] Pronounced **bidz-**.

min zamáan ? *where are the twelve pounds I lent you some time ago ?*; none of these examples are more emphatic in tone than, say, **ʕilʕaṣanṣéer féen ?** *where is the lift ?* or **ʕaláaʕi fákka féen ?** *where can I get change ?* Contrariwise, the placing of **ʕeeh** at the head of **ʕéeh illi-btiɛmilu(h) ?** *what are you doing ?* not only involves the necessary inclusion of **ʕilli** but once again is more emphatic than its counterpart **bitiɛmil éeh ?** Any such emphatic flavour is absent, however, from the following examples, in which the particle is regularly placed at the head of the sentence, **ʕéeh ʕáḥsan lukánda f-ilbálad di ?** *what's the best hotel in this town ?*, **ʕéeh ʕanwáaɛ illáḥma-lli ɛandúkum ?** *what have you got in the way of meat* (lit. *what* (*are the*) *kinds of meat, etc.*) *?*, **ʕéeh iṭṭúɛm illi bitṣṭid biih ?** *what bait do you use* (lit. *hunt*, sc. *fish, with*) *?*

Sentences with the specifically interrogative particles most frequently have the (falling) intonation of the declarative sentence. This is also so in English; contrast *when did he come ?* and *did he come ?* The falling pattern is by no means the only possibility for the specifically interrogative sentence in either English or Arabic but, broadly, there is a similarity of intonational usage between the two languages. Commonly enough, however, one hears examples of a pattern sounding very foreign to English ears; herein the final interrogative particle is pronounced on a monotone (no rise or fall) and on a higher pitch than the preceding syllable: **bitiɛmil éeh ?** uttered in this way may be represented graphically - ‾ _ -.

Those interrogative particles which are used pronominally are, of course, often preceded by prepositional particles, cf. **ɛamálti kida ɛalaʃan éeh ?** *why* (lit. *for the purpose of what*) *did you do so ?*, **bitittíkil ɛala miin ?** *whom do you count on ?* Derivationally, it may be noted, **leeh** = **li** + **ʕeeh, feen** = **fi** + **ʕeen, minéen** = **min** + **ʕeen.**

A few points of grammatical detail concerning individual members of the list of interrogative particles remain to be made. Word-order is sometimes relevant to the particle **miin** when associated with 3rd pers. sing. verbal forms. In colloquial Arabic word-order is fixed in noun-verb-noun sentences such as **ɛáli ʃáaf maḥámmad** *Ali saw Mohamed*, **maḥámmad ʃáaf ɛáli** *Mohamed saw Ali*; similarly, **miin** in **miin ʃáaf ?** *who saw ?* is marked as the subject of the verb by the fact that it immediately precedes the verbal form: contrast **ʃáaf míin ?** *whom did he see ?*, in which **míin** is marked as the object by its occupation of immediate post-verbal position. This position is generally reserved for the object; thus, with the typical interrogative sentence order already noted above, we may find **ʃáafu míin ?** *who saw him ?*, in which **míin** follows the verb but not immediately and is thus in subjective relation to it. There is an alternative form to the earlier **ʃáaf míin ?** *whom did he see ?*, viz. **míin illi ʃáafu(h) ?**, which is, in fact, ambiguous and might also mean *who saw him ?*; **ʕilli** may optionally be included after subjective **míin**, e.g. **míin illi kátab ittaʕríir da ?** *who wrote this report ?*, **míin illi wáaʕif hináak ?** *who's that standing over there ?*, **míin illi middíik ʕiznĭ tímʃi ?** *who gave you permission to go ?* The inclusion of **ʕilli** is the rule in participial (nominal) sentences of the kind illustrated in the last two examples but is not essential before verbal tense forms, cf. **míin (illi) ʕállak inn-ána miʃ ráayiḥ ?** *who told you I'm not going ?*

kaam requires a following noun in the singular, e.g. **ḥatistánna kam yóom ?** *how many days are you going to stay ?*, **baʕáalak kam sána-f máṣr ?** *how many years have you been in Egypt ?*, **ʕiṭṭayyáara di-btáaxud káam ráakib ?** *how many passengers does this plane take ?* In the sense of (pronominal) *how many* notice the association of **kaam** with **wáaḥid** as in **ʕixtáaru káam wáaḥid ?** *how many have they picked ?*

ʕánhu/ʕánhi/ʕánhum *which* behaves like the ordinal numerals in that it may precede or follow the noun it accompanies with similar implications as to the presence or absence of the definite article: if **ʕánhu** precedes, the noun does not take the article; if it follows, the article is included. Thus, **ʕánhu-ktáab ?** or **ʕikkitáab ánhu ?** *which book ?*, cf. **táalit kitáab** or **ʕikkitáab ittáalit** *the third book*. If the sentence is extended, then the second pattern (with the article) requires **ʕilli**, the first does not, i.e. either **ʕánhu-ktáab ɛáyzu(h) ?** or **ʕikkitáab anhú-ll-inta ɛáyzu(h) ?** *which book do you want ?*, cf. **táalit kitáab fi dóol** or **ʕikkitáab ittáalit illi-f dóol** *the third one among those books*. **ʕayy** may not be used pronominally in the way of **ʕánhu** in, say, **ʕanhú-ll-inta ɛáyzu(h) ?** *which one do you want ?*, cf. **ʕáyyĭ wáaḥid** in, say, **ʕáyyĭ wáaḥid ɛáyzu(h) ?** *which one do you want ?*

The form **ʕizzáyy**, not **ʕizzáay**, is used in the common greetings formulae **ʕizzáyyak, ʕizzáyy iṣṣíḥḥa, ʕizzáyy ilḥáal** *how are you ?*, **ʕizzáyy ilɛéela ?** *how's the family ?*, etc.

EXCLAMATIONS AND "OATHS"

(*a*) The following exclamations (**kilmáat ilʕistiɣráab**) are common: **ṣubḥáan alláah !**, (**ʃéeʕ**) **ɣaríib !**, (**ʃéeʕ**) **ɛagíib !**, (**ʃéeʕ**) **múdhiʃ !**, **yáa saláam !**, **ʕálla(h) !**, **ʕéhda** or **déhda !**, **fiih ʕéeh !**, **gára ʕéeh !**, **yígra ʕéeh !** The English equivalent of a given example will depend on the context and, to some extent, on individual taste. Selection may be made from *what !, well !, indeed !, well, I never !, fancy !, good heavens !, great Scott !, good lord !, bless my soul !*, etc.

Not only difference of intonation but also difference of association with other words will contribute to considerable difference of meaning for otherwise similar forms; for example, **ya saláam** is associated with **ɛala dámmak** in the exclamation of disgust or disapproval **ya saláam ɛala dámmak, ya ʕaxi !** roughly *what an unpleasant fellow you are !* but with **ɛala kída** in the exclamation of approval **ya saláam ɛala kída !** *how delightful !* The introductory particle **ya** is found quite commonly in exclamations, cf. **ya ḥaláawa !** *how nice !*, **ya-xṣáara !** *what a pity !*, **ya ḥáwl l-illáah !** *what a loss !* (said on hearing of the death of a highly respected person).

Other common exclamations are: **ɛáal, ɛáal !** *excellent !*, **wálla(h)** or **láʕ, ya ʃéex !** *really !, you don't say !*, **ɛéeb ɛaléek !** *shame on you !*, **ḥaráam ɛaléek !** *shame on you !* (in religious matter), **ʕamma . . .** *what a . . . !*, as in **ʕamma ráagil !** *what a man !*, **ʕamma ḥárr !** *isn't it hot !, what heat !* **ʕaɛúuzu b-illáah,** roughly *oh dear !*, is used as an exclamation of disapproval or displeasure; thus, for example, **ʕaɛúuzu b-illáah mínnak, ya ʕaxi !** *may God preserve us from you !* is an alternative to the earlier **ya saláam ɛala dámmak, ya ʕaxi. ʕiʃmíɛna** in, say, **ʕiʃmíɛna kida !** also relates to disapproval or surprise, i.e. *why do you do that ?* or *how can you say that ?* There seems to be little or no difference of meaning between **ʕiʃmíɛna kida !** and **léeh baʕa !** (notice in passing the very common colloquial form **báʕa,** which corresponds to the English parenthetic *then* at the end of sentences, e.g. *come on, then, let's see what you're made of, then*).

Finally, notice the exclamatory **yaréet** as in **yarétni rúḫt** ! *if only I had gone !*

(*b*) The " oaths " (**ḫulfáan**) are often used for exclamation or emphasis, e.g. **walláahi-lʕaẓíim** ! *good lord !*, **walláah-inta muʃ kuwáyyis** ! *how very unpleasant you are !*, **walláah-ana ʕándi ḫáẓẓ** ! *I'm indeed lucky !*

The " oaths " as such, i.e. to vouch for the truth of what is said, vary according to the educational standard and geographical origin of the speaker. Educated speakers use **walláahi-lʕaẓíim, walláahi,** and **w-innábi,** as in **walláahi-lʕaẓíim ma ʃúftu(h)** *I swear I didn't see him*, but the unsophisticated, especially in the countryside, use a greater range. They may, for example, swear to divorce or on the life of a member of the family as in **wi-ḫyáat íbni** *on my son's life* or **wi-ḫyáat abúuya** *on my father's life*, or local saints may be invoked as, for example, in the Cairene **wi-ḫyáat sayyídna-lḫuséen** or **wi-ḫyáat issayyída zéenab.** Such oaths are not, of course, used indiscriminately without reference to the personal background of the speaker. Only a married man with a son may swear by his son's life and swearing to divorce or on the good name of one's family are only used by married men as in the very strong oaths **ʕaláyya-ṭṭaláaʕ b-ittaláata** ! or **ʕaláyya-lḫaráam min béeti** ! For the single man, **walláahi-lʕaẓíim** ! is the strongest oath.

The oaths as such have virtually no binding force among educated people to-day ; in contrast, however, if the Bedouin swears to divorce his wife unless his guest continues to eat, then he may well do so in the event of the guest's refusal. Embarrassment, not to mention discomfort, is generally avoided on such occasions by a nice interchange of " oaths ", but the rules of the game are only known to the initiated. The non-Arab is strongly advised not to use the oaths except in their exclamatory function and then to limit himself to educated usage ; he is otherwise almost certain to offend or, at best, to amuse the Arabic speaker.

IV. USEFUL SENTENCES AND VOCABULARY

PASSPORT FORMALITIES

Vocabulary[1]

passport	gawáaz issáfar, gawazáat issáfar; paṣpóor, paṣporṭáat[1]
passport office	ʔidáarit iggawazáat
embassy	sifáara, sifaráat
consulate	ʔunṣulíyya, ʔunṣuliyyáat
passport section	qísm iggawazáat, ʔaqsáam iggawazáat
permit	taṣríiħ, taṣriħáat
visa	taʔʃíira, taʔʃiráat; víiza, vizáat
entry permit/visa	taṣríiħ/taʔʃíira b-idduxúul
exit permit/visa	taṣríiħ/taʔʃíira b-ilxurúug
transit permit	taṣríiħ b-ilmurúur
residence permit	taṣríiħ b-ilʔiqáama
stay	ʔiqáama
length of stay	múddit ilʔiqáama
temporary residence	ʔiqáama muʔaqqáta
permanent residence	ʔiqáama daaʔíma
the reason for the visit	ʔilɣáraḍ min izziyáara
business trip	ríħla l-ittigáara
holiday trip	ríħla l-ilfúsħa/l-issiyáaħa
personal matters	masáaʔil ʃaxṣíyya
family matters	masáaʔil ʕaʔilíyya
stamp	ṭáabiʕ, ṭawáabiʕ
fiscal stamp	wáraʔit dámɣa
consular (fiscal) fees	rásm iddámɣa
date of the passport's expiry	taríix intiháaʔ ilpaṣpóor
(an) official	muwáẓẓaf, muwaẓẓafíin
abroad	f-ilxáarig
to get a passport	ṭállaʕ, yiṭállaʕ[1] paṣpóor; ʔistáxrag, yistáxrag gawáaz issáfar

[1] Both singular and plural forms of nouns are given where appropriate, and in that order. Verbs are given in the 3rd person singular masculine forms, first in the perfect tense, then in the imperfect.

to take out a new passport	xád, yáaxud paspóor gidíid
to surrender the old passport	sállim, yisállim ilpaspóor ilʕadíim
to examine passports	ʃáaf, yiʃúuf gawazáat issáfar
to grant an entry visa	ʕídda, yíddi taʕʃíirit idduxúul

Sentences

Do foreigners need a visa to enter Egypt / Syria / Iraq / Lebanon / Morocco?	(ʕúlli min fádlak) humma-lʕagáanib biyiḥtáagu víiza ʒaʃan yidxúlu máṣr/súrya/ilʒiráaq/libnáan/murráakiʃ?
When can I collect my passport?	ʕímta ʕáaxud paspóori?
Please fill in these two forms and sign them.	min fádlak ʕímla-ṭṭalabéen dóol w-imdíihum.
You need two photographs for your visa.	yilzámlak/lazímlak/láazim tigíib[1] ṣurtéen ʒaʃan ilvíiza.
What is your purpose in visiting Egypt?	ʕéeh ilɣárad min ziyártak li máṣr?/ɣáradak ʕéeh min ziyáarit máṣr?
How long may I stay in the country?	ʕáʕdar astánna ʕaddéeh (or ʕaddí ʕéeh) f-ilbiláad?
Ninety days with a tourist visa.	tisʒíin yóom bi víizit issiyáaḥa.
I am only travelling through the country.	ʕana ʒáawiz amúrri f-ilbiláad báss.
I need a transit visa.	ʕana miḥtáag(a) li taʕʃíirit murúur.
You must have an entry and an exit permit.	labúddi lik min taʕʃíirit duxúul wi taʕʃíirit xurúug.
Must I get a permit to stay (to take up work)?	yilzámli taʕʃíirit ʕiqáama (ʒa(la)ʃan aʃtáɣal hináak)?
I want a tourist visa.	ʕana ʒáawiz taʕʃíirit siyáaḥa.
I would like to apply for a three months' extension of this visa.	min fádlak ʒawiz (áktib ṭálab ʒaʃan) amídd ittaʕʃíira díyya tálatt úʃhur.
You must have your passport renewed.	láazim tigáddid gawáaz issáfar bitáaʒak.
Your visa is valid until 31st October.	ʕittaʕʃíira-lli-mʒáak ṣa(a)líḥa-l listiʒmáal liɣáayit wáaḥid wi talatíin uktóobar.
Can I get a residence visa?	mumkin ʕáaxud, law samáḥt, taʕʃíirit ʕiqáama?

[1] The oblique stroke is used between alternative possibilities.

I wish to live and work in Egypt for some time; would you please inform me of the steps to take.	ʔana ʕáawiz aʕíiʃ w-aʃtáɣal fi máṣri múdda. tísmaħ tiʔúll(i ʔ)aʕmil ʔéeh.
Is the currency allowance stated in my passport?	hiyya-lfilúus ilmasmúuħ bíiha mawgúuda-f gawáaz issáfar bitáaʕi?/huwwa-ttaṣríiħ bi ʔáxdi-flúus mawgúud fi gawáaz issáfar bitáaʕi?
The passport officials will board the train at the frontier (-post).	ʔilmufattiʃíin ħayiṭláʕu f-ilʔáṭri ʕandi núʔṭit ilħudúud.
Have your passports ready.	gahhízu gawazáat safárkum.
Your passport is in order.	gawáaz sáfarak maẓbúuṭ.
There is a stamp missing in your passport.	fih ṭáabiʕ náaʔiṣ fi paṣpóorak/ paṣpóorak náʔṣu(h) ṭáabiʕ.
Please hand in your passports.	min faḍlúku sallímu gawazáat safárku.
Where is the British/American Consulate?	féen ilʔunṣulíyya-lʔingilizíyya/ lʔamrikíyya?
There is only a Vice-Consul in this town.	ma fiiʃ hína ʔílla wakíil ʔúnṣul báss.
What are the office hours of the passport department?	ʔéeh mawaʕíid fátħi máktab taftíiʃ ilpaṣporṭáat?/máktab taftíiʃ ilpaṣporṭáat biyíftaħ min káam li káam?
How much does the visa cost?	taʔʃíirit idduxúul/ilxurúug bitkállif káam?
I wish to seek employment in Egypt. Could you help me?	ʔana ʕáawiz aʃtáɣal fi máṣr. min fáḍlak tiʔdar tisaʕídni?
I would like to break the journey here for twenty-four hours.	ʕáawiz astánna hín-arbáʕa-w ʕiʃríin sáaʕa.
Do I need to report to the local police-station for a three days' stay?	lazim arúuħ núʔṭit ilbulíiṣ ilmaħálli ʕalaʃan astánna tálatt iyyáam?
Full name of passport holder.	ʔísmi ħáamil ilpaṣpóor b-ilkáamil.
Nationality at birth/at present.	ʔalginsíyya[1] ʕand ilmiláad/ f-ilwáʔt ilħáaḍir.
Date and place of birth.	taríix wi maħáll ilmiláad.
Profession.	ʔalmíhna.
Condition (single/married/ widow(-er)).	ʔalħáala ligtimaʕíyya (ʔáʕzab/ mutazáwwig/ʔármal(a)).

[1] The form ʔal for the definite article, rather than ʔil, is felt to be more appropriate to the utterance of written language, especially when initial in the utterance.

Description:	ʕalʕawṣáaf ilgismíyya:
Face: colour of the eyes; nose; complexion.	ʕalwágh: lóon ilʕaynéen; ʕal-ʕánf; lóon ilbáʃra.
Hair.	ʕaʃʃáʕr.
Distinctive marks.	ʕalʕalamáat ilmumayyíza.
Height.	ʕaṭṭúul.
Remarks.	mulaḥaẓáat.
Signature in full.	ʕalʕimḍáaʕ b-ilkáamil.

CUSTOMS

Vocabulary

customs, custom-house	ʕiggúmruk
custom-bond	máxzan iggúmruk
customs regulations	ʕilqawaníin iggumrukíyya; qanúun iggamáarik
customs officer	muwáẓẓaf iggúmruk, muwaẓẓafíin iggúmruk
customs inspector	mufáttiʃ iggúmruk, mufattiʃíin iggúmruk
customs duty	ʕiḍḍaríiba-ggumrukíyya
dutiable articles	ʕilḥagáat ilmafrúuḍ ʕaléeha ḍaríiba
luggage	ʕafʃ
tariff	ʕittaʕríifa-ggumrukíyya
clearance	tatmíim
luggage clearance	ʕittatmíim ʕa-lʕáfʃ
goods clearance	ʕittatmíim ʕa-lbaḍáayiʕ
customs declaration	bayáan ilmuḥtawayáat [1]
tobacco	duxxáan
cigarettes	sagáayir
cigars	sagáayir zanúbya
perfume	ʕiṭr, ʕuṭúur
liquor, spirits	xumúur; maʃrubáat ruḥíyya
camera	ʕáalit ittaṣwíir, ʕaláat ittaṣwíir; kámira, kamiráat
watch	sáaʕa, saʕáat
smuggling	tahríib
smuggler	muhárrib, muharribíin
fine	ɣaráama
export/import licence	taṣríiḥ ittaṣdíir/listiráad
consular declaration	ʕiqráar ilqunṣulíyya

[1] Lit. "description of the contents".

customs-free	**xáali (xálya, xalyíin) iḍḍaríiba**
to conceal	**xábba, yixábbi**
to levy duty	**ḥáddid, yiḥáddid ḍaríibit iggúmruk**
to clear	(goods) **xállaṣ, yixállaṣ** (**ʕala**) ; (passport) **támmim, yitámmim** (**ʕala**)
to smuggle	**hárrab, yihárrab**

Sentences

Where is the custom-house ?	(**ʕúlli min fáḍlak**) **ʕiggúmruk féen ?**
Please place your luggage on the counter.	**min fáḍlak ḥúṭṭi ʕáfʃak ʕala-lbánk.**
Here is my suitcase.	**ʃanṭít(i ʕ)ahéh !**
Will you examine my trunk, please.	**tísmaḥ tifáttiʃ ʃanṭíti (min fáḍlak).**
Your turn next, have the keys ready please.	**ʕiddóora ʕaléek, ḥáḍḍar mafatíiḥak min fáḍlak.**
Have you anything to declare ?	**ʕándak ḥáaga min ilmamnuʕáat ?**
Are you carrying any of the articles on this list ?	**maʕáak ḥáaga m-illi f-ilʕáyma di ?**
The new customs tariff comes into force on the 1st July.	**qanúun iggamáarik iggidíid ḥayitṭábbaʕ [1] min ʕáwwil yúlya.**
Have you any spirits, tobacco, new watches, or perfumes ?	**maʕáak ʕáyyi maʃrubáat ruḥíyya, walla** (or **ʕaw**) **duxxáan, walla saʕáat gidíida, walla ʕuṭúur ?**
I have this small bottle of perfume.	**maʕáaya-ʕzáazit ilʕiṭr iṣṣuɣay-yára di.**
This is free of duty.	**dí ma ʕalehaáʃ ḍaríiba/dí xálya-ḍḍaríiba.**
Is that all ?	**xaláaṣ ?/fíih ḥaga tánya ?**
You can close your suitcase.	**ṭáyyib, ʕiʕfil ʃanṭítak.**
Is my luggage passed ?	**ʕáfʃi xúluṣ ?**
I have an import licence for these goods.	**maʕáaya [2] taṣríiḥ istiráad b-ilbaḍáayiʕ di.**
You can take delivery of the case of liqueurs ; it has been cleared.	**tiʕdar táaxud ʃánṭit ilxumúur ; xúluṣ taftíʃha.**
Please get me a taxi and take the luggage to it.	**hátli táksi min fáḍlak wi wáddi-lʕáfʃi da fíih.**
You are fined for not having declared these articles.	**lazim tídfaʕ yaráama ʕaʃan ma ʕaʕlántiʃ ilḥagáat di.**

[1] Pronounce **ḥayiṭṭ-**.
[2] If carried on the person, otherwise **ʕándi.**

TRAVELLING

TRAVELLING BY ROAD

Vocabulary

road travel	ʕissáfar b-ilʒarabiyyáat
highway, road	ṭaríiʕ, ṭúruʕ ; síkka, síkak
motor-car	ʒarabíyya, ʒarabiyyáat ; sayyáara, sayyaráat ; ʕuṭumbíil, ʕuṭumbiláat[1]
private car	ʒarabíyya malláaki, ʒarabiyyáat malláaki
hired car	ʒarabíyyit ilʕúgra
taxi	táksi, taksiyyáat
coach, motor-bus	ʕutubíis, ʕutubisáat
overland coach	sayyáarit irriḥláat
lorry	lúuri, luriyyáat
truck	ʒarabíyyit náʕl, ʒarabiyyáat náʕl
van	ʒarabíyya muɣláqa ; ʒarabíyya maʕfúula ; ʒarabíyya búks
motor-cycle	mutusíkl, mutusikláat
gharry	ḥanṭúur,[2] ḥanaṭíir
two-wheeled trap	karétta, karettáat
bicycle ; wheel	ʒágala, ʒagaláat, ʒagal[3]
racing bicycle	ʒágalit sábaʕ (or sibáaʕ)
tandem	ʒágala mígwiz
moped	ʒágala buxxaríyya
cart	ʒarabíyya kárru, ʒarabiyyáat kárru
tram	ṭurmáay, ṭurmayáat
driver	sawwáaʕ, sawwaʕíin
conductor	kumsáari, kumsaríyya
cyclist	ráakib ʒágala
three cyclists	taláata rakbíin ʒágal
body	háykal (pl. hayáakil) ilʒarabíyya
chassis	ʃasée(h), ʃasehaat ; gísm issayyáara
bonnet	ɣáṭa-lʒídda, ɣuṭyáan ilʒídad
hood	kabbúud, kababíid
mudguard	ráfraf, rafáarif
wheel	ʒágala, ʒagaláat
hub	míḥwar, maḥáawir
tyre	kawítʃ, kawitʃáat

[1] In this and certain other sections below will be found a fairly large number of loan-words from European languages.

[2] Or ḥanṭúur.

[3] A collective form.

inner tube	kawitʃ guwwáani
rim	ṭáara, ṭaráat
brake	farmála, faráamil
gear-lever	vitíss
gear	tirs, turúus (or tirúus)
gear-box	ɛílbit ittirúus
gear-change (bicycle)	náaʕil itturúus
steering-wheel	diriksiyóon ; ɛágalit ilqiyáada ; ɛágalit issiwáaʕa
exhaust	ʕumbúubit ilɛáadim, ʕanabíib ilɛáadim ; ʃakmáan, ʃakmanáat
battery	baṭṭaríyya, baṭṭariyyáat
accelerator	baddáal ilbanzíin
carburettor	karburitéer, karburiteráat
starting-handle	manafílla, manafilláat
windscreen wiper	masáaḥit ilʕizáaz
speedometer	ɛaddáad issúrɛa
self-starter	márʃi ʕutumatíik
bumper	ʕaksidáam, ʕaksidamáat
horn	nifíir, nifiráat
windscreen	ʕizáaz iʃʃibbáak
crankshaft	ɛamúud ikkiránk
ball-bearings	bily
ball-bearing race	kúrsi-lbíly
handlebars	gadóon, gadunáat
straight/dropped handlebars	ʕiggadóon ilɛídil/ilmaɛwúug
saddle	kúrsi, karáasi
pedal	bidáal, bidaláat
chain	ganzíir, ganazíir
fork	furʃ (ilɛágala)
frame	háykal ilɛágala ; mawasíir [1]
crossbar	ʕilmasúura-lʕuddamaníyya
spoke	silk, ʕisláak
bell	gúras, ʕigráas
carrier	kúrsi warráani, karáasi warraníyya
front lamp	lámba ʕuddamaníyya
rear lamp	lámba warraníyya
spare parts	qíṭaɛ ilɣiyáar
spare wheel	ɛágala-stíbn
tools	ɛídad (sing. ɛídda)
tool-bag	ʃánṭit ilɛídad
jack	jaak, jakáat

[1] Lit. "tubes, pipes".

pump	munfáax, manáafix
screwdriver	mifákk ilʕaláawiẓ
hammer	ʃakúuʃ, ʃawakiiʃ
pincers	kammáaʃa, kammaʃáat
pliers	ẓarradíyya, ẓarradiyyáat
spanner	muftáaḥ iṣṣawamiil
adjustable spanner	muftáaḥ ingiliizi
repair	taṣliiḥ, taṣliḥáat
puncture	xurm ; xurʕ, xurúuʕ
patch	rúʕɛa, rúʕaɛ
solution	sirisyóon
fuel	waqúud
petrol	banziin
oil (lubricating-)	zeet (ittaʃḥiim)
water	máyya
distilled water	máyya-mʕaṭṭára
petrol pump	ṭurúmbit ilbanziin, ṭurumbáat ilbanziin
petrol station	maḥáṭṭit ilbanziin, maḥaṭṭáat ilbanziin
garage	garáaʃ, garaʃáat
lorry crane (*or* winch)	winʃ illúuri
speed limit	ḥádd issúrɛa
pot-hole	maṭább, maṭabbáat ; ḥúfra, ḥúfar (or ḥufráat)
collision	taṣáadum
accident	ḥádsa, ḥawáadis
level-crossing	muzliʕáan, muzliʕanáat
to drive	saaʕ, yisúuʕ
to start up	dáas, yidúus ɛa-lmárʃ ʕutumatiik
to overtake	ɛádda, yiɛáddi
to brake	fármil, yifármil
to slow down	hádda, yiháddi
to accelerate	dáas, yidúus banziin
to stop	wiʕif, yúʕaf (or yiʕaf)
to park	rákan, yirkin
to repair	ṣállaḥ, yiṣállaḥ
to collide	ṣáadim, yiṣáadim
to run over	daas, yidúus
to somersault	ʕitʃáɛlib (or ʕiʃʃ-), yitʃáɛlib
to overturn	ʕinʕálab, yinʕilib
to tow away	garr, yigúrr
to go uphill	ṭiliɛ, yiṭlaɛ ilɛilwáaya
to go downhill	nízil, yinzil
to ride a bicycle	rikib, yirkab ɛágala
to cycle, go by bicycle	ráaḥ, yirúuḥ b-ilɛágala

to pedal	báddil, yibáddil
to pump up a tyre	náfax, yínfux ilɛágala

Sentences

I have a tourer/saloon/sports car.	ʕana ɛándi ɛarabíyyit makʃúufa/ ɛarabíyya şalúun/ɛarabíyyit sábaʕ (or sibáaʕ).
Do you own a car?	ʕinta şáaḥib ilɛarabíyya?
My car is a two-seater.	ɛarabiyyíti-b kursiyyéen.
Who is going to drive to-day?	míin ḥaysúuʕ innahárda?
Have you got your driving-licence with you?	maɛáak rúxşit issiwáaʕa?
Hadn't we better let the hood down? It is getting hot.	miʃ níftaḥ (or niʃíil) ikkabbúud áḥsan? ʕiddínya ḥarrárit.
Look out for the bends, otherwise we shall skid.	xúd báalak min iddawaranáat, láḥsan nizzáḥlaʕ (or nidz-).
Did you see the traffic-lights?	ʃúfti ɛalamáat ilmurúur?
You have to pay a fine for speeding.	láazim tidfaɛ ɣaráama ɛalaʃáan súrɛit issiwáaʕa.
The traffic policeman has taken our number.	ɛaskári-lmurúur xád nímrit ɛarabiyyítna.
I had a breakdown on my last trip to Suez.	ɛarabiyyíti-tɛaţţálit w-ana ráayiḥ issuwées ilmárra-lli fáatit.
We've a puncture in one of the front wheels, but there's a spare.	fíih xúrmi-f wáḥda m-ilɛagaltéen ilʕuddamaniyyíin, lakin fíih ɛágala-stíbn.
The tool-box is under the seat.	sandúuʕ ilɛídad taḥt ikkúrsi.
If you are going to town I can give you a lift.	ʕiza kútti ráayiḥ máşr, ʕáʕdar awaşşálak.
Switch on the headlights.	wállaɛ ikkaʃʃafáat.
You ought to change gear.	láazim tiɣáyyar issúrɛa.
Where can I park my car?	ʕáʕdar árkin ɛarabiyyíti féen min fáḑlak?
The car park is over there.	máwʕaf ilɛarabiyyáat hináak aho(h)!
Where can I get this car repaired?	ʕáʕdar aşállaḥ ilɛarabíyya dí féen?
There is a garage around the corner.	fíih garáaʃ baɛd iddawaráan.
Where is the nearest petrol-station?	féen áʕrab maḥáţţiţ banzíin?
I must fill up with petrol and check the tyre-pressures.	ʕana láazim ámla-lɛarabíyya banzíin w-ákʃif ɛala-lɛágal.

How much are you going to charge for washing my car?	**táaxud** (or **ꜥáawiz**) **káam fi yasiil ilꜥarabíyya?**
Street signs:	**ʕiʃaráat** (or **ꜥalamáat**) **ilmurúur:**
Slow.	**háddi-ssúrꜥa.**
One-way street.	**ṭaríiq b-ittigáah wáaḥid.**
Speed limit: 80 kilometres.	**ḥádd issúrꜥa: tamaníin kelumítr.**
Slow. Major road ahead.	**ḥáaðir.**[1] **ʕiṭṭaríiq ilmuqáabil húwa-rraʕíisi.**
Halt.	**qif!**
Street repairs (roadworks).	**taṣlíiḥ iṭṭaríiq.**
Diversion.	**taḥwíid.**
Crossroads.	**taqáaṭuꜥ.**
I'm fond of cycling.	**ʕana baḥíbbi-rkúub ilꜥágal.**
Are your brakes in working order?	**ʕilfaráamil bitáꜥtak bitiʃtáɣal kuwáyyis?**
Yes, but the chain is a bit loose.	**ʕáywa, lakin igganzíir miráxrax ʃuwayya.**
You were riding on the pavement, you'll have to pay a fine.	**ʕinta kútti máaʃi b-ilꜥágala ꜥa-rraṣíif, láazim tidfaꜥ ɣaráama.**
I must pump the tyres up.	**ʕana láazim ánfux ilꜥágala.**
I've a puncture in my back tyre and shall have to mend it.	**ꜥagálti-lwarraníyya maxrúuʕa, láazim aṣalláḥha.**
The front wheel is out of centre.	**ʕilꜥágala-lʕuddamaníyya maꜥ-wúuga.**
I have to renew my licence for another year.	**lazim agáddid rúxṣit ꜥagálti li múddit sána tánya.**
I prefer the straight handlebar to the dropped one.	**ʕan-afáḍḍal iggadóon ilꜥídil ꜥan iggadóon ilmaꜥwúug.**
The brakes are worn.	**ʕilfaráamil xasráana.**
You can cycle on the by-path.	**tiʕdar tímʃi b-ilꜥágala f-iṭṭaríiʕ igganíbi.**
The road to the farm is full of pot-holes.	**ʕiṭṭaríiʕ illi ráayiḥ ilꜥízba malyáan maṭabbáat.**
You have to unfasten the bag from the carrier.	**lazim tifúkk iʃʃánṭa min ꜥala-kkúrsi.**
No cycling!	**mamnúuꜥ rukúub iddarragáat húna!**[2]

[1] These signs belong to the written language and contain many features peculiar to it. Pronounce **ð** as *th* in "the".
[2] Written language.

TRAVELLING BY RAIL

Vocabulary

rail travel	ʕissáfar b-issíkka-lḫadíid
railway	ʕissíkka-lḫadíid
transport	naʕl ; wasáaʕil innáql
station	maḫáṭṭa, maḫaṭṭáat
train	ʕaṭr, ʕuṭúra (or ʕuṭuráat)
freight train	ʕáṭr ilbiḍáaẓa
express train	ʕilʕiksibrées ; ʕissaríiẓ
slow train	ʕilʕaʃʃáaʃ
diesel train	ʕiddíizil
inquiry office	máktab listiẓlamáat
booking office	ʃibbáak ittazáakir [1]
fare	ʕúgra
ticket	tazkára, tazáakir
platform ticket	tazkárit raṣíif
ticket collector	kumsáari, kumsaríyya
waiting room	ḫúgrit lintiẓáar/ʕistiráaḫa
buffet	bufée(h)
restaurant	máṭẓam, maṭáaẓim
cloak-room, left-luggage department	ʕilʕamanáat
lavatory	dóorit ilmáyya
platform	raṣíif, ʕarṣífa
signal	ʕiʃáara, ʕiʃaráat
goods van	ẓarabíyyit ilbiḍáaẓa
coach, carriage	ẓarabíyyit irrukkáab, ẓarabiyyáat irrukkáab
compartment	ṣalóon, ṣalonáat
seat	kúrsi, karáasi
corner corridor-seat	ʕikkúrsi-lli-gámb ilmamárr
corner window-seat	ʕikkúrsi-lli gámb iʃʃibbáak
sleeping-car	ẓarabíyyit innóom
dining-car	ẓarabíyyit ilʕákl
engine	wabúur, waburáat
engine-driver	sawwáaʕ ilʕaṭr
stoker, fireman	ẓaṭáʃgi, ẓaṭaʃgíyya
signalman	miḫwálgi, miḫwalgíyya
stationmaster	náaẓir ilmaḫáṭṭa, nuẓẓáar ilmaḫaṭṭáat
ticket inspector	mufáttiʃ, mufattiʃíin
guard's van	sibínsa [2]

[1] Lit. " ticket-window ".
[2] The last carriage in any train is called sibínsa.

porter	**ʃayyáal, ʃayyalíin**
soot	**hibáab**
smoke	**duxxáan**
rail	**ʔaḍíib, ʔuḍbáan**
railway-sleeper	**falánka, falankáat**
tunnel	**náfaʔ**
arrival	**wuṣúul**
departure	**ʔiyáam**
speed	**súrʕa**
the 9.40 express	**ʔiksibrées issáaʕa ʕáʃra-lla tilt**
to reserve seats	**ḥágaz, yíḥgiz tazkára f-ilʔáṭr**
to lean out of the window	**ṭall, yiṭúll min iʃʃibbáak**
to get into the train	**ríkib, yírkab ilʔáṭr**
to get out of the train	**nízil, yínzil min ilʔáṭr**
to get out while the train is going	**nízil, yínzil w-ilʔáṭri máaʃi**

Sentences

Where do I get a ticket?	**ʔagíib tazkára-mnéen ?/féen ʃibbáak ittazáakir ?**
Is the booking-office open?	**ʃibbáak ittazáakir maftúuḥ ?**
Third return Cairo and a platform ticket, please.	**tazkára zihaab wa ʔiyáab dáraga tálta li máṣr wi tazkárit raṣíif, min fáḍlak.**
Are you travelling via al-Qanātir?	**ʔinta-msáafir ʕan ṭaríiʔ ilʔanáaṭir ?**
Which is the shortest way from Cairo to Alexandria?	**ʔéeh ʔáʔṣar ṭaríiʔ min máṣri l-iskindiríyya ?**
What is the fare from Cairo to Suez?	**ʔilʔúgra káam min máṣri l-issuwées ?/táman ittazkára káam min máṣri l-issuwées ?/ʔittazkára-b káam min máṣri l-issuwées ?**
You have to pay a supplement on your ticket.	**láazim tídfaʕ fárʔ [1] ʕala tazkártak.**
Have your money ready.	**ḥáḍḍar filúusak.**
Can I break the journey?	**ʔáʔdar atxállif f-iṭṭaríiʔ ?**
Where must I change?	**ʔaɣáyyar féen ?**
Where is the Station Hotel?	**féen lukándit ilmaḥáṭṭa ?**
Where is the nearest hotel?	**féen áʔrab lukánda ?**
Can you tell me if the train will be late?	**tiʔdar tiʔúlli min fáḍlak ʔiza káan ilʔáṭri ḥayitʔáxxar walla láʔ ?**

[1] Lit. "difference".

Porter, please register this luggage to Shibin Al-Kawm.	ya ʃayyáal, min fáḍlak sággil ilɛafʃída li-ʃbíin ilkóom.
You will have to pay excess luggage on this trunk.	láazim tídfaɛ ʕúgra-zyáada ɛala-ssandúuʕ da.
Please bring the registration slip to me in the train.	min fáḍlak hátli wáṣl ittasgíil f-ilʕáṭr.
Please leave the suitcases in the left-luggage department.	min fáḍlak ḥúṭṭ iʃʃúnaṭ f-ilʕamanáat.
From which platform does the slow train start?	ʕilʕáṭr ilʕaʃʃáaʃ ḥayʕúum min ʕáyyi raṣíif?
Platform No. 4.	ʕirraṣíif nímra-rbáɛa.
I was lucky—I got a seat near the window with my back to the engine.	ʕana kútti maḥẓúuẓ—laʕéet kúrsi gámb iʃʃibbáak wi káan ḍáhri l-ilwabúur.
Did you reserve it?	kútti ḥágzu(h)?
All change!	kúll irrukkáab yiɣayyáru!
I have left my coat in the compartment.	ʕana síbt ilbálṭu-btáaɛi f-iṣṣalóon.
Where is the Lost Property Office?	féen máktab ilmafqudáat?/féen máktab ilḥagáat illi-tkun ḍáyɛa?
Where is the buffet?	féen ilbuféе(h)?
Over there.	hináak aho(h)!
Is there a restaurant car on the train?	fiih ɛarabíyyit ʕáklī f-ilʕáṭr?
The sleeping car is in the middle of the train.	ɛarabíyyit innóom fi wíṣṭ ilʕáṭr.
Arrival and departure times of trains are in the guide.	mawaɛíid ʕiyáam ilʕuṭuráat wi wuṣúlha f-iddalíil.
Here is the summer time-table.	dalíil ilʕuṭuráat f-iṣṣéef ahó(h).
I bought my ticket at a travel agency.	ḥagázt ittazkára min máktab issiyáaḥa.
Take your seats, please.	kúllī wáaḥid yúʕɛud fi makáanu(h), min faḍlúku(m).
Your suitcase is too large for the luggage-rack.	ʃanṭítak kibíira ʕáwi ɛala-rráff.
The big trunk goes in the luggage van.	ʕissandúuʕ ikkibíir láazim yirúuḥ ɛarabíyyit ilɛáfʃ.
Don't lean out of the window.	ma-ṭṭúlliʃ min iʃʃibbáak.
How long do we stop here?	ʕilʕáṭri ḥayúʕaf hina ʕaddéeh?
You had better ask the ticket inspector when he comes to check the tickets.	ʕilʕáḥsan innak tíbʕa tísʕal ikkumsáari lamma yíigi yúṭlub ittazáakir.

TRAVELLING BY SEA

Vocabulary

sea travel	**ʕissáfar b-ilbáhr**
port, harbour	**miina, mawáani**
steamship company	**ʃirkit ilbawáaxir**
passenger-boat	**ba(a)xirat [1] irrukkáab**
liner	**ʒa(a)birat [1] ilmuhitáat**
one-class liner	**ba(a)xira-b dáraga wáhda**
first class	**dáraga ʕúula**
second class	**dáraga tánya ; sukáandu**
tourist class	**dáraga siyahíyya**
passage, crossing	**ríhla, rihláat**
bow	**muqáddam ilba(a)xíra**
stern	**muʕáxxar ilba(a)xira**
hull	**háykal ilba(a)xira**
fo'c'sle	**ʕáʒla muqáddam ilba(a)xira**
mast	**sáari, sawáari**
anchor	**mirsa, maráasi**
cable	**hábl ilmirsa**
funnel	**madxána, madáaxin**
railings	**suur ; darabziin**
deck	**dáhr ilmárkib/sáth ilmárkib, duhúur/sutúuh ilmárkib ; dekk**
bridge	**ʕódt [2] ilqiyáada**
rudder	**dáffa, daffáat**
porthole	**kúwwa, kuwwáat**
gangway	**síllim, saláalim**
engine-room	**ʒámbar ilʒidda**
dining-saloon	**máṭʒam**
smoking-room	**húgrit ittadxíin**
lounge, saloon	**salóon**
1st class saloon	**salóon iddáraga-lʕúula**
deck-chair	**ʃizlúng (or ʃizlóon), ʃizlungáat**
life-boat	**ʕáarib innagáah, ʕawáarib innagáah**
life-belt	**hizáam innagáah, ʕihzímit (or hizímit) innagáah**
cabin	**kabíina, kabáayin**
berth	**siríir, saráayir**
hammock	**murgéeha, maragíih**
passenger	**ráakib, rukkáab**

[1] A somewhat literary form.
[2] Pronounced ʕoṭṭ.

captain	kábtin, kabáatin
sailor	baħħáar, baħħáara
stoker	ʕaṭáʃgi, ʕaṭaʃgiyya
steward	farráaʃ, farraʃíin ; xáaḍim, xáḍam
purser	ṣarráaf
harbour pilot	múrʃid ilmíina, murʃidíin ilmawáani
lighthouse	fanáar, fanaráat
tug-boat	raffáaṣ ʔirʃáad ilbawáaxir, raffaṣáat ʔirʃáad ilbawáaxir
wake	mágra-lba(a)xira
seasickness	duwáar ilbáħr
to sail (depart)	ʔábħar, yúbħir[1]
to steer	wággih, yiwággih
to roll	ʔitmáayil, yitmáayil
to pitch	ʔitmárgaħ, yitmárgaħ
to book a passage	ħágaz, yíħgiz tazkára-f márkib
to embark	ṭiliʕ, yíṭlaʕ ʕa-lmárkib/ríkib, yírkab ʕa-lmárkib
to disembark	nízil, yínzil min ʕa-lmárkib
to cast anchor	ráma, yírmi-lmírsa
to weigh anchor	ʃaal, yiʃíil ilmírsa

Sentences

Have you booked your passage?	ħagázt ittazkára ʕa-lba(a)xira ?
Which route are you travelling by?	misáafir bi ʔáyyi ṭaríiʔ ?
When are you sailing?	ʔilba(a)xira-lli ħatsáafir ʕaléeha ħatíṭlaʕ ʔímta ?
I'm travelling first class.	ʔana-msáafir b-iddáraga-lʔúula.
This cargo boat takes some passengers.	márkib ilbiḍáaʕa dí-btáaxud (báʕḍ ir)rukkáab.
How many knots does she do?	bitsáafir bi súrʕit káam ʕúʔda ?
This steamer is not one of the fastest, but she is very comfortable.	ʔilba(a)xira dí miʃ min ʔásraʕ ilbawáaxir, láakin issáfar ʕaléeha muríiħ gíddan.
Where does this liner call?	ʔilba(a)xira di-btúʔaʕ féen fi riħlítha ?
Where is my cabin?	kabínti féen ?
I cannot stand the noise of the propellers.	ʔana miʃ ʔáadir astáħmil dáwʃit ilmuħarrikáat.
Where can I get a deck-chair?	ʔaláaʔi kúrsi féen, min fáḍlak ?
Is there a doctor on board?	fiih duktóor ʕa-lba(a)xira ?

[1] A "learned" form.

My wife has been seasick for some days.	ʕissítti-btáɛti ʕaṣábha duwáar ilbáḥr min káam yóom.
The English Channel crossing was very stormy.	ɛubúur ilkanáal lingilíizi kan ṣáɛbi gíddan.
Are you a good sailor?	ʕínta ma-btitɛábʃi m-issáfar f-ilbáḥr?
We had a rough passage.	ʕirríḥla káanit mutɛíba ʕáwi.
The ship is rolling and pitching a lot.	ʕilba(a)xíra-btitmárgaḥ ʕáwi.
The sea is very rough.	ʕilbáḥri háayig gíddan.
It's getting foggy.	ʕiḍḍabáab biyíktar.
Visibility is bad.	ʕirrúʕya ṣáɛba.
We are twenty miles off the coast.	bénna-w béen iʃʃáṭṭi ɛiʃríin míil.
Where can I send a cable?	minéen aʕdar ábɛat tiliɣráaf, min faḍlak?
In the wireless operator's cabin.	min ʕóḍt[1] illasílki.
Get your passports and landing cards ready, the coast is in sight.	ḥaḍḍáru gawazáat issáfar bitaɛítkum wi-bṭaʕáat innuzúul, ʕarrábna ɛala-ʃʃáṭṭ.
The harbour pilot has already come on board.	múrʃid ilmíina wíṣil ɛa-lba(a)xíra.
We shall soon be alongside.	ʕíḥna ʕarrábna níwṣal ilbárr.
They are lowering the gangway.	ʕilbaḥḥáara biynazzílu-ssiʕáala.
The crane is unloading a car on to the dock side.	ʕilwínʃi biynázzil ɛarabíyya ɛa-lmíina.

TRAVELLING BY AIR

Vocabulary

air travel	sáfar b-iṭṭayyáara
aeronautics	ɛílm iṭṭayaráan
air transport	ʕinnáql iggáwwi
aircraft, aeroplane	ṭayyáara, ṭayyaráat
seaplane	ṭayyáara-lmaʕíyya
jet aircraft	ṭayyáara naffáasa (or naffáaθa[2]), ṭayyaráat naffáasa
airship	munṭáad, manaṭíid
flight	ṭayaráan; sáfar b-iṭṭayyáara, ʕasfáar b-iṭṭayyáara
air-route	xáṭṭi gáwwi
air-lines	ʃarikáat iṭṭayaráan
Egyptian Airways	ʃírkit (or ʃárikat) máṣri l-iṭṭayaráan

[1] Pronounced ʕoṭṭ.
[2] Pronounce θ as *th* in English "think".

aerodrome, airport, airfield	maṭáar, maṭaráat
steward	muḍíif, muḍiffín
stewardess	muḍíifa, muḍifáat
pilot	ṭayyáar, ṭayyaríin
flight engineer	muhándis iṭṭayyáara, muhandisíin iṭṭayyaráat
wireless operator	muhándis illasílki
passenger	musáafir, musafríin
ground staff	muwaẓẓafíin ilmaṭáar
engine	mákana, makanáat ; ɛídda, ɛídad
airscrew, propeller	marwáḥa, maráawiḥ
cockpit	máqɛad iṭṭayyáar
wing	ginaáḥ (or ganáaḥ), ʕigníḥa
wingspan	ṭúul igginaḥéen
fuselage	gísm iṭṭayyáara
rudder	dáffa, daffáat
tail	deel, diyúul
fuel oil	mazúut (or mazútt)
wind direction	ʕittigáah irríiḥ
vibration	zabzába
safety belt	ḥizáam ilʕamáan
air pocket	maṭábbi hawáaʕi
air-conditioning system	gihaáz takyíif ilháwa
tank	xazzáan, xazzanáat
parachute	paraʃútt, paraʃuttáat
parachutist	ʕinnáazil b-ilparaʃútt
rate of climb	súrɛit iṣṣuɛúud
rate of descent	súrɛit ilhubúuṭ
forced landing	ʕinnuzúul liṭṭiráari
civil aviation	ʕiṭṭayaráan ilmádani
military aviation	ʕiṭṭayaráan ilḥárbi
to fly	ṭaar, yiṭíir
to take off	ʕaam, yiʕúum
to land	nízil, yínzil
to crash	wíʕiɛ, yúʕaɛ [1]
to climb	ɛíli, yíɛla [2]

Sentences

Which is the shortest way to the airport ?	ʕéeh ʕáʕrab ṭaríiʕ l-ilmaṭáar ?
When does the next plane leave for London ?	ʕiṭṭayyáara-lli gáyya ḥatʕúum li lándan waʕtéeh ?

[1] More often in the feminine forms, wíʕɛit, túʕaɛ.
[2] More often in the feminine forms, ɛílyit, tíɛla.

The time-table is in the waiting-room.	**gádwal ilmawaɛíid f-ilʕistiráaħa.**
I should like to travel without breaking the journey.	**ʕana ɛáawiz asáafir fi ṭayyáara miʃ ħatúʕaf fi ʕáyyi ħítta tanya/ ʕana ɛáawiz asáafir min γéer tawáqquf.**
How many passengers does this aircraft take?	**ʕiṭṭayyáara di-btáaxud káam ráakib?**
This plane carries fifty passengers and a crew of five.	**ʕiṭṭayyáara di-btáaxud xamsíin ráakib wi fíiha xámas ṭayyaríin.**
Where will they put my luggage?	**ħayħúṭṭu ɛáfʃi féen?**
In the luggage hold.	**fi máxzan ilɛáfʃ.**
The plane is just taxi-ing out of the hangar.	**ʕiṭṭayyáara ṭálɛa min iggaráaʃ.**[1]
There's a two-engined plane just coming in.	**ṭayyáara-b muħarrikéen gáyya.**
Jets have a limited range.	**ʕiṭṭayyaráat innaffáaθa bitsáafir masafáat ʕuṣayyára bass.**
The load-capacity of an aircraft is limited to a certain weight.	**ħumúulit iṭṭayyáara maħdúuda-b wázni maxṣúuṣ.**
Each passenger is allowed to carry twenty kilos of luggage free.	**masmúuħ li kúlli-msáafir innu yáaxud maɛáah ɛiʃríin kéelu maggáanan.**
You have to pay on excess luggage.	**láazim tídfaɛ ɛala-lɛáfʃ izziyáada.**
Are you liable to be airsick?	**ʕinta bitdúux**[2] **min rukúub iṭṭayyáara?**
The stewardess is serving a meal.	**ʕilmuḍíifa bitʕáddim ilʕákl.**
The meteorological station has announced a storm warning.	**maṣláħit ilʕarṣáad ilgawwíyya ʕaɛlánit taħðíir**[3] **min ɛa(a)ṣífa.**
The take-off has been delayed (because of fog).	**ʕiṭṭayyáara-tʕaxxárit ɛan máwɛid ʕiyámha (ɛaʃan iḍḍabáab).**
We landed at Al-Maza[4] at the scheduled time.	**nizílna-f maṭáar ʕalmáaẓa f-ilmaɛáad ilmuħáddad.**

[1] In educated speech this word is very often pronounced with the final sound of " rouge " in place of ʃ.

[2] Pronounced **bidd-**.

[3] Pronounce **ð** as *th* in English " the "; **ʕaɛlánit**, too, is essentially a written form.

[4] Cairo Airport.

THE TOWN

Vocabulary

town	**bálad,[1] biláad ; madíina**
city	**madíina, múdun**
village	**bálad, biláad ; qárya, qúra**
capital	**ʒa(a)ṣíma, ʒawáaṣim**
provincial town	**mudiríyya, mudiriyyáat ; márkaz,[2] maráakiz**
country(side)	**riif** (pl. **ʕaryáaf**)
in the country	**f-ilʕaryáaf**
in town and country	**f-ilbándar wi f-irríif**
country (nation)	**barr, burúur [3]**
land (as opposed to sea)	**barr**
on sea and land and in the air	**f-ilbáḥrí-w ʒa-lbárrí-w f-iggáww**
suburb	**ḍa(a)ḥíya, ḍawáaḥi**
slum	**ḥáyyi faqíir, ʕaḥyáaʕ faqíira**
market (square)	**suuʕ, ʕaswáaʕ**
main square	**midáan raʕíisi**
street	**ʃáariʒ, ʃawáariʒ**
quarter	**ḥayy, ʕaḥyáaʕ**
lane	**ḥáara, ḥawáari**
blind-alley	**ʃáariʒ mazdúud**
side-street	**ʃáariʒ ga(a)níbi**
street corner	**náṣya, nawáaṣi ; rúknī ʃáariʒ, ʕirkáan ʃawáariʒ**
crossing	**ʒubúur ilmuʃáah, ʕamáakin ʒubúur ilmuʃáah ; taqáaṭuʒ**
road-junction	**taqáaṭuʒ ʃáariʒ . . .** (e.g. **fuʕáad) maʒa ʃáariʒ . . .** (e.g. **ʒimáad iddíin)**
private road	**ʃáariʒ maxṣúuṣi**
pavement	**raṣíif, ʕarṣífa**
kerb	**ḥáffit irraṣíif**
traffic lights	**ʕanwáar ilmurúur**
traffic signs	**ʕiʃaráat ilmurúur**
garden	**ginéena, ganáayin**
park	**muntázah, muntazaháat**
bridge	**kúbri, kabáari ; ʕanṭára, ʕanáaṭir [4]**
river	**nahr, ʕanháar**
railway station	**maḥáṭṭit issíkka-lḥadíid**
hospital	**mustáʃfa, mustaʃfayáat**
town hall	**baladíyya**
cemetery	**gabbáana, gabbanáat**

[1] A feminine form.

[2] An administrative division, strictly.

[3] Cf. **bárrī máṣr** "Egypt".

[4] Or **ʕanáaṭir.**

post office	máktab ilbariid ; ʕilbúṣṭa
police station	márkaz ilbulíiṣ ; núʕṭit ilbulíiṣ ; karakóona, karakonáat
public library	maktába ɛá(a)mma
school	madrása, madáaris
college	kullíyya, kulliyyáat
university	gámɛa, ga(a)miɛáat
museum	mátħaf, matáaħif
Museum of Antiquities	ʕantikxáana ; dáar ilʕaθáar ilmaṣríyya
Cairo General Library	ʕilkutubxáana
exhibition	máɛraḍ, maɛáariḍ
mosque	gáamiɛ, gawáamiɛ
church	kiníisa, kanáayis
cathedral	katidraʕíyya, katidraʕiyyáat
synagogue	kiníst ilyahúud
fire station	ʕilmaṭáafi ; maħáṭṭit ilħaríiʕ
block of flats	ɛimáara, ɛimaráat
shop	dukkáan, dakakíin
restaurant	máṭɛam, maṭáaɛim
café	ʕáhwa, ʕaháawi
bar, wine-shop	baar, baráat ; xammáara, xammaráat
flat, apartment	ʃáʕʕa, ʃúʕaʕ
shop-window	batríina, batrináat
policeman	ɛaskári bulíiṣ, ɛasáakir bulíiṣ
traffic policeman	ɛaskári-lmurúur
night-watchman	yafíir, yúfara
pedestrian	máaʃi, maʃyíin
street cleaner	kannáas, kannasíin
bus	ʕutubíis, ʕutubisáat
tramcar	turmáay, turmayáat
lorry	lúuri, luriyyáat ; kámyun, kamyunáat
car	ɛarabíyya, ɛarabiyyáat ; ʕuṭumbíil, ʕuṭumbiláat ; sayyáara, sayyaráat
private car	ɛarabíyya malláaki
cart	ɛarabíyya kárru, ɛarabiyyáat kárru
gharry	ħanṭúur, ħanaṭíir
gharry-driver, cart-driver	ɛarbági, ɛarbagíyya
taxi	táksi, taksiyyáat ; ɛarabíyyit ʕúgra
taxi-rank	máwʕaf taksiyyáat
stopping-place	máwʕaf, mawáaʕif ; maħáṭṭit ilʕutubíis (or maħáṭṭit itturmáay)
palace	ʕaṣr, ʕuṣúur ; saráaya, sarayáat
night-club	kázinu (or kazíinu), kazinuháat

houseboat	ʕawwáama, ʕawwamáat
Nile steamer	ba(a)xíra nilíyya
Tourist police	ʔilbulíiṣ issiyáaḥi
dragoman	turgumáan, tarágma
beggar	ʃaḥḥáat, ʃaḥḥatíin
terminus	ʔáaxir ilxáṭṭ, ʔawáaxir ilxuṭúuṭ
entrance	duxúul, ṭúruʔ idduxúul ; baab, ʔabwáab
exit	báab ilxurúug, ʔabwáab ilxurúug
standing	wáaʔif, wáʔfa, waʔfíin [1]
sitting	ʔáaʕid, ʔáʕda, ʔaʕdíin [1]
3 standing (places)	tálat maḥalláat l-ilwuʔúuf
on foot	ʕa-lʔádam
first class	dáraga ʔúula
second class	dáraga tánya
to ride, get in *or* on a vehicle	ríkib, yírkab (ilʕarabíyya, etc.)
to get on a horse	ríkib, yírkab ʕala-lḥuṣáan
to get off	nízil, yínzil (min)
to walk	míʃi, yímʃi
to take a walk	ʔitmáʃʃa, yitmáʃʃa ; ʔitfássaḥ, yitfássaḥ

Sentences

How far is it to the shopping centre?	ʔilmasáafa ʔaddéeh min hína-l ʃáariʕ issúuʔ (or l-iddakakíin) ?
Which is the shortest way to the town centre?	ʔéeh ʔáʔrab ṭaríiʔ li wiṣṭ ilbálad ?
Can you tell me the way to the theatre?	tiʔdar tiʔúlli min fáḍlak ilmásraḥ féen ?
Where is the post office?	féen ilbúṣṭa/máktab ilbaríid ?
The second turning on the right.	ʔittaḥwíida-ttánya ʕa-lyimíin.
Don't cross the street unless the green light is on.	ma-tʕaddíiʃ iʃʃáariʕ ílla lamma-ykúun innúur láxḍar minúwwar.
There are the traffic lights.	ʔanwáar ilmurúur ahé(h).
Don't step off the pavement.	ma tinzílʃi min ʕa-rraṣíif.
The traffic is very heavy.	ʔilmurúur záḥma ʔáwi.
Mind the lorry!	ḥáasib (ḥásba, ḥasbíin[1]) illúuri ; xud (xúdi, xúdu [1]) báalak (báalik, bálkum) m-illúuri.
There is a traffic jam at the corner of Suliman Pasha Street.	fiih ʕáṭala (f-ilmurúur) fi ʔáwwil ʃáariʕ silimáan baaʃa.
The streets are narrow.	ʔiʃʃawáariʕ dayyáʔa.
I've lost my way.	ʔana táayih (ʔana táyha, ʔiḥna tayhíin [1]).

[1] Masculine singular, feminine singular, and plural forms, in that order.

Turn to the left.	ḥáwwid ɛa-ʃʃimáal.
Straight on.	ɛala ṭúul ; dúɣri.
Where is the main entrance to the hospital ?	féen ilmádxal irraʕíisi bitaɛ ilmustáʃfa ?
Where does Mr. Ali Fathi live ?	ʕissáyyid ɛáli fátḥi sáakin féen ?
On the top floor.	fi ʕáaxir dóor f-ilɛimáara.
They have a flat on the ground floor.	lúhum ʃáʕʕa f-iddóor ilʕárḍi.
Can I get to Liberation Square by bus ?	ʕáʕdar arúuḥ midáan ittaḥríir b-ilʕutubíis ?
Take the lift. Or do you prefer the stairs ?	ʕiṭlaɛ f-ilʕaṣanṣéer. walla-tḥíbbi tiṭlaɛ b-issíllim ?
You have to get a ticket.	láazim tiʕṭaɛ tazkára.
Get your ticket at the ticket-office.	háat tazkártak min ʃibbáak ittazáakir.
You can also take the bus.	tiʕdar táaxud ilʕutubíis bárḍu(h).
The buses are crowded.	ʕilʕutubisáat záḥma.
Let the passengers off first, please.	ʕinnáazil ilʕáwwal, min faḍlúku(m).
We are full up. Next bus, please.	ʕilʕutubíis malyáan. xúd illi báɛdu(h).
In Alexandria there are both single- and double-decker trams.	fiih turmayáat bi doréen wi turmayáat bi dóor wáaḥid f-iskindiríyya.
Standing room only.	fiih maḥalláat wuʕúuf báss.
Pass down inside.	ʕidxúlu gúwwa min faḍlúku.
Don't push.	ma-tzúʕʕiʃ.[1]
Is there no queue ?	ma fiiʃ ṭabúur ?
Keep a passage clear.	wassáɛu síkka min faḍlúkum.
Fares, please.	tazáakir min faḍlúkum.
I've lost my ticket.	tazkárti ḍáaɛit.
Don't get off while the train is going.	ma tinzílʃi w-ilʕáṭri máaʃi.
When does the last bus leave ?	ʕáaxir ʕutubíis biyʕúum issáaɛa káam ?
Sunday traffic is limited.	ma fiiʃ ɛarabiyyáat kitíir yóom ilḥádd.
Where do I have to get off ?	ʕánzil féen ?
No thoroughfare.	ṭaríiq masdúud.[2]
Closed to pedestrians.	mamnúuɛ murúur ilmuʃáah.[2]
No admittance (private).	mamnúuɛ idduxúul (xaaṣṣ).[2]

[1] Pronounced **ma-dz . . .**

[2] Written language.

Have you seen the illuminated advertisements in the centre of the city?	ʃúft ilʕiɛlanáat ilminawwára-lli-f wiṣṭ ilbálad?
They are hosing down the roadways.	biyiɣsílu-ʃʃawáariɛ b-ilxaraṭíim.[1]

HOTELS

Vocabulary

hotel	lukánda, lukandáat; fúnduq, fanáadiq
single room	ʕóoḍa-l ʃáxṣi wáaḥid
double room	ʕóoḍa l-itnéen
private bathroom	ḥammáam xuṣúuṣi
reception desk	ɣúrfit listiqbáal; listiqbáal
key	muftáaḥ, mafatíiḥ
lounge	ʕistiráaḥa, ʕistiraḥáat
dining-room	ʕóḍt[2] ilʕákl; ɣúrfit iṭṭaɛáam
writing-room	ʕóḍt[2] ikkitáaba
lobby	hool
gentlemen's cloakroom	dáwrit miyáah irrijáal[3]
ladies' cloakroom	dáwrit miyáah issayyidáat[4]
corridor	mamárr, mamarráat
service stairs	síllim ilxádam
lift	ʕaṣanṣéer, ʕaṣanṣeráat
fan	marwáḥa, maráawiḥ
air conditioning	takyíif háwa
bell	gáras, ʕagráas
bell-boy	farráaʃ, farraʃíin
chambermaid	xaddáama, xaddamáat
boots	massáaḥ iggízam
waiter	garsóon, garsonáat
waitress	garsóona, garsonáat
hall-porter	farráaʃ, farraʃíin
doorman	bawwáab, bawwabíin
manager	mudíir, mudiríin
proprietor	ṣáaḥib ilmílk, ʕaṣḥáab ilmílk
cook	ṭabbáax, ṭabbaxíin
to book (a room/accommodation)	ḥágaz, yíḥgiz (ʕóoḍa/maḥáll)
to lodge	síkin (or sákan), yúskun

[1] Singular xarṭúum.
[2] Pronounced ʕoṭṭ.
[3] Written language. Pronounce j as in English "jeep".
[4] Written language.

to stay at (a hotel)	nízil, yínzil (fi lukánda)
to cancel (a booking)	láɣa, yílɣi (ħágz ilʕóoḍa)
to settle (the bill)	dáfaɛ, yídfaɛ (ilħisáab)

Sentences

Which hotel are you staying at?	ʕinta náazil fi ʕáyyi lukánda?
The service is good (bad).	ʕilxídma ṭayyíba (wíħʃa).
Can I have a single room?	ɛáawiz ʕóoḍa-l wáaħid.
Is there central heating and running hot and cold water in the rooms?	fíih tadfíya-w máyya súxna-w sáʕɛa f-ilʕíwaḍ?
Here is the key to your room.	ʕitfáḍḍal muftáaħ ʕóḍtak.[1]
The lift boy will take your luggage up.	ɛáamil ilʕaṣanṣéer ħayṭállaɛ ʃúnaṭak fóoʕ.
Can I have breakfast in my room?	múmkin tigíbli fuṭúuri-f ʕoḍti?[1]
Where is the bathroom, please?	féen ilħammáam, min faḍlak?
Please give me another towel and some soap.	ʕiddíini min fáḍlak fúuṭa tánya-w ṣabúuna.
I have ordered a room with bath.	ʕana ṭalábti ʕóoḍa-b ħammáam.
Please enter your name and address in the visitors' book.	min fáḍlak ʕíktib ísmak wi ɛunwáanak fi dáftar izzuwwáar.
Will you please fill in this form.	ʕímla-lbayanáat di min fáḍlak.
How long do you intend to stay?	ħaḍrítak [2] ħatistánna f-illukánda ʕaddéeh?
What are your terms?	ħádfaɛ káam, min faḍlak?
How much is bed and breakfast?	ʕilmabíit w-ilfuṭúur bi káam?
I should like another blanket.	ʕana ɛáawiz baṭṭaníyya tánya min faḍlak.
Have you reserved a room for me?	ʕintu ħagzíin ʕóoḍa líyya?
Where is the bar?	féen ilbáar?
I want to lodge a complaint with the manager.	ʕana ɛáawiz akállim ilmudíir.[3]
Any letters for me?	fíih gawabáat ɛaʃáani?
Can you call me to-morrow at six o'clock?	ṣaħħíini búkra-ssáaɛa sítta, min faḍlak.
Ring twice for the chambermaid.	ʕíḍrab iggáras marritéen li ṭálab ilxaddáama.
Where did you put my brush and comb?	ħaṭṭéet ilfúrʃa w-ilmíʃṭi-btúuɛi féen?

[1] Pronounced ʕoṭṭ-.
[2] Term of polite address.
[3] Lit. "... to talk to the manager".

When can you let me have my laundry back?	ħatrággaɛ ilɣasíil waʕtéeh ?
Here is my laundry list:	ʕáymit ilɣasíil bitáaɛ(i)-ahó(h) :
4 white shirts.	ʕárbaɛ ʕumṣáan bíiḍ.
3 coloured shirts.	tálat ʕumṣáan milawwiníin.
6 collars (starched).	sítti yaʕáat (minaʃíyya).
5 soft collars.	xámas yaʕáat miʃ minaʃíyya.
5 detached collars.	xámas yaʕáat munfáṣila.
2 vests.	fanillitéen.[1]
2 pairs of underpants.	libaséen.
1 pair of pyjamas.	bijáama.
10 handkerchiefs.	ɛáʃar manadíil.
5 pairs of socks.	xámast igwáaz ʃarabáat.
2 blouses.	biloztéen.[2]
3 slips.	tálat ʕumṣáan ħaríimi.
2 nightdresses.	ʕamiṣéen nóom.
3 pairs of stockings.	tálatt igwáaz ʃarabáat ħaríimi.
1 linen dress.	fustáan tíil wáaħid.
1 dressing gown.	róob wáaħid.
Is there a barber's shop in the hotel?	fíih dukkáan ħalláaʕ f-illukánda ?
I've forgotten my razor.	ʕana-nsíit mákanit ilħiláaʕa-btáɛti.
Can I have this suit pressed?	múmkin tikwíili-lbadláadi, min faḍlak.
Let me have the bill, please.	ʕiddíini ʕáymit ilħisáab, min faḍlak.
I stayed at the Misr for a week.	ʕana-nzíltī-f lukándit máṣrī-l múddit ʕusbúuɛ.
Is there anywhere to stay there?	fíih lukandáat hináak ?
I'm looking for a hotel which is not too expensive.	ʕana ɛáawiz lukánda mutawaṣṣiṭa.[3]
Do you like your hotel?	ʕillukánda ɛagbáak ?
The food is good and plentiful.	ʕilʕáklī-ktíir wi-kwáyyis.
The cooking is excellent.	ʕiṭṭóbxi mumtáaz.
Can I book rooms for August?	ʕáʕdar áħgiz ʕóoḍa-l ʕaɣúṣṭuṣ ?
Sorry, we are booked up till October.	ʕáasif, ʕilʕúwaḍ kulláha maħgúuza-lɣáayit ʕuktóobar.
You should have booked long in advance.	kan láazim tíħgiz min bádri ʕáwi.

[1] Sing. fanílla.
[2] Sing. bilóoza.
[3] Lit. "average"

RESTAURANTS AND MEALS

Vocabulary

restaurant	**máṭʕam, maṭáaʕim**
café	**ʕáhwa, ʕaháawi**
bar	**baar, baráat**
breakfast	**fuṭúur**
lunch	**ɣáda**
dinner	**ʕáʃa**
meal	**ʔákla, ʔakláat**
plate, dish	**ṭábaʔ, ʔiṭbáaʔ**
knife	**sikkíina, sakakíin**
fork	**ʃóoka, ʃíwak** (or **ʃúwak**)
spoon	**maʕláʔa, maʕáaliʔ**
tea-spoon	**maʕláʔit ʃáay**
cup	**fingáal, fanagíil**
saucer	**ṭábaʔ fingáal**
glass	**kubbáaya, kubbayáat**
tea-pot, coffee-pot	**barráad, bararíid**
milk-jug	**ʔabríiʔ lában, ʔabaríiʔ lában**
sugar-basin	**sukkaríyya, sukkariyyáat**
water-jug	**ʔabríiʔ máyya**
tray	**ṣiníyya, ṣiniyyáat** (or **ṣawáani**)
saucepan	**kasaróola, kasaroláat**
menu, bill of fare	**ʔilʔáyma ; ʔáymit ilʔasʕáar** [1]
course	**ṣanf, ʔaṣnáaf**
vegetarian	**nabáati, nabatiyyíin**
meat dish	**ʔáklit láhma**
wine	**xamr**
spirits	**maʃrubáat ru(u)híyya**
hors d'œuvre	**muʃahhiyáat**
dessert	**fákha**
sweet	(course) **hilw ;** (sweetmeat) **túufi, tufiyyáat**
sandwich	**sándawitʃ** (or **sandi-**), **sandawitʃáat**
salt	**malh**
pepper	**filfil**
chilli	**ʔárni filfil, ʔurúun filfil**
parsley	**baʔdúunis**
mustard	**mustárda**
vinegar	**xall**
oil	**zeet, ziyúut**
butter	**zíbda**

[1] Lit. " price-list ".

clarified butter, ghi	samn
lard	díhni xanzíir
fat	ʃaħm
bread	ʕeeʃ
French bread	ʕéeʃ afrángi
local bread	ʕéeʃ báladi
loaf	riɣíif, ʔirɣíifa
toast	tust
tinned meat	láħma maħfúuẓa
ham (*also* pork *and* bacon)	xanzíir
sausage	sugúʔʔ (c.),[1] ṣubáaʕ sugúʔʔ, ṣawáabiʕ sugúʔʔ
egg	beeḍ (c.), béeḍa, beḍáat [2]
fried eggs	béeḍ máʔli
scrambled eggs	béeḍ maḍrúub
boiled egg	béeḍa maslúuʔa
omelette	ʕígga, ʕiggáat
soup	ʃúrba
vegetable soup	ʃúrbit xuḍáar
lentil soup	ʃúrbit ʕáts
chicken soup	ʃúrbit firáax
tomato soup	ʃúrbit ṭamáaṭim
joint	fáxda
veal	láħma-btíllu ; ʕaggáali
beef	láħma báʔari
beefsteak	filée
mutton	láħma ḍáani
lamb	láħma ʔúuzi
fish	sámak (c.), sámaka, samakáat
pond fish	búlṭi
mullet	búuri
sole	sámak múusa [3]
vegetables	xuḍáar
potatoes	baṭáaṭiṣ (c.), baṭaṭṣáaya, baṭaṭṣáat
potato crisps	baṭáaṭiṣ maʔlíyya ; baṭáaṭiṣ maħammára
rice	ruzz
lettuce	xaṣṣ (c.), xaṣṣáaya, xaṣṣáat
salad	ṣálaṭa, ṣalaṭáat
cabbage	kurúmb (c.), kurúmba, kurumbáat
cauliflower	ʔarnabíiṭ (c.), ʔarnabíiṭa, ʔarnabiṭáat

[1] (c.) = collective noun.

[2] Cf. ṭúurit béeḍ or ʔárbaʕ beḍáat "4 eggs", dástit béeḍ or ʔiṭnáaʃar béeḍa "a dozen eggs".

[3] The names of other fish are given on p. 202.

carrots	gáẓaṛ (c.), gaẓaráaya, gaẓaráat
spinach	sabáanix (or si-)
beans	fuul (c.), ḥabbáayit fúul, ḥabbáat fúul
peanuts	fúul sudáani
green beans	faṣúlya (c.), ḥabbáayit faṣúlya, ḥabbáat faṣúlya
peas	bisílla (c.), ḥabbáayit bisílla, ḥabbáat bisílla
onions	báṣal (c.), baṣaláaya, baṣaláat
garlic	toom (c.), ráas tóom, rúus tóom
pumpkin	ʕarɛ (c.), ʕarɛáaya, ʕarɛáat
marrow (small)	kúusa (c.), kusáaya, kusáat
melon	ʃammáam (c.), ʃammáama, ʃammamáat
Jew's mallow	muluxíyya
ladies' fingers	bámya
fruit	fákha, fawáakih
stewed fruit	fákha maṭbúuxa
cheese	gíbna
minced meat	láḥma mafrúuma ; kúfta
beer	bíira
cider	sáydar
mineral waters	miyáah fawwáara [1]
lemonade	lamunáatu
lemon juice	ɛaṣíir lamúun
orange juice	ɛaṣíir burtuʕáan
coffee	ʕáhwa
tea	ʃaay
cocoa	kakáaw
milk	lában
cream	ʕíʃṭa
pigeon	ḥamáam
duck	baṭṭ
turkey	díik rúumi
chicken	fárxa ; firáax
breast of chicken	sídri fárxa
leg of chicken	wírki fárxa
pastry, pastries	gatóo, gatoháat
cake	kaḥk (c.), káḥka, kaḥkáat
biscuits	baskawíit (c.), baskawíita, baskawitáat
jam	mirábba
table napkin	fúuṭit ṣúfra, fúwaṭ ṣúfra
tablecloth	máfraʃ, mafáariʃ
bill, check	ḥisáab
tip	baʕʃíiʃ

[1] A "learned" form.

A FEW EGYPTIAN DISHES

kiʃk	dish of which yoghourt and flour are important ingredients
túrli	fried meat and vegetables in layers
ṭaɛmíyya	fried bean purée
kíbad wi kaláawi	liver(s) and kidneys
láḥma kustaléeta	chops (usually lamb)
ʃiiʃ kabáab	meat grilled on a spit
kúfta	minced meat similarly grilled
kabáab ḥálla	braised, stewed meat
láḥma-mḥammára	fried meat, lemon, onions, salt and pepper
láḥma rústu b-ilbéet	roast meat and egg pie served in slices
siníyyit baṭáaṭis b-illáḥm	tray of roast meat and potatoes (often obtainable from butcher's)
láḥma buftéek	escalope [1]
ḥamáam máʃwi	roast pigeon
ḥamáam máḥʃi	pigeon stuffed with rice and/or minced meat and fried in ghi
láḥma-b tarbíya	meat with white sauce and mixed vegetables
láḥma-b jáli	jellied meat
láḥma maslúuʕa	boiled meat
fáttit láḥma	bread and meat soup
sámak máʕli	fried fish
sámak máʃwi	baked fish
kúftit sámak	minced fish
kúftit gambári	minced prawns
siníyyit sámak	fish baked in tomato sauce
sámak ʕámama	fish, onions, raisins, salt, pepper, mustard, dipped in oil and baked
sámak ma(a)yunáyz	boiled fish with mayonnaise; ail-au-lit
sálaṭit ṭaḥíina	sesame oil, salt, pepper, vinegar, spices
sálaṭit ṭamáaṭim	tomato salad
sálaṭit zabáadi	yoghourt (**zabáadi**) with the addition of salt, garlic, and dry mint
sálaṭit bidingáan (or **bitingáan**)	aubergine salad
báaba ɣánnu	aubergine and "**ṭaḥiina**" salad together
máḥʃi-krúmb	stuffed cabbage
máḥʃi waraʕ ɛínab or **ḍúlma**	stuffed vine leaves

[1] **buftéek** relates to the method of frying in crumbs.

máḥʃi bidingáan	stuffed brinjals
máḥʃi ṭamáaṭim	stuffed tomatoes
máḥʃi waraʕ xáss	stuffed lettuce leaves
máḥʃi kúusa	stuffed marrows
máḥʃi baṭáaṭis	stuffed potatoes
misaʕáaɛa	aubergine cooked in tomato sauce
ʕilḥággi rúẓẓ	rice, raisins, liver or kidney of poultry casseroled
fúul midámmis	baked beans
fúul náabit	boiled beans

Sentences

Have you booked a table in advance?	**ʕinta ḥáagiz ṭarabéeẓa ?**
Waiter, a table for four, please.	**ya garsóon, ṭarabéeẓa l-arbáɛa, min faḍlak.**
Here is the menu.	**ʕitfáḍḍal ilʕáyma.**
What would you like?	**tiḥíbbi ʕéeh ?**
There are many courses to choose from.	**fiih ʕaṣnáaf kitiira tiʕdar tixtáar minha.**
Does the menu appeal to you or would you prefer to eat *à la carte*?	**tiḥíbbi táaxud ʕákli káamil walla tixtáar ilʕaṣnáaf illi tiɛgíbak ?**
I can recommend our fish.	**ɛandína sámak kuwáyyis xáaliṣ.**
The special dish to-day is mutton and spinach.	**ʕilʕákli-lmaxṣúuṣa-nnahárda sabáanix b-illáḥma-ḍḍáani.**
What have you in the way of meat?	**ʕéeh ʕanwáaɛ illáḥma-lli ɛandúkum ?**
Anything you like; we have all kinds.	**ʕilli yiɛgíbak; ɛandína kúlli ḥáaga.**
I would like a lettuce and tomato salad dressed with oil and vinegar.	**ʕana ɛáawiz sálaṭa xáḍra min faḍlak wi ɛaléeha xálli-w zéet zetúun.**
What can I order for you?	**ʕáṭlub li siyádtak[1] ʕéeh ?**
Could I have some kidneys or liver with rice and onions?	**tiʕdar tigíbli min fáḍlak kaláawi walla kíbda b-ilbáṣal w-irrúzz ?**
What alternative is there?	**ɛandúku ʕéeh táani ?**
What would you like to follow?	**tiḥíbbi táaxud ḥáaga tánya ?**
Are there any sweets?	**ɛandúku ḥilw ?**
Would you like me to bring you some fruit?	**tiḥíbb agíblak fákha ?**

[1] **siyáada + ak**; pronounced **siyáttak.**

There is no more fruit.	ma ʕátʃi fiih fákha or ma-fḍilʃi fákha.
Would you like something to drink?	tiḥíbbi tiʃrab ḥáaga?
Would you like Turkish or French coffee?	tiḥíbbi tiʃrab ʔáhwa túrki walla ʔáhwa faransáawi?
How would you like it? Very sweet, sweet, a little sugar, or unsweetened?	tiḥibbáha-zzáay? ziyáada, maẓbúuṭa, ʕa-rríiḥa walla sáada?
I prefer Turkish coffee.	ʔan-afáḍḍal ilʔáhwa-ttúrki.
Have a cigarette.	tifáḍḍal sigáara.
Thank you but may I smoke my pipe?	mutaʃákkir ʔáwi, ʔana ḥadáxxan ilbíiba-ḅtáʕti, law samáḥt?
Where have I put my matches?	ʔana ḥaṭṭéet ikkabríit féen?
Here we are, I've a lighter.	ʔitfáḍḍal, ʔana-mʕáaya walláaʕa-hé(h)!
Pass the ashtray, please.	nawílni iṭṭaʔṭúuʔa, min faḍlak.
Let me have the bill, please.	ʔiddíini-lḥisáab, min faḍlak.
Would you like a drink at the bar?	tiḥíbbi tiʃrab ḥáaga ʕa-lbáar?
I would like to sit at a table outside in the fresh air.	ʔana ʕáawiz áʔʕud ʕala ṭarabéeẓa bárra f-ilháwa.
Come and have supper with us.	ʔitfáḍḍal ilʕáʃa ʕandína.
Come and take pot-luck with us.	taʕáala náakul ilmawgúud.
Heavy meals do not agree with me.	ʔilʔákli-ttiʔíil biyitʕábni.
Shall I get you something light?	ʔagíblak ḥáaga xafíifa?
What would you like for breakfast?	tiḥíbbi tifṭar ʔéeh?
Can I have a boiled egg, bread and butter, and honey?	ʔiddíini béeḍa maslúuʔa, wi ʕéeʃ wi zíbda wi ʕásal ábyaḍ?
Something cold.	ḥáaga sáʔʕa.
Iced drinks.	maʃrubáat muθallága.[1]
No gratuities.	mamnúuʕ ʔiʕṭáaʔ ʔáyyi nuqúud l-ilxádam.
I have no appetite.	ʔana ma líiʃ níyya/nífsi mazdúuda.
He has a hearty appetite.	huwwa ʔakúul.
Here's health!	fiṣiḥḥítak!
Would you like to share our meal?	ʔitfáḍḍal kúl maʕáana?
No, thank you. I have already eaten. *Bon appétit.*	mutaʃákkir giddan, ʔana kált ʔábli kída. b-ilhána w-iʃʃífa.

[1] Written language. Pronounce θ as *th* in "think".

SHOPPING

Vocabulary

shop	dukkáan, dakakíin
wholesaler's	dukkáan ilgúmla
retailer's	dukkáan ilʔɑṭṭáɑʕi
stores	maḥáll ilʔumáaʃ, maḥalláat ilʔumáaʃ
store, depot	máxzan, maxáazin
baker's shop	máxbaz, maxáabiz
pastrycook('s)	ḥalawáani, ḥalawaníyya
butcher('s)	gɑẓẓáɑr, gɑẓẓɑríin
fishmonger('s)	sammáak, sammakíin
poulterer('s)	farárgi, farargíyya
grocer('s)	baʔʔáal, baʔʔalíin
greengrocer('s)	xúḍɑri, xuḍɑríyya
fruiterer('s)	fakaháani, fakahaníyya
stationer's, bookseller's	maktába, maktabáat
men's outfitter('s)	xayyáɑṭ, xayyɑṭíin
haberdasher('s)	xirdawáati, xirdawatíyya
hardware dealer('s)	bayyáaʕ ʔadawáat ilḥidáada, bayyaʕíin ʔadawáat ilḥidáada
cleaner's and dyer's	maḥálli tɑnẓíif ilmaláabis ; tintiraríi
tobacconist('s)	daxáxni, daxaxníyya
dispensing chemist('s)	ṣɑyḍáli, ṣɑyḍɑlíyya
chemist's shop	ṣɑyḍɑlíyya ; ʔagzaxáana, ʔagzaxanáat
cigarette kiosk	kúʃki sagáayir, ʔikʃáak sagáayir
shop assistant	ṣábi (or ṣɑby), ṣubyáan
customer	zibúun, zabáayin
to buy	ʔiʃtára, yiʃtíri
to sell	baaʕ, yibíiʕ
to choose	ʔixtáɑr, yixtáɑr
to order	ṭálɑb, yúṭlub
to cancel	láɣa, yílɣi
to exchange	báddil, yibáddil ; ɣáyyɑr, yiɣáyyɑr
to deliver	sállim, yisállim
to fetch	gaab, yigíib
to bargain	fáɑṣil, yifáɑṣil
to wrap up	laff, yilíff

Sentences

At the baker's:	ʕand ilxabbáaz:
What can I get for you?/Are you being served?	ʔáyyi xídma?

I want two fresh loaves of European bread.	**ʔana ɛáawiz riɣiféen ɛéeʃ afrángi ṣabħíin.**[1]
6 rolls, please.	**sitt iryífa-frángi-ṣɣayyaríin, min faḍlak.**
At the fruiterer's:	**ɛand ilfakaháani:**
Have you any apples, please?	**ɛándak tiffáaħ, min faḍlak?**
I should like three pounds of pears, please.	**ʔana ɛáawiz tálatt irṭáal**[2] **kummítra, min faḍlak.**
Could you send me a dozen tangerines, half a dozen lemons, two pounds of bananas, and a pound of grapes?	**ʔibɛátli min fáḍlak iṭnáaʃar yusafandíyya, wi sítti lamunáat, wi raṭléen móoz wi ráṭli ɛínab?**
The walnuts and almonds are too dear. I'll take some peanuts instead.	**ʔiggóoz w-illóoz ɣalyíin ʔáwi.**[3] **ħáaxud ʃuwáyyit fúul sudáani badálhum.**
Strawberries are out of season, madam/sir.	**múusim ilfaráwla fáat, ya sitt/ħáḍrit** (or **sáyyid**).
Have you any figs or plums?	**ɛándak tiin walla barʔúuʔ?**
Will you be having any cherries in to-morrow?	**ħaykúun ɛandúkum kiréez búkra, min faḍlak?**
Shall I keep some for you, madam?	**ʔaħgízlik ʃuwáyya** (or **tiħíbb(i) aħgízlik ʃuwáyya**)**, ya sitt.**
At the grocer's:	**ɛand ilbaʔʔáal:**
I want a packet of raisins and a pound of almonds.	**ɛáawiz báaku-zbíib wi ráṭli lóoz.**
Half a pound of ground coffee and a quarter of a pound of tea, please.	**núṣṣi ráṭli búnni maṭħúun wi rúbɛi ráṭli ʃáay, min faḍlak.**
Will you have granulated or lump sugar?	**tiħíbbi súkkar náaɛim walla súkkar mákana?**
Half a litre of vinegar, please.	**núṣṣi lítri xáll, min faḍlak.**
I want a litre of olive oil and three pounds of flour.	**ʔiddíini min fáḍlak lítri zéet zetúun wi tálatt irṭáal diʔíiʔ.**
Have you any tinned fruit?	**ɛándak** (or **ɛandúku(m)**) **fákha maħfúuza** (or **fákha f-ilɛílab**)**?**
At the market:	**f-issúuʔ:**
I want five pounds of tomatoes, please.	**ɛáawiz xámast irṭáal ṭamáaṭim, min faḍlak.**

[1] Cf. also **ṭáaza** (invariable) = "fresh" (of fruit, vegetables, etc.).
[2] Strictly, 1 rotl = approx. ⅞ lb.
[3] Arabic has nothing corresponding to the distinction between *too dear* and *very dear*.

The tomatoes and radishes are cheap and fresh.	ʔiṭṭamáaṭim w-ilfígli-rxáaṣ wi ṣabḥíin (or ṭáaẓa).
Could you please weigh this chicken for me?	ʔiwzínli [1]-lfárxa di, min faḍlak?
Have you a small cabbage or lettuce and carrots?	ɛándak kurúmba-ṣγayyára walla xaṣṣáaya-w gáẓar?

At the stores: | **f-iddakakíin ikkibíira:**

There is a sale on at the stores.	fíih taxfíiḍ f-ilmaḥalláat.
What sort of woollen material have you in stock?	ʔéeh ʔanwáaɛ ilʔaṣwáaf illi ɛandúkum, min faḍlak?
Can you show me your designs in silks?	warríini min fáḍlak ʔanwáaɛ ilḥaríir illi ɛandúku?
We have a large selection.	ɛandína magmúuɛa-kbíira.
Four metres of red velvet, please.	ʔárbaɛt imtáar ʔaṭíifa ḥámra (or ḥumr), min faḍlak.
That will do.	dá-ll-ana ɛáwzu(h).
A reel of black cotton.	bákara sóoda.
A reel of black silk (thread).	bákarit xéet ḥaríir ásmar.
Three metres of that white elastic.	tálatt imtáar min ilʔástik lábyaḍ dá.
I also want a zip-fastener.	ʔana ɛáawiz sústa.
Do you stock scissors?	ɛandúku-mʔaṣṣáat?
I want a thimble and some tape.	ʔana ɛáwza [2] kuʃtubáan wi-ʃwáyyit ʃiríiṭ.
I want a plain blue tie and a coloured handkerchief to match.	ʔana ɛáawiz karafíṭṭa [3] zárʔa wi mandíil miláwwin yiwafíʔha (or yimʃi-mɛáaha).
Does this material wash well?	ʔilʔumáʃda-byíbhat? [4]/ʔillónda sáabit walla-byíṭlaɛ f-ilγasíil?
It's fast, it does not fade in the wash.	sáabit, ma-byibhátʃi f-ilγasíil.
Our van calls in your neighbourhood to-morrow.	ʔilɛarabíyya-btaɛítna ḥatwáṣṣal biḍáaɛa ligránkum búkra.

At the cleaner's: | **f-ittintiraríi:**

I want these flannel trousers dry cleaned.	ʔana ɛáawiz ilbanṭalóon ilfaníila dá yitnáḍḍaf ɛa-nnáaʃif.
When can I fetch them?	ʔag(i)-axúdhum waʔtéeh?

[1] Pronounced ʔiwzílli.
[2] All other examples have assumed a man speaking.
[3] Or **karafáṭṭa, karafítta, karaváṭṭa.**
[4] **báhat, yíbhat** "to fade"

Can this coat be dyed brown?	múmkin tuṣbúɣu-lbálṭu dá búnni ?
Do you do mending?	ʕintu-btirfu [1] ṣúuf ?
At the chemist's:	**f-ilʕagzaxáana (or f-iṣṣaydalíyya):**
Do you keep razors and blades?	ɛandúku-mwáas wi makanáat ḥiláaʕa ?
I want a shaving-brush and some shaving-soap.	ʕana ɛáawiz fúrʃit ḥiláaʕa-w ṣabúun ḥiláaʕa.
I also want a tube of tooth-paste and a tooth-brush.	ʕana ɛáawiz kamáan ʕumbúubit maɛgúun isnáan wi fúrʃit isnáan.
How much will that be altogether?	káam táman ilḥagátdi kulláha ?
Have you anything for headaches?	ɛandúku ḥáaga l-iṣṣudáaɛ ?
Can you recommend a gargle?	tiʕdar tiʕúlli ɛala ɣarɣára-kwayyísa ?
I want some adhesive plaster, please, and a box of cough lozenges.	ʕana ɛáawiz biláastar, min faḍlak, wi ɛílbit bastílya min bitáaɛit ilkúḥḥa.
A big packet of cotton-wool, please.	wáraʕit ʕúṭni-kbíira, min faḍlak.
Please have this prescription made up for me.	min fáḍlak ḥaḍḍárli-rruʃítta díyya.
I want a good tonic.	ʕana ɛáawiz dáwa-mʕáwwi, min faḍlak.
Can you let me have some cream for sunburn?	tiʕdar tiddíini-ʃwáyyit kiríim ɛaʃan ḥurúuʕ iʃʃáms ?
At the tobacconist's:	**ɛand iddaxáxni:**
Can you recommend a mild cigar?	tiʕdar tiʕúlli ɛala núuɛ sigáar xafíif ?
What kind of cigarettes do you stock?	ʕéeh ʕanwáaɛ issagáayir illi ɛandúkum ?
Have you any lighter-flints (wicks, petrol)?	ɛandúku-ḥgáarit (ʃaráayiṭ, banzíin) wallaɛáat ?
Sorry, we've only boxes of matches left.	ʕáasif, ma ɛátʃi ɛandína-lla ɛílab kabríit.
At the confectioner's:	**ɛand ilḥalawáani:**
A large box of chocolates, please.	sandúuʕ ʃukuláaṭa-kbíir, min faḍlak.

[1] ráfa, yírfi "to darn, mend".

How much is this bar (or packet) of chocolate?	**ʔiʃʃukulaṭáaya dí-b káam ?**
Please wrap up the cake and pastries for me.	**min fáḍlak liffli-ṭṭúrṭa w-ilḥalawiyyáat.**
Do not touch goods displayed on the counter.	**mamnúuʕ láms ilbaḍáaʔiʕ ilmaʕruuḍa.**[1]
In the Muski[2]:	**fi xáan ilxalíili :**
Do come in, is there anything I can do for you?	**ʔitfáḍḍal, láazim xídma ?**
I want a few small things.	**lazímni ḥagáat basíiṭa.**
You've come to the right place.	**ʔitfáḍḍal, da maḥállak** (lit. *this is your place*).
I'm at your service.	**ʔúṭlub w-ana táḥti ʔámrak** (lit. *ask and I am under your order*).
But do sit down.	**báss itfáḍḍal istaráyyaḥ ʕa-lkúrsi.**
Thank you.	**mutaʃákkir.**
Do you like (your) coffee very sweet, half and half, or without sugar?	**tiḥíbbi tiʃrab ʔáhwa súkkar ziyáada walla maẓbúuṭa walla sáada ?**
No coffee, thank you all the same.	**láʔ, káttar xéerak, ʔahwítak maʃrúuba, ʕiʃt.**
What are you looking for?	**ʔéeh ṭalabáatak ?** (lit. *what are your requests ?*).
How much are you selling it (fem.) at?	**bi káam tibíʕha ?**
Do you want to bargain or do you want a fixed price?	**ḥaḍritak ʕawiz tifáaṣil walla ʕáawiz kaláam wáaḥid ?**
Give me a fair price, there's no need for bargaining.	**min fáḍlak ʔúlli ʕa-ttáman b-ilḥáʔʔ, ma fiiʃ luzúum l-ilfiṣáal.**
We don't put our prices either up or down.	**láa binzáwwid wala binnáʔʔaṣ.**
What's the price, then?	**ʔittáman káam baʔa ?**
Well now, to be fair, four pounds.	**ʔittáman b-iṣṣála ʕa-nnábi** (lit. *by praying on the Prophet*), **ʔarbáʕa-gnéeh.**
You've put me off.	**ya ʃéex inta xaḍḍétni.**
What sort of a price is that?	**ʔéeh ittáman dá ?**

[1] Written form. Cf. the spoken **ma tilmísʃ ilbiḍáaʕa-lmaʕrúuḍa.**

[2] The eastern bazaar in Cairo where the customer should bargain for his purchases.

I'll give you two and a half pounds.	**ʕan-adfáɛlak itnéen ginéeh wi núṣṣ.**
No, no, you're a long way off my price (said by shopkeeper).	**láa, láa, líssa bádri** (lit. *it is still early*).
Let's split the difference.	**niʕsim ilbálad nuṣṣéen** (lit. *let's divide the town in two halves*).
Done!	**mabrúuk!** (lit. *congratulations*).
All right. Here's the money.	**ʕalláah yibarik fiik** (answer to **mabrúuk**). **ʕitfáḍḍal ilfilúus.**
an you change me a £1 note?	**tiʕdar tifukkíli-gnéeh, min fadlak?**
ould you change me 50 piastres?	**min fáḍlak, fukkíli xamsíin ʕirʃ?**
ood morning, may I just take a look round?	**ṣabáaḥ ilxéer, múmkin báṣṣ atfárrag?**

THE POST OFFICE

Vocabulary

he General Post Office	**ʕilbúṣṭa-lɛumumíyya**
tter box	**sandúuʕ ilbúṣṭa**
tter	**gawáab, gawabáat**
nswer	**gawáab, ʕagwíba**
ostcard	**kárti bustáal, kurúut bustáal**
rinted matter	**maṭbuɛáat**
egistered letter	**gawáab musággal**
xpress letter	**gawáab mustáɛgal**
elegram	**tiliɣráaf, tiliɣrafáat**
ample having no commercial value	**ɛayyína láysa l-ilbíiɛ** [1]
irmail letter	**gawáab b-ilbaríid ilgáwwi**
nvelope	**ẓárfi gawáab, ẓurúuf gawabáat**
ddress	**ɛunwáan, ɛanawíin**
ddressee	**ʕalmúrsal ʕiléeh**
ender	**múrsil, mursilíin; ráasil, rásliin**
ounter	**bank, bunúuk**
ost-office official	**miɛáawin ilbúṣṭa**
ostman	**buṣṭági, buṣṭagíyya; sáaɛi, suɛáah; ɛáamil ilbaríid, ɛummáal ilbaríid**
tamp	**wáraʕit baríid; ṭáabiɛ búṣṭa**
vrapper, wrapping paper	**wáraʕ láff**

[1] Written form.

sealing wax	ʃámʒ-áḥmar
postage	ʕúgrit ilbaríid
string	dubáara
postal order	ʕízni baríid, ʕuzúun baríid
telegraphic transfer	ḥiláawa tiliyrafíyya
fees, charges	dámya ; táman
post-free	min γéer wáraʕ búṣṭa
by airmail	b-iṭṭayyáara ; b-ilbaríid ilgáwwi
by seamail	b-ilmárkib
abroad	f-ilxáarig
country	ʕirríif ; ʕilʕaryáaf
poste restante	yantáðir b-iʃʃibbáak ilbaríid [1]
collection times	lámm ilbúṣṭa ; máwʒid, mawaʒíid
ordinary letter	gawáab ʒáadi
parcel	ṭard, ṭurúud
money order	ḥiwáala
receipt-slip	ḥáfẓa, ḥawáafiẓ
distribution window	ʃibbáak ittawzíiʒ
to post	ráma, yírmi gawáab (fi sandúuʕ ilbúṣṭa)
to receive	ʕistálam, yistílim
to stamp a letter	ḥaṭṭ, yiḥúṭṭ wáraʕit búṣṭa ʒa-ggawáab
to frank a letter	xátam, yíxtim gawáab
to send	báʒat, yíbʒat
to register	ṣóogar, yiṣóogar ; sággil, yisággil

Sentences

Has the postman been?	ʕilbuṣṭági fáat (or ʒádda or gih)?
He delivered two letters and a postcard this morning.	huwwa gáab gawabéen wi kárt bustáal innahárda-ṣṣúbḥ.
The postman has left this form.	ʕilbuṣṭági sáab ilwaṣlída.
Letters are delivered three times a day.	ʕiggawabáat bititwázzaʒ tálat marráat f-ilyóom.
Where can I collect this parcel?	ʕáʕdar astílim iṭṭárdi da-mnéen?
Take this letter to the post-box, please.	ʕísʕiṭ iggawábda-f sandúuʕ ilbúṣṭa, min faḍlak.
The next collection is at six.	ḥaylímmu-ggawabáat baʒdi kída ssáaʒa sítta.
You must pay excess-postage.	lazim tídfaʒ fárʕi ʒa-ggawábda.
Return to sender, address not known.	yuráddu ʕila-lmúrsil, ʕalʒunwáan γéer maʒrúuf.

[1] Written form. Pronounce ð as *th* in "thus" but with "emphasis"; ð is the emphatic counterpart of ð.

Please forward.	**yuħáwwal ʔiléeh.**
What is the postage for an air-mail letter to England?	**ʔiggawáab b-iṭṭayyáara l-ingiltíra-b káam?**
Where can I inquire for poste restante letters?	**ʔaʔdar ásʔal féen min faḍlak ʔiza káan fiih gawabáat maħgúuza líyya?**
Where can I get postage stamps?	**ʔáʔdar aʃtíri ṭawáabiɛ bariid minéen, min faḍlak?**
Two one-piastre stamps.	**waraʔtéen búṣṭa min ʔábu ʔirʃi sáay.**
Could I have a cable form, please?	**ʔiddíini min fáḍlak fúrmit tiliγráaf?**
I want to send these things cash on delivery.	**ʔana ɛáawiz ábɛat ilbaḍáayiɛ dí-b ṭaríiʔit iddáfɛi ɛand ittasliim.**
Would you register this letter for me, please?	**saggílli-ggawábda, min faḍlak?**
Do you want to register this parcel?	**ɛawiz tibɛat iṭṭárdi dá b-ilbaríid ilmusággal?**
You must complete the special form that has to accompany the parcel.	**láazim tímla ilfúrma-lmaxṣúuṣa-lli ħatitbíɛit maɛa-ṭṭárd.**
Please give me an international form to send money to England.	**ʔiddíini fúrma dawlíyya ʔábɛat bíiha-flúus l-ingiltíra.**
You have to seal a registered parcel.	**lazim tiʃámmaɛ iṭṭárd ɛaʃan asaggilhúulak.[1]**
I want to send a telegram.	**ʔana ɛáawiz ábɛat tiliγráaf, min faḍlak.**
Don't forget to put the name and address of sender.	**ma tinsáaʃ tíktib ísm ilmúrsil wi ɛunwáanu(h).**
If it cannot be delivered, it will be returned.	**ʔíza ma waṣalítʃ (or wiṣlítʃ), ħatitráddi l-ilmúrsil.**
A telegram with prepaid reply.	**tiliγráaf wi ráddi xáaliṣ.**
What is the telegram rate to England?	**ʔittiliγrafáat bi káam l-ingiltíra?**
Greetings telegrams are dearer.	**tiliγrafáat ittaháani ʔáγla.**
This letter is dated the 12th, but the post-stamp shows it was sent off on the 14th.	**ʔiggawábda maktúub bi taríix iṭnáaʃar, lakin xitmi wáraʔit ilbúṣṭa bi taríix ʔarbaɛṭáaʃar.**
How long does a surface-mail letter take from here to America?	**ʔiggawáab ilɛáadi yáaxud ʔaddéeh min hína-l ʔamríika.**

[1] Lit. "so that I may register it for you".

THE TELEPHONE

Vocabulary

public telephone	**tilifóon ɛumúumi**
receiver, instrument	**sammáaɛa, sammaɛáat**
exchange	**sintiráal**
automatic exchange	**sintiráal utumatíiki**
extension	**nímra da(a)xilíyya, nímar da(a)xilíyya**
operator	**ɛáamil ittilifóon**
subscriber	**ṣáaḥib ittilifóon**
telephone booth	**kabíinit ittilifóon**
telephone directory	**dalíil ittilifonáat**
call	**mukálma, mukalmáat**
local call	**mukálma maḥallíyya**
trunk call	**mukálma xa(a)rigíyya**
night call	**mukálma laylíyya**
connection	**tawṣíil**
engaged	**maʃɣúul**
button	**ẓuráar, ẓaráayir**
slot	**tuʕb, ʕitʕáab**
to phone, ring up	**kállim, yikállim f-ittilifóon; ḍárab, yíḍrab tilifóon li . . .**
to ring (intr.)	**rann, yirínn**
to dial	**dáwwar, yidáwwar ittilifóon**
to connect	**wáṣṣal, yiwáṣṣal**
to book a call	**ḥágaz, yíḥgiz mukálma**
to cancel a call	**láɣa, yílɣi mukálma**

Sentences

Hello!	**ʕalóo!**
Are you on the phone?	**ɛándak tilifóon?**
Please give me a ring to-morrow evening.	**ʕiḍrábli-tlifóon búkra b-illéel, min faḍlak.**
How do I use the phone?	**ʕizzáay astáɛmil ittilifóon?**
Lift the receiver.	**ʕírfaɛ issammáaɛa.**
Then dial the number required.	**wi baɛdéen dáwwar innímra-ll-inta ɛawízha.**
Have you any change for the telephone?	**maɛáak fákka ɛaʃan ittilifóon?**
Put the money in before dialling.	**ʕísʕiṭ ilfilúus ʕáblí ma titkállim.**
Could I use your phone, please?	**ʕáʕdar astáɛmil tilifóonak, min faḍlak?**
Hello, could I speak to Mr. Mahmoud Ali?	**ʕalóo, múmkin akállim issáyyid maḥmúud ɛáli, min faḍlak?**

Speaking.	ʔána maħmúud.
Are you 1563?	ʔíntu (nimrit) ʔálfi xumsumíyya taláata-w sittíin?
Number engaged.	ʔinnímra maʃɣúula.
There's no answer.	ma ħáddiʃ biyrúdd.
Put the receiver down and call again.	ħúṭṭ issammáaɛa w-íḍrab táani.
I can't get through.	miʃ ɛáarif attíṣil b-innímra.
Inquiries, please.	ʔiddíini listiɛlamáat, min faḍlak.
Can you give me the number of Mr. Muhammad Salim, of 10 Station Road?	tiʔdar tiddíini nímrit issáyyid muħámmad sáalim illi sáakin fi nímra ɛáʃara, ʃáariɛ ilmaħáṭṭa?
I have tried several times to ring the hotel, but there is no reply.	ʔana ħawílt attíṣil b-illukánda-ktíir láakin ma ħáddiʃ biyrúdd.
Sorry, wrong number.	ʔáasif, ʔinnímra ɣálaṭ.
The telephone is out of order.	ʔittilifóon ɛaṭláan.
Is that the Travel Agency?	da máktab issiyáaħa, min fáḍlak?
Just a minute, hold the line, please.	daʔíiʔa wáħda, xallíik ɛa-lxáṭṭ, min faḍlak.
Isn't there a public call-box around here?	ma fiiʃ kabíinit tilifóon ɛumúumi f-ilħítta di?
Miss, I want to book a call to Alexandria, please.	ɛáawiz áħgiz mukálma l-iskindiríyya, min fáḍlik, ya ʔa(a)nísa (or madmuwazáll).
Where can I wait until my trunk call comes through?	ʔáʔdar astánna féen liɣáayit ilmukálma ilxarigíyya-btáɛti tíigi?
Alexandria, booth No. 7.	ʔiskindiríyya, fi kabíinit nímrit sábɛa.
Sorry, we were cut off.	ʔáasif, ʔilxáṭṭ itʔáṭaɛ.
Could you please give a message to Mr. Fareed Abdalla?	tiʔdar min faḍlak táaxud risáala ɛaʃan issáyyid faríid ɛabdálla?
You are wanted on the phone.	ʔinta maṭlúub ɛa-ttilifóon.

CORRESPONDENCE

Vocabulary

letter	gawáab, gawabáat
business letter	gawáab maṣláħi, gawabáat maṣlaħíyya
letter of congratulation	gawáab tahníya
letter of condolence	gawáab taɛzíya
postcard	kárti bustáal, kurúut bustáal
handwriting	xaṭṭ ; kitáaba yadawíyya (manuscript)
pen	ríiʃa, ríyaʃ

fountain-pen	ʕálam ḥíbr, ʕiʕláam ḥíbr; ʕálam ʕabanóos, ʕiʕláam ʕabanóos
ball-pen	ʕálam ḥíbri gáaf, ʕiʕláam ḥíbri gáaf
pencil	ʕálam ruṣáaṣ, ʕiʕláam ruṣáaṣ
nib	sinn irríiʃa, ʕasnáan irríiʃa
penholder	ʕíid irríiʃa, ʕayáad irríyaʃ
copying-ink pencil	ʕálam kúbya, ʕiʕláam kúbya
coloured pencil	ʕálam miláwwin, ʕiʕláam milawwína
gum, glue	samɣ
letter-file	duséeh iggawabáat, dusehéat; miláff, milaffáat
card-index	fíhris, fahárris
paper	wáraʕ (c.), wáraʕa, waraʕáat, ʕawráaʕ
notepaper	karráasa, karrasáat (or kararíis)
cardboard	kartúun
envelope	ẓarf, ẓurúuf
writing-pad, writing-paper	wáraʕ kitáaba
blotting-paper	naʃʃáafa, naʃʃafáat
ink	ḥibr
inkstand, inkwell	dawáaya, dawayáat (or díwy)
sealing wax	ʃámɛ áḥmar
stationer's	maktába, maktabáat
writing-desk	máktab, makáatib
stationery	ʕadawáat ilkitáaba
shorthand	ʕixtizáal
typewriter	ʕáala kátba, ʕaláat kátba
carbon-paper	wáraʕit karbúun
string	dubáara
folder	duséeh, dusehéat
sender	múrsil, mursilíin
addressee	ʕalmúrsal ʕiléeh, ʕalmúrsal ʕiláyhim
address	ɛunwáan, ɛanawíin
enclosures	ʕilmurfaqáat
heading, reference	mawḍúuɛ
signature	ʕimḍáaʕ (or ʕímḍa), ʕimḍaʕáat
commercial term	ʕiṣṭiláaḥ tugáari
trade mark	márka musaggála
clerk	káatib, kátaba
typist	káatib (kaatíba) ɛala-lʕáala-lkátba
secretary	(male) sikirtéer, sikirteríyya; (female) sikirtéera, sikirteriyyáat
book-keeper	máasik iddafáatir, maskíin iddafáatir; muḥáasib, muḥasbíin

book-keeping	**másk iddafáatir**
partner	**ʃariik, ʃúraka**
owner	**ṣáaḥib, ʕaṣḥáab**
staff	**muwaẓẓafiin**
to write	**kátab, yíktib**
to type	**kátab, yíktib ʒala-lʕáala-lkátba**
to copy	**náʕal, yínʕil**
to answer	**gáawib, yigáawib; radd, yirúdd (gawáab)**
to stick	**lázaʕ, yílzaʕ**
to seal	**xátam, yíxtim**
to fold	**ṭáwa, yíṭwi**
to tie	**rábaṭ, yúrbuṭ**
to send	**báʒat, yíbʒat**

Sentences

Where is the writing-room?	**féen ʕóḍt[1] ikkitáaba?**
There are envelopes and note-paper on the writing-desk.	**fiih ẓurúuf wi karráasa ʒala-lmáktab hináak.**
I have to write an urgent letter.	**láazim áktib gawáab mistáʒgil.**
Shall I type it?	**ʕaktíbu ʒa-lʕáala-lkátba?**
I am expecting important news.	**ʕana muntáẓir ʕaxbáar muhímma.**
I have to answer some letters.	**ʕana láazim arúddi ʒala báʒḍi gawabáat.**
I owe my friend a letter.	**ʒaláyya ʕáktib li ṣáḥbi gawáab.**
Can you lend me your fountain-pen?	**tísmaḥ tisallífni ʕálamak ilḥíbr?**
My fountain-pen is broken. Where can I get it repaired?	**ʕálam ilḥíbri-btáaʒi maksúur. ʕaṣalláḥu féen?**
He writes a very clear hand.	**xáṭṭu-kwáyyis ʕáwi.**
Take this letter down in shorthand.	**ʕíktib iggawábda b-ilʕixtizáal.**
He can neither read nor write. He is illiterate.	**húwwa ma-byiʕdárʃi láa yíʕra wala yíktib. huwwa ʕúmmi.**
Get this letter done quickly, it must catch the evening post.	**xállaṣ iggawábda-b súrʒa, lazim yílḥaʕ búṣṭit ilmísa.**
Make three carbon copies of this invoice.	**ʕíʒmil tálat núsax min ilfatúura di.**
Have you filed the letters?	**ḥaṭṭéet iggawabáat f-iddusehåat?**
I told you all about it in my last letter.	**ʕana ʕultílak kúlli ḥáaga ʒan il-ḥikáaya-f ʕáaxir gawáab líyya.[2]**
I read your letter with great pleasure.	**qaráʕtu xiṭaabáka bi báaliɣ issurúur.[3]**

[1] Pronounced ʕoṭṭ.

[2] Notice the use of **li**, with **gawáab** already defined by the preposed ordinal numeral.

[3] Written language.

My sincere congratulations.	ʔáxlaṣ ittaháani.
Many happy returns of the day.	kúlli sána w-ínta ṭáyyib.
I was very pleased to hear of your engagement (marriage).	(spoken) ʔana-nbaṣáṭṭi [1] giddan lamma-wṣílni xábar xuṭbítak (gawáazak); (written) laqad surírtu jíddan [2] ɛindáma waṣalánii nábaʔu xuṭbátik (zawáajik [2]).
My sincere condolences.	ʔáxlaṣ ittaɛáazi (or ʔáxlaṣ ittaɛzíya); (spoken) ʔilbaʔíyya-f ħayáatak.
May I express my deep sympathy.	laqad taʔaθθártu jiddan bi muṣaabíkumu-lʔalíim.
In reply to your letter of the 16th June.	ʔijaabátan ɛalaa xiṭaabíkum bi taaríix siṭṭáaʃar yúnya.
In receipt of your favour I am pleased to inform you that . . .	ʔijaabátan ɛalaa xiṭaabíkum yasurrúnii ʔan ʔuxbírakum ʔanna . . .
I herewith acknowledge receipt of your circular.	ʔistalámtu xiṭaabákum iddáwrii.
My dear father.	waalídi-lɛazíiz.
Dear Ahmad.	ɛazíizi ʔáħmad.
Dearest Susan.	ħabi(i)bátii sáwsan.
Dear Professor/Doctor/Captain Fikri (Abdurrahman).	ɛazíizi-lʔustáaz/-dduktóor/-lyuzbáaʃi fíkri (friendly); (more formal) ʔassáyyid il-muħtáram ilʔustáaz fíkri ɛabd irraħmáan.
Dear Mr. Fahmy.	(friendly) ɛazíizi-ssáyyid fáhmi; (more formal) ʔassáyyid il-muħtáram ilʔustáaz fáhmi ɛabdálla.
Dear Mrs. Fathiya Hilmy.	ʔassayyída-lfaaḍila-lʔustáaza fatħíyya ħílmi.[3]
Dear Miss Fawzia Ahmad.	ʔalʔaanísa (-lmuhaððába) fawzíyya ʔáħmad.
The Manager, Cotton Ginning Co.	ʔassáyyid mudíir ʃírkit ħálg il-ʔaqṭáan.
Dear Sir.	ʔassáyyid mudíir ʃírkit . . .
Yours sincerely.	ʔalmúxliṣ.

[1] Pronounced ʔimbaṣáṭṭ.
[2] Pronounce j as in English "jeep".
[3] Or ʔassayyída-lmuħtárama fatħíyya háanim ħílmi.

I remain, Yours faithfully. — wa tafaḍḍálu bi qabúul fáaʔiq liħtiráam.

With kind regards. — maɛa ʔáṭyab attaħiyyáat.

With all good wishes. — maɛa ʔáṭyab ilʔamáani.

Your affectionate son. — ʔibnúka-lbáar.

Your affectionate brother. — ʔaxúuka-lmúxliṣ.

A personal letter: — gawáab ʃáxṣi :

Alexandria, 4th May, 1953

ʔalʔiskandaríyya, fi ʔarbáɛa máayu, sanat ʔálfi tusɛumíyya tamánya-w xamsíin [1]

Dear Mrs. Ahmad Hilmy,

ʔassayyída ħáram ilʔustáaz ʔáħmad ħílmi [2]

Many thanks for your kind invitation to dinner. I am sorry to say I shall be away this week-end, but I shall be very pleased to spend one evening next week with you if convenient.

ʃúkran jazíilan ɛala daɛwátikum l-ilɛaʃáaʔ. ʔana ʔáasif liʔanni saʔáqḍi ɛúṭlat nihaayit ilʔusbúuɛ xáarij ilmadíina, wala(a)kinnáhu yasurrúnii jíddan ʔan ʔaqḍíya ʔumsíyatan máɛakum filʔusbúuɛ ilmúqbil ʔiða(a) wa(a)fáqakum ðáalik.

With kind regards,
Yours sincerely,
Mohamed Abu Al-Farag.

maɛa ʔáṭyab attaħiyyáat
ʔalmúxliṣ
muħámmad abu-lfárag.

(The same message as it might be communicated by 'phone.)

mutaʃákkir giddan ɛala daɛwítkum l-ilɛáʃa. láakin ʔana ʔáasif ʔáwi liʔánni ħaʔáḍḍi nihaayit ilʔusbúuɛ bárra-skindiríyya. ʔiza káan yiwafíʔkum ʔáyyi yóom f-ilʔusbúuɛ illi gáyy ʔakúun mabṣúuṭ gíddan ʔinn-aʔáḍḍi ʔumsíya ɛandúkum.[3]

[1] This is, of course, simply an indication of the way in which the figures denoting the year would be uttered.

[2] The following few short letters have been included, together with other material in this section, in order to illustrate the difference between written language and that which is elsewhere the concern of this book. Vocabulary apart, the grammar is substantially that of written Arabic and cannot be accounted for in a book dealing exclusively with the very different colloquial language.

[3] Notice the polite use of the *plural* pronominal suffix.

A short business note:

Cairo, 8th June, 1959.

The Manager,
Municipal Electricity Co.
Dear Sir,

I beg to inform you that our electric meter is not working. Please send someone to attend to it. With thanks in anticipation.

Yours faithfully,
So-and-so.

xiṭáab maṣláḥi qaṣiir:

ʔalqa(a)híra, fi tamánya yúnya, sanat ʔálfi tusɛumíyya tísɛa-w xamsíin.

ʔassáyyid ilmudíir
ʃírkat innúur
sayyídi

ʔáktub háaða li ʔuxbírakum ʔanna ɛaddáad ilkahrabáaʔ ɛindána taɛáṭṭal, wa ʔárgu ʔan tursílu mán yuṣlíḥuh. wa fi(i) lintið̣áar[1] lákum jazíil iʃʃúkr.

muqaddímu
fuláan.

A business letter:

Suez, 10th August, 1959.

Dear Sir,

We have pleasure in sending you herewith invoice for two hundred pairs of best-quality men's shoes bought for your account and to be shipped to you on the 22nd inst. We hope you will be pleased with the goods, as the make is strong and serviceable and the manufacturers guarantee the goods to stand any climate.

You will gather from the invoice that we have been able to obtain a special cash discount of five per cent.

I am,
With compliments,
Yours faithfully,
So-and-so.

xiṭáab maṣláḥi:

ʔissuwées, fi ɛáʃara ʔayúṣṭuṣ, sanat ʔálfi tusɛumíyya tísɛa-w xamsíin.

ʔassáyyid mudíir ʃírkit (kaza ...)[2]

surrúna ʔan nursíla ʔiláykum maɛa háaða qa(a)ʔímati-lʔasɛáar bi miʔatay záwjin min ʔaḥsáni-lʔaḥðíya-lxáaṣṣa b-irrijáal ʔiʃtúriyat li ḥisa(a)bíkum wa satuʃḥánu ʔiláykum f-iθθáani wa-lɛiʃríin mina-ʃʃáhr ilḥáali. naɛmúlu ʔan tanáala-lbiḍa(a)ɛátu ʔiɛja(a)bákum liʔanna-ṣṣináaɛa matíina wa tataḥammálu kaθíiran wa-lmuntijúuna yaḍmanúuna ṣala(a)ḥíyat albiḍáaɛa li ʔáyyi jáww.

wa sataɛlamúuna min qa(a)ʔímati-lʔasɛáar ʔannána ḥaṣúulna ɛala xáṣmin xáaṣṣin lákum qi(i)mátuhu xámsa(tun) f-ilmíʔah.

wa tafaḍḍálu bi qabúuli fáaʔiq liḥtiráam.

fuláan.

[1] ð̣ is only associated with written Arabic and is the "emphatic" counterpart of ð.
[2] Lit. "The Manager (of the so-and-so company)".

Addresses on envelopes:	ɛanawíin iggawabáat:
. . ., Esq./Professor . . .,	ʔassáyyid ilmuħtáram
	ilʔustáaz fuláan,
4 Station Road,	4 (ʔɑrbáɛa) ʃáariɛ ilmaħáṭṭɑ,
Port Said.	bur saɛíid.
Miss . . .	ʔalʔaanísa (-lmuhaððába)
	fuláana,
5 Mo'iz Street, Flat 9, Cairo.	5 (xámsa) ʃáariɛ ilmuɛízz,
	ʃíʔʔa nimrit 9 (tísɛa),
	ʔalqɑ(ɑ)hírɑ.

NUMERATION

Vocabulary

Cardinals:	ʔilʔaɛdáad ilʔasasíyya:
nil, nought	ṣifr
one	wáaħid, wáħda
two	ʔitnéen
three	tálat, taláata
four	ʔárbɑɛ, ʔɑrbáɛa
five	xámas, xámsa
six	sitt, sítta
seven	sábaɛ, sábɛa
eight	táman, tamánya
nine	tísaɛ, tísɛa
ten	ɛáʃɑr, ɛáʃɑrɑ
eleven	ħiḍáaʃɑr
twelve	ʔiṭnáaʃɑr
thirteen	talaṭṭáaʃɑr
fourteen	ʔɑrbaɛṭáaʃɑr
fifteen	xɑmɑsṭáaʃɑr
sixteen	siṭṭáaʃɑr
seventeen	sabaɛṭáaʃɑr
eighteen	tamɑnṭáaʃɑr
nineteen	tisɑɛṭáaʃɑr
twenty	ɛiʃríin
twenty-one	wáaħid wi ɛiʃríin
twenty-two	ʔitnéen wi ɛiʃríin
twenty-three	taláata-w ɛiʃríin
twenty-four	ʔɑrbáɛa-w ɛiʃríin
thirty	talatíin
forty	ʔɑrbiɛíin
fifty	xamsíin
sixty	sittíin

seventy	**sabɛíin**
eighty	**tamaníin**
ninety	**tisɛíin**
hundred	**míyya, miyyáat**
one hundred and one	**míyya-w wáaḥid**
two hundred	**mitéen**
three hundred	**tultumíyya**
four hundred	**rubɛumíyya**
five hundred	**xumsumíyya**
six hundred	**suttumíyya**
seven hundred	**subɛumíyya**
eight hundred	**tumnumíyya**
nine hundred	**tusɛumíyya**
thousand	**ʔalf, ʔaláaf**
eleven hundred	**ʔálfi-w míyya**
one hundred and sixty-three	**míyya taláata-w sittíin**
two thousand one hundred and ninety-two	**ʔalféen míyya-tnéen wi tisɛíin**
five thousand five hundred and seventy	**xámast aláaf xumsumíyya-w sabɛíin**
million	**milyóon, malayíin**
two million	**ʔitnéen milyóon**

Ordinals:	**ʔilʔaɛdáad ilwaṣfíyya:**
first	**ʔáwwil; ʔawwaláani, ʔawwalaníyya, ʔawwalaniyyíin**
second	**táani, tánya**
third	**táalit, tálta**
fourth	**ráabiɛ, rábɛa**
fifth	**xáamis, xámsa**
sixth	**sáatit, sátta; sáadis, sádsa**
seventh	**sáabiɛ, sábɛa**
eighth	**táamin, támna**
ninth	**táasiɛ, tásɛa**
tenth	**ɛáaʃir, ɛáʃra**
(the) fifteenth	**ʔilxamastáaʃar**
(the) twentieth	**ʔilɛiʃríin**
(the) hundredth	**ʔilmíyya**
(the) twenty-fourth	**ʔilʔarbáɛa-w ɛiʃríin**
last	**ʔáaxir; ʔaxráani, ʔaxraníyya, ʔaxraniyyíin**

Fractions:	**ʔilkusúur:**
vulgar fraction	**kásr iɛtiyáadi**
decimal fraction	**kásri ɛúʃri**

half	nuṣṣ, ʕanṣáaṣ/ʕinṣáaṣ
third	tilt, ʕatláat/ʕitláat
quarter	rubʕ, ʕarbáaʕ/ʕirbáaʕ
fifth	xums, ʕaxmáas/ʕixmáas
sixth	suds, ʕasdáas/ʕisdáas
seventh	subʕ, ʕasbáaʕ/ʕisbáaʕ
eighth	tumn, ʕatmáan/ʕitmáan
ninth	tusʕ, ʕatsáaʕ/ʕitsáaʕ
tenth	ʕuʃr, ʕaʕʃáar/ʕiʕʃáar
(a) twentieth	wáaḥid ʕala ʕiʃriin
three twentieths	taláata ʕala ʕiʃriin
hundredth	wáaḥid ʕala míyya
3·5 (three point five)	taláata-w xámsa min ʕáʃara
4·75	ʕarbáʕa-w xámsa-w sabʕíin min míyya
2·01	ʕitnéen wi wáaḥid min míyya
figure	raqm, ʕarqáam
number	ʕádad, ʕaʕdáad ; nímra,[1] nímar
mathematics	riyáaḍa
arithmetic	ḥisáab
algebra	(ʕil)gabr
geometry	handása
addition	gamʕ
subtraction	ṭarḥ
multiplication	ḍarb
division	qísma
sum	gúmla
multiplication table	gádwal iḍḍárb, gadáawil iḍḍárb
percentage	nísba miʕawíyya
once	márra
twice	marritéen
three times	tálat marráat
to add	gámaʕ, yígmaʕ
to subtract	ṭáraḥ, yíṭraḥ
to multiply	ḍárab, yíḍrab
to divide	ʕásam, yíʕsim
to calculate	ḥásab, yíḥsib
to estimate	ʕáddar, yiʕáddar
to deduct	xáṣam, yíxṣim

[1] Especially as a means of identifying an object or place, e.g a house or flat.

Sentences

Twice two are four.	**ʔitnéen f-itnéen b-arbáɛa.**
Three (times) two(s) are six.	**taláata f-itnéen bi sítta.**
Two into six goes three.	**sítta ɛala-tnéen yisáawi [1] taláata.**
Two and three make five.	**ʔitnéen záaʔid taláata yisáawi xámsa.**
Three from five leaves two.	**xámsa náaqiṣ taláata yisáawi-tnéen.**
How long have you been waiting?	**ʔinta mistánni baʔáalak ʔaddéeh?**
Three-quarters of an hour.	**tálatt írbaɛ [2] sáaɛa.**
What are your office hours?	**ʔinta-btiʃtáɣal min káam li káam?**
From nine to five.	**min tísɛa-l xámsa.**
I had ten days' leave.	**ʔana kan ɛándi ɛáʃart iyyáam ʔagáaza.**
I spent a year and a half in Egypt.	**ʔana maḍḍéet fi múṣri sána-w núṣṣ.**
How far is it to Cairo?	**ʔilmasáafa ʔaddéeh min hína-l múṣr?**
It is 26 kilometres from here.	**sítta-w ɛiʃríin kelumítri min hína.**
How long does it take to get there?	**táaxud ʔaddéeh min hína li-hnáak?**
About an hour and a half.	**sáaɛa-w núṣṣi taʔríiban.**
The train will leave for Shibin el Qanatir in thirty minutes.	**ʔilʔáṭr illi ráayiḥ ʃibíin ilʔanáaṭir ḥayʔúum baɛdi núṣṣi sáaɛa.**
My seat is row ten, number twelve.	**ʔikkúrsi-btáaɛi nimra-ṭnáaʃar f-iṣṣáff ilɛáaʃir.**
This ring is worth more than a pound.	**ʔilxáatim da-ysáawi ʔáktar min ginéeh.**
There were hundreds of children in that school.	**ʔilmadrasáadi kan fíiha talámza b-ilmiyyáat.**
It is the last day of my holidays.	**ʔinnahárda ʔáaxir yóom fi ʔagázti.**
He inherited a hundred acres from his father.	**wáras ɛan abúuh míit faddáan.**
Two-thirds of the book are uninteresting.	**tiltéen m-ikkitáab malúuʃ máɛna.**
He sold half of his property.	**báaɛ núṣṣi ʔamláaku(h).**
A year and a half ago I was in hospital.	**ʔana kútti f-ilmustáʃfa min sána-w núṣṣ.**

[1] Lit. "equals".
[2] Notice the unexpected stress and short vowel in the final syllable (cf. the isolated form ʔirbáaɛ).

Their boy is six months old.	ʕibnúhum ʒandu sitt úʃhur.
He stayed abroad over three months.	ʕáɖɖa ʕáktar min tálat ʃuhúur f-ilxáarig.
In nineteen hundred and fourteen.	fi sanat ʕálfi tusʒumíyya w-arbaʒṭáaʃar.
The percentage of pupils studying mathematics is larger than that studying languages.	ʕinnísba-lmiʕawíyya l-ittalámza-lli-byidrísu-ryáaɖa ʕáktar m-illi-byidrísu luɣáat.

COINAGE, WEIGHTS, MEASURES

Vocabulary

(the) coinage	(ʕal)ʒúmla [1]
weights and measures	ʕalʕawzáan w-almaqaayíis [1]
coin	ʒúmla, ʒumláat
money	filúus [2]
change	fákka
small change	ʒúmla ṣaɣíira
foreign currency	ʒúmla ʕagnabíyya
£1 note	wáraʕa-b ginéeh
50-piastre note	wáraʕa-b xamsíin ʕírʃ
25-piastre note	wáraʕa-b xámsa-w ʒiʃríin ʕírʃ
10-piastre note	wáraʕa-b ʒáʃara sáaɣ
5-piastre note	wáraʕa-b xámsa sáaɣ
£10 note	wáraʕa-b ʒáʃara-gnéeh
£5 note	wáraʕa-b xámsa-gnéeh
20-piastre piece	riyáal (fáɖɖa [3]), riyaláat (fáɖɖa)
10-piastre piece	ʒáʃara sáaɣ (fáɖɖa), ʒaʃaráat sáaɣ (fáɖɖa)
5-piastre piece	xámsa sáaɣ fáɖɖa, xamsáat sáaɣ fáɖɖa
2-piastre piece	núṣṣi-fránk, núṣṣi-frankáat
1-piastre piece	ʕírʃi sáaɣ, ʕurúuʃ sáaɣ
½-piastre piece	ʕírʃi taʒríifa
milleme ($\frac{1}{10}$ piastre)	mallíim, malalíim
1½ piastres (not a coin)	taláata taʒríifa ; taláat-ábyaɖ
2½ piastres (not a coin)	xámsa taʒríifa ; xáms-ábyaɖ
pound sterling	ginéeh istirlíini, ginehäat istirliníyya

[1] The vowel a is commonly associated with the article in such borrowings from Modern (written) Arabic.

[2] A feminine form.

[3] fáɖɖa = "silver".

Weights:	**ʔilʔawzáan:**
ton	**ṭinn, ʔaṭnáan**
cantar (approx. 75 lb.), quintal	**ʔinṭáar, ʔanaṭíir**
oke (approx. 2¾ lb.)	**wíʔʔa, wíʔaʔ**
kilogram (2⅕ lb.)	**kéelu, keluwáat; kilugráam, kilugramáat**
pound, rotl (¾ lb.)	**raṭl, ʔirṭáal**
ounce	**wiʔíyya, wiʔiyyáat**
dram (400 drams = 1 oke)	**dárhim, daráahim**
gramme	**giráam, giramáat**
Liquid measures:	**makayíil issawáaʔil:**
litre (4½ litres = 1 gal.)	**litr, litráat**
gallon	**galúun, galunáat**
Linear measures:	**ʔalmaqa(a)yíis:**
kilometre (⅝ mile)	**kéelu, keluwáat; kilumítr, kilumitráat**
metre (approx. 39 in.)	**mitr, ʔimtáar**
centimetre	**santimítr** (or **ṣ-**), **santimitráat**
millimetre	**millimítr, millimitráat**
league	**fársax, faráasix**
mile	**miil, ʔamyáal**
yard	**yárda, yardáat**
foot	**ʔádam, ʔiʔdáam**
inch	**búuṣa, buṣáat** [1]
Square measures:	**ʔilmaqa(a)yíis ilmirabbáɛa:**
acre	**faddáan, fadadíin**
square metre	**mítri-mrábbaɛ**
square yard	**yárda-mrabbáɛa**
100 square metres	**míit mítri-mrábbaɛ**
qirat (1/24 faddaan)	**ʔiráaṭ, ʔararíiṭ** [2]
busa (1/144 qirat, i.e. approx. 3 square metres)	**búuṣa-mrabbáɛa, buṣáat mirabbáɛa**
Cubic measures:	**ʔilmaqa(a)yíis ilmukaɛɛába:**
cubic metre	**mítri mukáɛɛab**
cubic inch	**búuṣa mukaɛɛába**

[1] In the agricultural context of the measurement of fields, **búuṣa** = approx. 3 metres.

[2] The context is again that of land measurement; elsewhere **ʔiráaṭ** = "the width of a finger".

Grain measurement:

kéela, keláat (the standard measuring canister and the amount it contains)

ʕardább, ʕaradíbb (12 **kéelas** = 1 **ʕardább**)

wéeba, webáat (used only in countryside) (2 **kéelas** = 1 **wéeba**)

ʕádah, ʕiʕdáah (¼ **kéela**)

armspan	**baaɛ, ʕibwáaɛ**
handspan	**ʃibr, ʕiʃbáar**
fingerspan (between thumb and index finger)	**fitr, ʕiftáar**
high	**ɛáali, ɛálya, ɛalyíin**
wide	**ɛaríiḍ, ɛaríiḍa, ɛuráaḍ**
long	**ṭawíil, ṭawíila, ṭuwáal**
deep	**ɣawíiṭ, ɣawíiṭa, ɣuwáaṭ**
scales	**mizáan, mawazíin**
ruler	**maṣṭára, maṣáaṭir**
tape measure	**mazúura, mazuráat**
to measure	**ʕaas, yiʕíis**
to weigh	**wázan, yíwzin**
to measure out	**káyyil, yikáyyil**

Sentences

Can you lend me 50 piastres?	**tiʕdar tisallífni xamsíin ʕirʃ, min faḍlak?**
I have no change on me.	**ma-mɛíiʃ fákka.**
Can I borrow a pound till to-morrow?	**tismah tisallífni-gnéeh li búkra?**
I have only a little silver.	**ma-mɛíiʃ illa-ʃwáyyit fákka-ṣɣayyaríin.**
Are there silver coins in Egypt?	**fiih ɛúmla fáḍḍa-f máṣr?**
Yes, but they are really an alloy.	**ʕáywa, lakinnáha f-ilhaʕíiʕa sabíika.**
Put a one-piastre piece in the slot.	**húṭṭi ʕirʃ sáaɣ f-ittúʕb.**
I've lost £5.	**ráah minni xámsa-gnéeh.**
I have to pay £3.	**lazim ádfaɛ taláata-gnéeh.**
You can repay me next week.	**tiʕdar tídfaɛ illi ɛaléek ilʕusbúuɛ illi gáay.**
He has run into debt.	**huwwa madyúun.**
What do I owe you?	**ɛaláyya káam lik?**
He's a black marketeer.	**huwwa-byiʃtáɣal f-issúuʕ issóoda.**
Have you paid your income tax?	**dafáɛti ḍaríbt iddáxl illi ɛaléek?**
It is deducted from my salary.	**ʕiḍḍaríiba-btitxíṣim min mahiyyíti** (or **murattábi**).

Did you weigh yourself on the scales?	ʕinta wazántī náfsak ʢa-lmizáan?
I weigh 65 kilos.	wázni xámsa-w sittíin kéelu.
How many okes of oranges do you want me to buy?	ʢawízn(i)-aʃtíri káam wíʕʕit burtuʕáan?
Two kilograms will be enough.	ʕitnéen kéelu bi-kfáaya.
How much is a ton of charcoal?	ṭinn ilfáḥmi-b káam?
We have bought 50 lb. of potatoes.	ʕiʃtaréena xamsíin ráṭlī baṭáaṭis.
We want twelve "bushels" of wheat.	ʕíḥna ʢawzíin ʕardábbī ʕámḥ.
How far is Alexandria from Cairo?	ʕilmasáafa ben máṣrī w-iskindiríyya ʕaddéeh?
I was driving at 50 kilometres an hour.	ʕana kúttī sáayiʕ bi súrʢit xamsíin kéelu f-issáaʢa.
Let me have three metres of this ribbon.	ʕiddíini tálatt imtáar min iʃʃiríiṭ da, min faḍlak.
The garden is 35 metres long and 20 metres wide.	ʕigginéena ṭúlha xámsa-w talatíin mítr wi ʢarḍáha ʢiʃríin mítr.
Will you take my measurements for a suit?	tismaḥ táaxuḍ maʕáasi ʢalaʃan bádla?
These shoes are made to measure.	ʕiggazmáadi tafṣíil.
Have you a measure to see how long this cloth is?	ʢándak mítrī ʢalaʃáan tiʕíis ilʕumáaʃa di.
Does your ruler show inches and centimetres?	maṣṭártak mitʢállim ʢaléeha-lbuṣáat w-iṣṣantimitráat?
How many miles is it from Suez to Port Said?	ʕilmasáafa min issuwées li bur saʢíid káam míil?
I don't know the figure in miles, only in kilometres, but I'll work it out presently for you.	ʕana miʃ ʢáarif ilʢádad b-ilʕamyáal, ʕana ʢárfu b-ilkeluwáat báss — ʕana ḥaḥsibháalak ḥáalan.
Half a litre of milk, please.	núṣṣī lítrī lában, min faḍlak.
I have ordered two cubic metres of wood.	ʕana ṭalábt itnéen mítrī xáʃab mukaʢʢabíin.

THE HUMAN BODY, HEALTH

Vocabulary

head	raas,[1] ruus
face	wiʃʃ, wiʃúuʃ
skull	gumgúma, gamáagim

[1] A feminine noun.

forehead	ʔúura, ʔúwar
eye	ɛeen,[1] ɛuyuun (or ɛi-)
eyelid	gifn, gufúun
eyebrow	ḥáagib, ḥawáagib
eyelash	rimʃ, rumúuʃ
ear	widn,[1] widáan
nose	manaxíir
mouth	buʔʔ ; ḥának
lip	ʃíffa, ʃafáayif
cheek	xadd, xudúud
chin	daʔn,[1] duʔúun
jaw	ḍábba, ḍubúub
tooth	sínna, ʔasnáan
neck	ráʔaba, raʔabáat (or raʔáabi)
gum	láθa [2] (or lása)
tongue	lisáan, ʔilsína
throat	zoor, ʔizwáar
tonsil	lóoza, líwaz
gland	γúdda, γúdad
hair	ʃaɛr (c.), ʃáɛra, ʃaɛráat
skin	gild, gulúud
bone	ɛaḍm (c.), ɛáḍma, ɛaḍmáat
rib	ḍálɛ, ḍulúuɛ
spine	silsílit iḍḍáhr
chest	sidr, sudúur
stomach	baṭn,[1] buṭúun
lung	ríʔa, riʔáat
heart	ʔalb, ʔulúub
bowels	ʔamɛáaʔ
liver	kibd (or kábid)
kidney	kílwa, kaláawi
shoulder	kitf, ʔiktáaf
arm	diráaɛ, ʔidríɛa
elbow	kuuɛ, kiɛáan
hand	ʔiid,[1] ʔidéen
wrist	xúnʔit ilʔíid
finger	ṣubáaɛ, ṣawáabiɛ
thumb	ʔiṣṣubáaɛ ikkibíir
middle finger	ʔiṣṣubáaɛ ilwiṣṭáani
little finger	ʔiṣṣubáaɛ iṣṣuγáyyar
joint	máfṣal, mafáaṣil
nail	ḍufr, ḍawáafir

[1] A feminine noun.
[2] Pronounce θ as *th* in English " think ".

thigh	**faxd, ʕifxáad ; wirk, ʕiwráak**
leg	**rigl,[1] rigléen**
knee	**rúkba, rúkab**
ankle	**bízz irrígl**
foot	**rigl,[1] rigléen**
toe	**ṣubáaʕ irrígl**
sole	**káff irrígl**
blood	**damm**
vein	**ʕirʕ, ʕurúuʕ**
blood circulation	**ʕiddáwra-ddamawíyya**
blood pressure	**ḍáɣṭ iddámm**
illness, disease	**máraḍ, ʕamráaḍ**
hygiene	**qawáaʕid iṣṣíḥḥa**
nutrition	**taɣzíya**
food	**ʕakl**
malnutrition	**súuʕ taɣzíya**
dirt	**wasáaxa**
refuse	**wásax**
flies	**dibbáan** (c.), **dibbáana, dibbanáat**
pain	**wágaʕ, ʕawgáaʕ**
headache	**ṣuḍáaʕ**
sore throat	**ʕiltiháab f-ilḥangára**
cold	**bard**
influenza	**ʕinfilwánza**
catarrh	**zukáam**
cough	**kúḥḥa**
inflammation	**ʕiltiháab**
pneumonia	**ʕiltiháab ríʕawi**
gastric trouble	**táʕab f-ilmíʕda**
tuberculosis	**sull**
bruise	**xadʃ, xudúuʃ**
cut	**ʕaṭʕ, ʕuṭúuʕ**
fracture	**kasr, kusúur**
medical examination	**fáḥṣ ṭíbbi**
treatment	**ʕiláaʕ**
medicine	**dáwa, ʕadwíya**
prescription	**ruʃítta, ruʃittáat**
injection ; syringe	**ḥúʕna, ḥúʕan**
vaccination, inoculation	**taṭʕíim ; taxtíin**
smallpox	**gúdari**
cholera	**kúlira**
typhus	**taayfúus**
typhoid	**taayfúud**

[1] A feminine noun.

paratyphoid	taayfuʕiid
dysentery	dusintárya
trachoma	tiraxóoma
international certificate of vaccination against smallpox	ʃiháada dawlíyya bi taṭɛíim ḍidd iggúdari
ambulance	ɛarabíyyit ʕisɛáaf, ɛarabiyyáat ʕisɛáaf
hospital	mustáʃfa, mustaʃfayáat
ward	ɛámbar, ɛanáabir
doctor	duktúur (or duktóor), dakátra
nurse	mumarríḍa, mumarriḍáat
microbe	gurθúuma (or gursúuma), garaθíim (or -s-)[1]
blood test	fáḥṣi dámm
analysis	taḥlíil
toothache	wágaɛ lisnáan
contagious	múɛdi, muɛdíya
healthy	salíim, salíima, suláam; fi ṣíḥḥa gayyída (of person); ṣíḥḥi (of climate, country, food)
convalescent	fi dóor innaqáaḥa
to cure, heal	ɛáalig, yiɛáalig
to anaesthetize	xáddar, yixáddar; bánnig, yibánnig
to clean	náḍḍaf, yináḍḍaf
to extract	ʕálaɛ, yíʕlaɛ
to fill	mála, yímla

Sentences

What are Dr. Rushdi's consulting hours?	ɛiyátt[2] idduktúur rúʃdi-btíftaḥ ʕímta?
Send for a doctor.	ʕíṭlub duktúur.
Did you consult a surgeon for the operation?	ʕinta-staʃárti garráaḥ ɛaʃan ilɛamalíyya?
What is the matter with you?	ʕinta ɛayyáan bi ʕéeh?
I don't feel well.	ʕana taɛbáan/ɛayyáan.
I feel very ill.	ʕana ɛayyáan ʕáwi.
I feel sick.	ʕálbi biyyúmmi ɛaláyya.
I feel giddy.	ʕana dáayix.
I feel weak.	ʕana hamdáan.
You have a sore throat.	ɛándak iltiháab f-ilḥangára.

[1] Pronounce θ as *th* in English " think ".
[2] = ɛiyáadit.

Your tonsils are swollen.	líwazak wárma.
I'm hoarse.	ʕana maḍbúuḥ.
I've caught a cold.	ʕana xátti bárd.
I keep sneezing and coughing.	ʕana báɛṭaṣ w-akúḥḥi dáyman.
You must gargle and take a cough mixture.	láazim titɣárɣar (or titráɣraɣ) wi táaxud dáwa l-ilkúḥḥa.
Stay in bed for a day or two and take your temperature regularly.	láazim tistánna f-issiríir yoméen taláata w-itʕíis ḥarártak b-intiẓáam.
You are feverish, put the thermometer under your tongue.	ʕinta ɛándak ʕirtifáaɛ fi dáragit ilḥaráara — ḥúṭṭ ittirmumítri táḥti-lsáanak.
The temperature is going up (down).	ʕilḥaráara murtáfiɛa (munxáfiḍa).
Your pulse is very irregular.	nábḍak muṭṭárib (or míʃ maẓbúuṭ).
His heart is very weak.	ʕálbu ḍaɛíif gíddan.
He has pneumonia.	ɛándu iltiháab riʕawi.
You must be taken to hospital.	láazim tirúuḥ ilmustáʃfa.
I prefer a private clinic.	ʕan-afáḍḍal ɛiyáada xáaṣṣa.
The patient must not be disturbed.	láazim ilɛayyáan yitánni mistaráyyaḥ.
What are the fees for a visit to an ear, nose, and throat specialist?	duktúur ilʕánf w-ilʕúzun biyáaxud káam f-ikkáʃf ?
I shall have to give you a thorough examination.	ʕana láazim ákʃif ɛaléek káʃfi káamil.
We shall have to take an X-ray.	láazim níɛmil káʃfi ʕaʃíɛɛa.
Is your digestion all right?	háḍmak kuwáyyis ?
The medicine was no good.	ʕiddáwa ma nafáɛʃ.
Take these pills and a teaspoonful of this powder after meals.	xúd ilḥugúbda wi maɛláʕit ʃáay min ilmasḥúʕda baɛd ilʕákl.
Shake the bottle.	rúgg ilʕizáaza.
For external use only.	li listiɛmáali-lxaarígi fáqaṭ.[1]
Poison.	summ.
You have broken your arm.	diráaɛak ikkásar.
We shall have to keep your leg in plaster.	láazim niḥúṭṭi ríglak f-iggíbs.
He has fractured his skull.	ráasu-tɛawwárit.
You have had a bad concussion.	kan ɛándak ʕirtigáag f-ilmúxxi-ʃdíid.
I am injured.	ʕana-ggaráḥt.
I've sprained my ankle.	rígli-ltáwaḥit.
His illness got worse.	ʕilɛáya túʕul ɛaléeh.
He is better.	huwwa xáff.

[1] Written language.

The cut is healed but you can still see the scar.	ʕiggárḫi ṭáab láakin ʕásaru líssa mawgúud.
I must dress your wounds.	láazim arbúṭlak iggárḫ.
I cannot hear well.	ʕana ma baʕdárʃ ásmaɛ kuwáyyis.
He is deaf and dumb.	huwwa ʕáṭraʃ wi ʕáxras.
Your inner ear is inflamed.	wídnak multáhiba min gúwwa.
I am short-sighted (long-sighted).	ʕana ɛándi ʕíṣar náẓar (ṭúul náẓar).
Do you know a good oculist?	tiɛraf ṭabíib ɛiyúun kuwáyyis?
He is blind.	huwwa ʕáɛma.
I need a pair of glasses.	ʕana ɛáawiz naḍḍáara.
He squints a little.	huwwa ʕáḫwal ʃuwayya.
At the dentist's:	ɛandi ṭabíib ilʕasnáan:
Please come into the surgery.	min fáḍlak taɛáala-lɛiyáada.
This tooth hurts me.	ʕiddirsída-byiwgáɛni.
This front tooth hurts me.	ʕissínna-lʕuddamaníyya di-btiwgáɛni.
This tooth must be stopped.	ʕissinnáadi láazim titḫáʃa.
The gums are bleeding.	ʕillása bitxúrri dámm.
I shall give you a local anaesthetic.	ʕana ḫaɛṭíik bingi maḫálli.
The root is decayed.	gídr issinnáadi-msáwwis.
Can't you manage without drilling?	ma tiʕdárʃi tiɛmílha min γéer táʕb.
The tooth must be extracted.	ʕissínna láazim titxálaɛ.
I have a gumboil.	ɛándi xurráag.
What tooth-paste do you use?	bitistáɛmil ʕáyyi maɛgúun ʕasnáan?
I'm afraid you must have a denture.	láazim tiɛmíllak ṭáʕm isnáan.
You must have a gold crown on your tooth.	láazim niḫúṭṭi ṭarbúuʃ dáhab ɛala sinnítak.
I shall have to get a new tooth-brush.	ʕana láazim agíib fúrʃit isnáan gidíida.
Is the treatment finished?	ʕilɛiláag xúlus?

AT THE HAIRDRESSER'S

Vocabulary

gentlemen's hairdresser's	mizáyyin (or ḫalláaʕ) l-irrigáal
ladies' hairdresser's	mizáyyin (or ḫalláaʕ) l-issayyidáat
safety razor	mákanit ḫiláaʕa
razor blade	múus ḫiláaʕa, ʕamwáas ḫiláaʕa
shaving brush	fúrʃit ḫiláaʕa

shaving lotion	**kulúnya l-ilḫiláaʕa**
shaving soap/stick	**ṣabúun ḫiláaʕa**
shaving cream	**maɛgúun ḫiláaʕa**
hair-cream	**diháan l-iʃʃáɛr**
eau-de-cologne	**kulúnya**
haircut	**ḫiláaʕa**
beard	**daʕn,[1] duʕúun**
moustache	**ʃánab, ʃanabáat**
wave	**tamwíiga, tamwigáat**
parting	**farʕ, furúuʕ**
wash	**ɣasl**
shampoo	**ʃampúu**
hair-net	**ʃábakit iʃʃáɛr**
hairpin	**dabbúus iʃʃáɛr**
comb	**miʃṭ, ʕimʃáaṭ**
hairbrush	**fúrʃit ʃáɛr**
perfume	**ɛiṭr, ɛuṭúur ; ríiḫa, rawáayiḫ**
nail varnish	**diháan ḍawáafir**
talcum powder	**búdrit tálk**
face powder	**búdrit wiʃʃ**
lipstick	**ʕáḫmar ʃafáayif**
tweezers	**mulʕáat**
manicure	**manikéer**
manicurist	**ɛa(a)míllit ilmanikéer**
to shave	**ḫálaʕ, yíḫlaʕ**
to cut	**ḫálaʕ, yíḫlaʕ** (hair) ; **ʕáṣṣar, yiʕáṣṣar**
to trim	**sáawa, yisáawi**
to lather	**ráɣɣa, yiráɣɣi**
to wave	**máwwig, yimáwwig**
to dry	**náʃʃif, yináʃʃif**
to dye	**sábaɣ, yúsbuɣ**
to massage	**ɛámal, yiɛmil masáaj li . . .**

Sentences

Is there a gentlemen's hair-dresser near here?	**fíih ḫalláaʕ l-irrigáal ʕuráyyib hína ?**
How do you want it, sir?	**ʕaɛmíllak ʕéeh fi ʃáɛrak ?**
A haircut, please, trim back and sides.	**ʕuṣṣʃli ʃáɛri, min faḍlak, wi ʕaṣṣarhúuli m-iggawáanib wi min wára.**
Not too short, please.	**ma-tʕaṣṣarúuʃ ʕáwi, min faḍlak.**
A two-days-old beard.	**dáʕni baʕálha yoméen min. ɣéer ḫiláaʕa.**

[1] A feminine noun.

Please trim my moustache.	min fáḍlak, wáḍḍab ʃánabi.
I should like a shampoo.	ʕana ɛáawiz ʃampúu, min faḍlak.
You can give me a shave, too.	ʕiħláʕli dáʕni kamáan, min faḍlak.
Does this shaving-cream give a good lather?	maɛgúun ilħiláaʕa da-byiɛmil ráγwa-kwayyisa?
Here is a hot towel, sir.	ʕitfáḍḍal fúuṭa súxna-(a)héh!
He is getting bald.	huwwa-byiṣlaɛ.
He is turning grey.	ʃáɛru biyʃíib.
Have you a hair-restorer?	ɛándak ħáaga ma-txallíiʃ iʃʃáɛri yiṣʕaṭ?
Have you any good hair-oil?	ɛándak zéet ʃáɛri-kwáyyis?
Should I leave a tip for the assistant?	láazim asíib baʕʃíiʃ ɛaʃan iṣṣábi?
I would like to make an appointment with my usual assistant for to-morrow at eleven.	ʕana ɛáwz(a)-áħgiz maɛáad maɛa-lħalláaʕa-btáɛti búkra-ssaɛa-ħḍáaʃar.
Everything is booked up for to-morrow, I am sorry.	ʕiħna maʃγulíin búkra, ʕana ʕáasif.
Can I come for a perm on Monday?	ʕáʕdar áagi ɛaʃan amáwwig ʃáɛri yóom litnéen?
Don't cut off too much, please.	ma-tʕaṣṣárʃi ʃáɛri ʕáwi, min faḍlak.
I should like to try a new hair-style.	ʕana ɛáwz(a)-aγáyyar listáyl bitaɛ ʃáɛri.
What colour do you want your hair dyed?	ɛáwza tisbúγi ʃáɛrik bi ʕáyyi lóon?
I should like a dark brown shade.	ʕana ɛáwza lóon búnni γáamiʕ.
Do you sell lipsticks and nail varnish to match?	ʕíntu bitbiíɛu ʕáħmar ʃafáayif wi-dháan ḍawáafir yiwáfʕu(h)?
For your make-up we have cream and face powder, eyebrow pencils and rouge.	ɛandína-kriim wi búdra l-ilwiʃʃ w-iʕláam l-ilħawáagib wi ʕáħmar ɛaʃan ittuwalítt.
Have you a manicure service?	ɛandúkum manikéer hína?
Have you any toilet soap?	ɛandúkum ṣabúun wiʃʃ?

CLOTHING [1]

Vocabulary

men's clothing	miláabis l-irrigáal
pyjamas	bijáama, bijamáat
dressing-gown	roob, ʕirwáab
slippers	ʃíbʃib, ʃabáaʃib

[1] Only European-style clothing is dealt with in this section.

socks	ʃaráab, ʃarabáat
shoes	gázma (pair) : fárdit gázma (one)
suspenders	ḥammaláat ʃarabáat ; ḥammáalit ʃaráab (one)
garters	ʕasáatik ʃarabáat ; ʕástik ʃaráab (one)
drawers, pants	libáas, ʕilbísa
vest	faníila, fanilláat
shirt	ʕamíiṣ, ʕumṣáan
braces	ḥammáalit banṭalóon
belt	ḥizáam, ʕiḥzíma
collar	yáaʕa, yaʕáat ; liyáaʕa, liyaʕáat
stud	ẓuráar liyáaʕa, ẓaráayir liyaʕáat
cuff-links	ẓaráayir ʕasáawir ilʕamíiṣ
tie	garafíṭṭa, garafiṭṭáat ; karafítta, karafittáat ; karavátta, karavattáat
suit, lounge-suit	bádla, bídal
jacket	jakétta, jakettáat
trousers	banṭalóon, banṭalonáat
waistcoat	sidéeri, sadáari
evening-dress	bádlit issáhra
overcoat	bálṭu, baláaṭi (or balṭuwáat)
cap	kaskítta, kaskittáat
hat	barníiṭa (or burnéeṭa), baraníiṭ
beret	biréе(h), birеháat
gloves	gawánti, gawantiyyáat ; fárdit gawánti (one)
stick	ʕáṣa, ʕuṣy
umbrella, parasol	ʃamsíyya, ʃamsiyyáat
scarf	talfíiḥa, talafíiḥ ; kufíyya, kufiyyáat
handkerchief	mandíil, manadíil
raincoat	bálṭu máṭar, baláaṭi máṭar
suit material	ʕumáaʃ bádla
sports wear	maláabis irriyáaḍa
cardigan	kardigáan, kardiganáat
pullover	bilóovar, bilovráat
stockings	ʃarabáat
underwear	maláabis daxilíyya
brassiere	sutiyáan, sutiyanáat
slip	ʕamíiṣ, ʕumṣáan
briefs	kalsúun, kalsunáat
night-dress	ʕamíiṣ nóom
girdle, roll-on	kurséе(h), kursеháat
dress, gown	fustáan, fasatíin
blouse	bilóoza (or bilúuza), bilozáat
suit, costume	tayyéer, tayyeráat
apron	ʕéeprun (or ʕáprun), ʕeprunáat

fur coat	**bálṭu fárw, baláaṭi fárw**
veil	**búrʕuʔ, baráaʕiʔ ; béeʃa, beʃáat** (on hat)
square, headkerchief	**ʕiʃáarb, ʕiʃarbáat**
shawl	**ʃaal, ʃiláan**
high-heeled shoe	**gázma-b káʔbi ʔáali**
walking-shoe	**gázma-b káʔbi wáaṭi**
sole (of shoe)	**naʔl**
fashion	**móoḍa, moḍáat**
design	**tafṣíila, tafṣiláat**
material	**ʕumáaʃ, ʕumaʃáat**
silk	**ḥaríir**
velvet	**vílvit**
wool	**ṣuuf**
linen	**kittáan**
jewels, jewellery	**migawharáat**
ring	**xáatim, xawáatim**
necklace	**ʔuʕd, ʔuʕúud**
bracelet	**ʕiswíra, ʕasáawir**
ear-rings	**ḥálaʕ** (pair), **ḥulʕáan** (pairs) ; **fárdit ḥálaʕ** (one)
tailor	**xayyáaṭ, xayyaṭíin**
dressmaker	**xayyáaṭa**
coat-hanger	**ʃammáaʔa, ʃammaʔáat**
red	**ʕáḥmar, ḥámra, ḥumr**
blue	**ʕázraʕ, zárʕa, zurʕ**
green	**ʕáxḍar, xáḍra, xuḍr**
yellow	**ʕáṣfar, ṣáfra, ṣufr**
brown	**búnni** [1]
grey	**ruṣáaṣi**
black	**ʕíswid, sóoda, suud**
white	**ʕábyaḍ, béeḍa, biiḍ**
purple	**banafsígi**
orange	**burtuʕáani**
silver	**fáḍḍi**
golden	**dáhabi**
light (in colour)	**fáatiḥ, fátḥa, fatḥíin**
dark	**ɣáamiʕ, ɣámʕa, ɣamʕíin**
to dress	**líbis, yílbis ; lábbis, yilábbis** (transitive)
to undress	**ʕálaʔ, yiʕlaʔ**
to put on	**líbis, yílbis** (e.g. **iggázma**)
to take off	**ʕálaʔ, yiʕlaʔ** (e.g. **ilbarníiṭa**)

[1] Also "coffee-coloured".

to sew	xáyyaṭ, yixáyyaṭ
to mend	ṣállaḥ, yiṣállaḥ
to darn	ráfa, yirfi

Sentences

Do you know a good tailor ?	tiɛraf xayyáaṭ kuwáyyis ?
I want a suit made to measure.	ɛáawiz afáṣṣal bádla.
I prefer a suit made to measure to a ready-made one.	ʔan-afáḍḍal ilbádla-ttafṣíil ɛan iggáhza.
What sort of material do you stock ?	ʔéeh nóoɛ ilʔumáaʃ illi ɛandúkum ?
I want a lounge suit.	ʔana ɛáawiz bádla, min faḍlak.
Single-breasted or double-breasted ?	bi ṣáffi wáaḥid walla-b ṣafféen ?
Do you wear a belt or braces ?	ʔinta-btilbis ḥizáam walla ḥammaláat ?
The sleeves are too short.	ʔilʔikmáam ʔuṣayyára ʔáwi.
The trousers are too long.	ʔilbanṭalóon ṭawíil ʔáwi.
The lapels are too wide.	tányit ijjakétta ɛaríiḍa ʔáwi.
The jacket does not fit.	ʔijjakétta miʃ ɛala ʔáddi.
To-morrow is your first fitting.	ʔilburúuva-lʔawwalaníyya búkra.
I should like a dark sports jacket and a pair of light grey flannel trousers.	ɛáawiz jakétta lónha yáamiʔ wi banṭalóon fanílla-rṣáaṣi fáatiḥ.
The suit is well cut.	ʔilbádla maẓbúuṭa.
Show me some check shirts, please.	warríini-lʔumṣáan ilmurabbaɛáat illi ɛándak, min faḍlak.
Six starched collars.	sittí yaʔáat minaʃʃíyya.
Have you a blue silk tie ?	ɛándak karavátta ḥaríir zárʔa ?
Half a dozen coloured and a dozen white handkerchiefs.	núṣṣi dástit manadíil milawwína wi dástit manadíil béeḍa.
The hat is too big for me.	ʔilbarníiṭa wáasɛa ʔáwi ɛaláyya.
I must send my grey hat to be cleaned.	ʔana láazim ábɛat barníṭti-rmáadi titnáḍḍaf.
This suit must be repaired, the lining is torn.	ʔilbadláadi láazim tiṣṣállaḥ, ʔilbiṭáana mitʔaṭṭáɛa.
Please send these shoes to be half-soled.	wáddi-ggazmáadi yiḥuṭṭúulha núṣṣi náɛl.
The slippers need new heels.	ʔiʃʃíbʃib ɛáawiz náɛli-gdíid.
I like plain socks.	ʔiʃʃarabáat issáada tiɛgíbni.
The woollen socks have shrunk.	ʔiʃʃarabáat iṣṣúuf káʃʃu.
The colours have run.	ʔilʔalwáan báhatit.
Do you prefer brown or black shoes ?	tifáḍḍal gázma búnni walla gázma sóoda ?

The shoes are too tight.	ʔiggázma dayyáʔa.
The toes of these boots pinch.	ʔiggázma dayyáʔa min ʔuddáam.
A pair of brown laces, please.	rubáaṭ gázma ʔásmar, min faḍlak.
Which lasts longer, silk or nylon clothes ?	ʔilhudúum ilḥariir tiɛiiʃ ʔáktar walla-lhudúum innáylun ?
Have you any pink slips which are not too expensive ?	ɛándak ʔumṣáan lábani ma-tkúnʃi yálya ʔáwi ?
Where can I get the ladders in my stockings repaired ?	ʔáʔdar aṣállaḥ ilʔáṭɛ illi-f ʃaráabi féen ?
The stockings are laddered and holed.	ʔiʃʃaráab maʔṭúuɛ wi-mxárraʔ.
I want a blue-striped blouse with long sleeves.	ʔana ɛáwza-blóoza zárʔa-mxaṭṭáṭa bi-kmáam ṭawiila.
The brown skirt is very smart.	ʔiggunilla-lbúnni gamiila ʔáwi.
It is too large for me.	di wásɛa ɛaláyya ʔáwi.
You can have it altered/taken in/let out.	múmkin tiṣṣállaḥ/tiddáyyaʔ/titwássaɛ.
I need a light woollen winter dress.	ʔana ɛáwza fustáan ṣúuf xafiif l-iʃʃita.
Have you any low-necked evening dresses ?	ɛandúku fustáan sáhra-b ṣidra makʃúuf ?
I want a black-lace veil.	ʔana ɛáwza béeʃa dantilla sámra.
This green dress really does suit you.	ʔilfustáan láxḍar da láayiʔ ɛaléeki ʔáwi.
This cardigan is nice and warm.	ʔilkardigáan da biydáffi-kwáyyis.
You can find leather goods in that shop.	tiláaʔi-f maḥálli da baḍáayiɛ gild.
I need a handbag and purse.	lazimni ʃánṭit yáddi-w maḥfáẓa.
I am looking for a pair of shoes size five.	ʔana badáwwar ɛala gázma maʔáas xámsa.
I am sorry, madam, in Egypt sizes are numbered differently. I should say yours is (number) 35.	ʔáasif, ya háanim, ʔiggizam mitnammára-b ʃákli táani hina-f máṣr. ʔaẓúnni maʔáasik yibʔa xámsa-w talatiin.
The hat with the black feathers does not match your brown coat.	ʔilbarniiṭa di ʔúmmi riyaʃ sámra miʃ máʃya maɛa-lbálṭu-lbúnni-btáaɛik.
I will take this silver watch with the leather strap.	ʔana ḥáaxud issáaɛa-lfáḍḍa di ʔúmmi ʔástik gild.
Have you any small gold earrings ?	ɛandúkum ḥulʔáan dáhab ṣuyayyára ?

ENTERTAINMENTS, PASTIMES, SPORTS

THE THEATRE

Vocabulary

the theatre and other entertainments	ʕilmásraħ w-almaláahi [1]-lʕúxra
the Opera House	dáar ilʕúpra
concert hall	qáaɛit ilmusíiqa
entertainment guide	dalíil ilmaláahi
play	riwáaya, riwayáat
comedy	kummídya ; malháah
tragedy	tira(a)jíidya ; maʕsáah
drama	diráama ; qíṣṣa
variety show	másraħ mutanawwaɛáat
show	ɛarḍ ; ɛárḍi nímar ; tamsíil
concert	musíiqa sinfuníyya ; ħáfla musiqíyya
circus	sark
folk songs	ɣúna báladi
musical instrument	ʕáala musiqíyya
public, audience	ʕinnáas
seating capacity	ɛádad ikkaráasi
late-night performance	ʕilħáfla-lʕaxíira ; ʕissuwarée(h)
early evening performance	ʕilħáfla-lʕawwalaníyya (or -lʕúula)
matinée	ʕilmatinée(h) [2]
foyer	mádxal
cloakroom, toilet	dó(o)rt ilmáyya
refreshment room	bufée(h)
auditorium	ṣáala
box	looj ; buks
circle	balkóon
gallery	ʕáɛla-lmásraħ
stage	másraħ
footlights	ʕanwáar ilmásraħ
wings	kawalíis
dressing-room	ʕúgrit taɣyíir ilmaláabis
national theatre	ʕilmásraħ ilqáwmi
scenery	manáaẓir
background	mánẓar xálfi ; báakgirawnd
prompter	muláqqin
props-man	mutaɛáhhid ilmaláabis

[1] The form (ʕ)al of the article marks what is essentially a literary form.

[2] Often a morning performance in cinemas.

company (theatrical)	gamɛíyyit ilfanniyyíin ; ʕittiħáad
producer	múxrig
author ; composer	muʕállif
playwright	riwáaɛi
poet	ʃáaɛir, ʃúɛara
cast	ʕilmumassilíin
actor	mumássil (-a, -iin, -aat)[1]
leading man	báṭal, ʕabṭáal
leading lady	báṭala, baṭaláat
ballet	balée(h)
dancer (male)	ráaqiṣ, raqṣíin
dancer (female)	ra(a)qíṣa, raqṣáat (or raqqáaṣa, raqqaṣáat)
ballerina	ra(a)qíṣat ilbalée(h)[2]
understudy	ʕilbádal
scene	mánẓar, manáaẓir
part	door, ʕidwáar
song	ʕuɣníya, ʕaɣáani
interval	ʕistiráaħa
curtain	sitáara
safety curtain	sitáarit ilʕamáan
singer	muɣánni, muɣanníyya, muɣanniyyíin, muɣanniyyáat[1]
acrobat	ʕaragóoz, ʕaragozáat
conjurer	ħáawi, ħuwáah
clown	muhárrig, muharrigíin
tamer	muráwwiḍ, murawwiḍíin
finale	niháayit ilɛárḍ
applause	taṣfíiq (or tasʕíif)
booing	tahzíiʕ
to tour (the provinces)	laff, yilíff (f-ilmudiriyyáat)
to watch a performance	ħáḍar, yíħḍar ittamsíil
to bow	ʕinħána, yinħíni (or yinħáni)
to play the piano	líɛib, yílɛab ɛa-lbiyáanu

Sentences

What's on at the theatre tonight?	fiih ʕéeh f-ilmásraħ illéela?
There's a drama by a modern author at the State Theatre.	fiih riwáaya katíbha muʕállif ħadíiθ f-ilmásraħ ilwáṭani.

[1] See footnote on p. 192.

[2] The form **ra(a)qíṣat** is marked as literary in many ways, including **-at** for **-it**.

We shan't get any tickets.	**miʃ ḥanláaʔi tazáakir.**
The house is sold out.	**ʔittazáakir xilṣit** (or **xúluṣit**).
Can I order tickets by telephone ?	**ʔáʔdar áḥgiz tazáakir b-ittilifóon ?**
Can you see all right from that seat ?	**ʃáayif kuwáyyis min ikkúrsi da ?**
I need some opera-glasses.	**ʔana ʕáawiz tiliskóop.**
I'd like some coffee in the interval.	**ʕáawiz áʃrab ʔáhwa fi listiráaḥa.**
You can only have it in the refreshment room.	**láazim tirúuḥ ilbuféeh ʕalaʃan tiʃrábha.**
The curtain's going up/coming down.	**ʔissitáara-btirtáfaʕ/btínzil.**
What a marvellous setting !	**manáaẓir ilmásraḥ gamíila gíddan.**
The lead hasn't learned his part very well.	**ʔilbáṭal miʃ ḥáafiẓ dóoru-kwáyyis.**
The play was enthralling/boring/amusing.	**ʔirriwáaya kanit mumtáaza/báyxa/laṭíifa.**
The footlights are too bright.	**ʔanwáar ilmásraḥ qawíyya** (or **ʃidíida**) **ʔáwi.**
There was a lot of/very little applause.	**ʔittasʔíif kan ḥá(a)ddi/basíiṭ gíddan.**
Have you seen the new show at the Rihani Theatre ?	**ʃúft irriwáaya-ggidíida-f másraḥ irriḥáani ?**
The songs are by a well-known composer.	**ʔilʔaɣáani-btáaʕit wáaḥid maʃhúur.**
I don't understand Arab/Eastern music, and I don't always like what I hear.	**ʔana ma bafhámʃ ilmusíiqa-lʕarabíyya/ʃʃarqíyya wi ma-btiʕgibníiʃ ilḥagáat illi basmáʕha**[1] **minha.**
Have you been to Umm Kalsuum's[2] recital this month ?	**rúḥti ḥáflit ʔúmmi kalsúum bitaʕt iʃʃáhri da ?**
I'd like to take the children to the circus.	**ʔana ʕáawiz awáddi-lʔawláad issárk.**
Did they enjoy the performance ?	**ʔittamsíil ʕagábhum ?**

[1] Pronounced **-ḥḥa.**
[2] A popular woman singer.

CINEMA

Vocabulary

cinema	**sínima, sinimáat**
local cinema	**ʕissínima-lmaḩallíyya**
film	**film, ʕafláam**
screen	**ʃáaʃa, ʃaʃáat**
talking film	**fílmi náatiʕ**
silent film	**fílmi ṣáamit**
plot	**qíṣṣa, qíṣaṣ**
cartoon	**kartúun**
newsreel	**film ilʕaxbáar**
Western	**fílmi kawbóoyz**
detective film	**fílmi bulíisi**
comedy	**fílmi kóomdi**
documentary	**fílmi wa(a)qíɛi**
film studio	**ʕistúdyu, ʕistudyuwáat** (or **ʕistudyuháat**)
projector	**ʕáalit ɛárḍ**
slides	**siláaydz**
dubbing	**dubláaj**
subtitles, translation	**targáma**
cut	**ʕatɛ, ʕutúuɛ**
sound-track	**mágra-ṣṣóot**
script	**riwáaya**
script writer	**káatib riwáaya, kuttáab riwayáat; riwáaʕi, riwaʕiyyíin**
director	**múntig, muntigíin; mudíir ilʕintáag**
producer	**múxrig, muxrigíin**
revival	**ɛárḍi táani**
re-make	**ʕixráag gidíid**
cinema-goers	**ruwwáad issínima** [1]
cinema programme	**birnáamig** [2] **issínima**
supporting programme	**ʕilbaráamig iθθanawíyya**
U-certificate film	**fílmi l-ilgamíiɛ**
X-certificate (adults only)	**fílmi l-ilkibáar fáqat**
continuous performance	**ɛárḍi mustamírr**
separate performances	**ɛárḍi ɛáadi**
doorman	**bawwáab**
cash-desk, cashier	**kays**
booking office, box office	**ʃibbáak ittazáakir**

[1] The corresponding singular requires the particle **min**, i.e. **fuláan** ("so-and-so") **min ruwwáad issínima.**

[2] Plural **baráamig.**

usher	**ɛáamil issínima, ɛummáal issínima**
usherette	**ɛa(a)míl̇at issínima, ɛa(a)miláat issínima**
operator	**ɛáamil mákanit ilɛárḍ**
choc-ice	**ʔáays kiríim bi ʃukuláaṭa**
sweets	**ḥalawiyyáat**
film-fan	**múɣram b-issínima**
cast	**ʔilmumassilíin**
hero	**báṭal, ʔabṭáal**
heroine	**báṭala, baṭaláat**
male star	**nágmi sinimáaʔi**
female star	**nágma sinimaʔíyya**
villain	**ʃirríir**
colour film	**fílmi-mláwwin; fílmi b-ilʔalwáan**
the end	**ʔinniháaya**
anthem	**ʔissaláam ilwáṭani**
to film, shoot, photograph	**ṣáwwar, yiṣáwwar**
to go to the pictures	**ráaḥ, yirúuḥ issínima**

Sentences

When does the next performance start?	**ʔilɛárḍ ittáani ḥayibtídi-ssaɛa káam?**
The news-reel is shown at 3.30.	**ʔilʔaxbáar ḥatúɛraḍ [1] f-issínima-ssáaɛa taláata-w núṣṣ.**
Is it a continuous performance?	**da ɛárḍi mustamírr?**
When is the film's first night going to be?	**ʔilɛárḍ ilʔáwwal l-ilfilmída yóom ʔéeh?**
Look at the programmes in the evening papers.	**ʃúuf ilbaráamig f-iggaráayid ilmasaʔíyya.**
Two stalls for the last performance, please.	**tazkartéen ṣáala l-ilɛárḍ ilʔaxíir, min faḍlak.**
We had better sit at the back.	**ʔáḥsan núʔɛud f-ilʔáaxir.**
Is there any emergency exit?	**fíih báab maxṣúuṣ l-ilxurúug ɛánd ilxáṭar?**
Can tickets be booked in advance?	**múmkin ḥágzi tazáakir muʔad-dáman?**
I know you know the plot, but please don't tell me.	**ʔana ɛáarif innak ɛáarif ilqíṣṣa láakin ma-tʔullíiʃ, min faḍlak.**
A new film is being shown.	**fíih fílmi-gdíid biyúɛraḍ.**
I've seen this film before.	**ʔana ʃúft ilfilmída ʔabli kída.**

[1] **-tuɛraḍ** exhibits the shape of the Classical passive but is commonly used in educated colloquial.

It's only a revival.	**da bássi tagdíid l-ilfilm.**
Don't miss it!	**ma-yfutákʃ ilfilmída !**
Did you read the review?	**ʕaréet ittaɛlíiq ɛa-lfílm?**
It's a slow-moving film.	**ʕilfílmi da-yzáhhaʕ.**
It's a thriller [1]—very exciting.	**da fílmi bulíisi múrɛib giddan.**
The criminal is always the last one you suspect.	**ʕilmúgrim húwwa-lli-nta dáyman tiftíkir innu ʕáħsan wáaħid.**

BROADCASTING

Vocabulary

broadcasting	**ʕizáaɛa**
broadcasting station	**maħáṭṭit ʕizáaɛa**
transmission	**ʕizáaɛa**
reception	**ʕistaqbáal**
radio	**rádyu, radyuwáat**
loudspeaker	**mukábbir iṣṣóoṭ**
earphone(s)	**sammáaɛa, sammaɛáat**
battery set	**rádyu baṭṭaríyya**
valve	**lámbit rádyu, lúmaḍ rádyu [2]**
condenser	**kundánsa (or kundánsar); mukáθθif, mukaθθifáat**
volume	**ʃíddit iṣṣóoṭ**
cabinet	**sandúuʕ irrádyu**
knob	**muftáaħ, mafatíiħ**
mains	**kahrába**
power-point	**fíiʃa, fiʃáat**
aerial	**ʕéeryal**
frame aerial	**ʕéeryal ʕiṭáari**
inside aerial	**ʕéeryal da(a)xíli**
flex, wire	**silk**
adjustment	**ẓabṭ**
direct current	**tayyáar mustamírr**
alternating current	**tayyáar mutaqáṭṭiɛ**
disturbances, "atmospherics"	**ʕiṭṭiráab gáwwi, ʕiṭṭirabáat gawwíyya**
interference	**tadáxxul**
short wave	**móoga ʕuṣayyára**
medium wave	**móoga mutawaṣṣíṭa**
long wave	**móoga ṭawíila**

[1] Or "detective story".

[2] Notice the unexpected plural form. **lambáat** also occurs; so, too, do the singular/plural forms **lánḍa/lúnaḍ** (or **lanḍáat**).

selectivity	ḥasa(a)síya
microphone	mikrufóon
announcer	mu(u)zíiɛ, muziɛíin
programme parade	birnáamig ilʕizáaɛa
disc, record	ʕisṭuwáana, ʕisṭuwanáat
news	ʕilʕaxbáar
weather forecast	ʕinnáʃra-lgawwíyya
talk	muḥáḍra, muḥaḍráat ; ḥadíiθ, ʕaḥadíiθ
serial	silsíla ; qíṣṣa musalsála
listener	mustámiɛ, mustámiɛa, mustamiɛíin, mustamiɛáat[1]
television set	tilivizyóon, tilivizyonáat
screen	ʃáaʃa
tape-recorder	giháaz tasgíil, ʕaghízit tasgíil
to switch on	wállaɛ, yiwállaɛ irrádyu ; ṭáfa, yíṭfi irrádyu
to tune in	dáwwar, yidáwwar irrádyu
to listen in	símiɛ, yísmaɛ irrádyu
to earth	wáṣṣal, yiwáṣṣal b-ilʕárḍ

Sentences

Can you pick up foreign stations with your set?	tiʕdar tigíib ilmaḥaṭṭáat ilʕagnabíyya b-irrádyu-btáaɛak ?
My set is out of order.	ʕirrádyu-btáaɛi mitɛáṭṭal.
There's a lot of disturbance and fading on my set.	ʕirrádyu-btáaɛi fíih xarwáʃa-w laxbáṭa f-iṣṣóoṭ kitíir.
Reception is poor.	ʕilmaḥáṭṭa di ḍaɛíifa.
Can you recommend a good wireless repair shop?	tíɛraf maḥálli-kwáyyis li taṣlíiḥ irradyuwáat ?
Can you send someone round to have a look at it?	tiʕdar tíbɛat ḥáddi-yʃúufu(h) ?
The valves want renewing.	ʕillúmaḍ bitaɛ irrádyu lazim tiggáddid.
Where do I take out a licence for my set?	ʕagíib rúxṣa l-irrádyu-mnéen ?
You can get the licence at the (local) telegraph office.	tiʕdar táaxud irrúxṣa min máktab ittiliɣráaf.
Do you often listen in?	ʕinta-btísmaɛ irrádyu-ktíir ?
Only when they broadcast concerts.	lamma biyzíiɛu mu(u)síiqa sinfuníyya báss.
Is there a talk on the radio this evening?	fíih muḥáḍra f-irrádyu-lléela ?

[1] The series is borrowed from the written language, whence a gender distinction between plural forms.

My neighbours' wireless disturbs me.	**rádyu-ggiráan biyiʕlíʕni.**
I like listening to music programmes.	**ʕana baḫíbb ásmaع ilmuxta(a)ráat ilmu(u)si(i)qíyya** (or **birnáamig ilmutanawwiعáat ilmu(u)si(i)qíyya**).
Did you hear the news?	**simíعt ilʕaxbáar?**
There's a play on the radio tonight at eight.	**fíih riwáaya f-irrádyu-lleláadi-ssáaعa tamánya.**
What was the weather forecast?	**ʕalu ʕéeh f-innáʃra-ggawwíyya?**
Did you buy your set on hire-purchase?	**ʕiʃtaréet irrádyu-btáaعak b-iṭṭaʕsíiṭ?**
Our neighbours come to us to hear the children's programmes.	**ʕiggiráan biyíigu عandína yismáعu birnáamig ilʕaṭfáal.**
Would you like to hear the gondola-song of Abd al-Wahhaab?	**عáawiz tísmaع ʕuɣníyit ilgundúul bitaعit عábd ilwahháab?**
The station has closed down.	**ʕilmaḫáṭṭa di xallágit ʕizáaعa.**
They always close down with the national anthem.	**biyínhu-lʕizáaعa dáyman b-issaláam ilwáṭani.**

PHOTOGRAPHY

Vocabulary

photography	**taṣwíir**
camera	**futuɣráfya, futuɣrafyáat**
box camera	**kámira búks**
folding camera	**kámira bi munfáax**
miniature camera	**kámira ṣuɣayyára**
ciné camera	**kámira sinimaʕíyya**
film	**fílm, ʕafláam**
plate	**looḫ, ʕalwáaḫ**
lens	**عádasa, عadasáat**
spool	**bákara, bakaráat**
aperture	**fátḫa**
diaphragm	**ḫáagib innúur**
shutter	**ḫáagib ilعádasa**
filter	**fíltar, filtaráat**
flash	**nuur**
self-timer	**kámira biṣṣáwwar bi nafsáha**
exposure meter	**maʕáas innúur**
leather case	**ʃánṭa gild**
tripod	**ḫáamil**

photograph	ṣúura, ṣúwar
snapshot	láʕṭa, laʕṭáat
slow motion	taṣwíir baṭiiʕ
light	nuur
focus	búʕra
stereoscopic picture	ṣúura mugassáma
three-dimensional film	fílmi-b tálat ʕabɛáad
negative	ɛafriita, ɛafariit
positive	ṣúura, ṣúwar
developer	ḥáamiḍ
fixer	sáaʕil muθábbit
print	ṭábɛa, ṭabɛáat
printing paper	wáraʕ ṭibáaɛa
dark room	ʕilʕóoḍa-ḍḍálma
cameraman, photographer	muṣawwaráati, muṣawwaratíyya
street photographer	muṣawwaráati f-iʃʃáariɛ
under-exposed	(ṣúura) miḍallíma ; (ṣúura) náʕṣa núur
over-exposed	(ʕiṣṣúura) xádit núur ; (ṣúura) minawwára ʕáktar m-illáazim
to expose	ɛárraḍ, yiɛárraḍ
to focus	ẓábaṭ, yíẓbuṭ ilɛádasa
to develop	ḥámmaḍ, yiḥámmaḍ
to enlarge	kábbar, yikábbar
to retouch	wáḍḍab, yiwáḍḍab
to make copies	ɛámal, yíɛmil núsax

Sentences

May I take a photograph here?	ʕáʕdar áaxud ṣúura hína?
You must hand in your camera.	láazim tisállim ilkámira-btáɛtak.
Where can I get photographic materials?	ʕáʕdar aʃtiri ʕadawáat[1] taṣwíir minéen?
I want a roll film, size 6 by 9 cm.	ʕana ɛáawiz fílmi maʕáas sítta-f tísɛa, min faḍlak.
Could you put it in for me?	tiʕdar tirakkibúuli, min fáḍlak.
Do you develop plates and films?	bitḥámmaḍ ʕalwáaḥ taṣwíir wi ʕafláam?
Please let me have a proof.	ɛáawiz aʃúuf birúuva, min faḍlak.
These photos are under-exposed.	ʕiṣṣúwar di-mḍallíma-ʃwayya.
Could you intensify them?	tiʕdar tiwaḍḍáḥhum?
Is the light too bright?	tiftíkir innúur ʃidíid ʕáwi?
I should like to have this snap enlarged.	ʕana ɛáawiz iṣṣúura di titkábbar.

[1] Sing. ʕadáah.

How much would an enlargement cost?	**ʕittakbíir yikállif káam?**
This portrait is out of focus.	**ʕiṣṣúura di míʃ maẓbúuṭa.**
Can you recommend a good photographer?	**tiʕdar tiʕúlli ʒala-mṣawwaráati-kwáyyis?**
I am going to have my photo taken.	**ʕana ḥaṣṣáwwar.**
I shall keep the photographs in an album.	**ʕana ḥálfaẓ iṣṣúwar fi ʕalbúum.**
Are you a keen photographer?	**ʕinta múɣram b-ittaṣwíir (or ʕinta bitḥíbb ittaṣwíir or ʕinta ɣáawi taṣwíir)?**

FOOTBALL

Vocabulary

football	**kúrat ilʕádam**
match	**liʒb; mu(u)ba(a)ráah, muba(a)ra(a)yáat**
team	**fírʕa, fíraʕ; faríiʕ**
the backs	**ʕilbakáat**
the half-backs	**ʕilhafbakáat**
the forwards	**ʕilʕamamiyyíin**
goalkeeper	**goon, ʕigwáan**
(right/left) back	**ʕilbáak (ilyimíin/iʃʃimáal)**
(right/left/centre) half	**ʕilháafbaak (ilyimíin/iʃʃimáal/ilwiṣṭáani)**
forward line	**ʕilxáṭṭ ilʕamáami**
home team	**ʕilfírʕa-lmaḥallíyya**
away team	**ʕilfírʕa-lɣaríiba**
ground	**málʒab, maláaʒib**
shot, free kick, penalty	**ʃóota, ʃotáat**
corner	**kóornar, kornaráat**
cup	**kaas**
classification, league	**tartíib**
football association	**ʕittiḥáad kúrat ilʕádam**
first half	**ʕilháaf táayim ilʕawwaláani**
second half	**ʕilháaf táayim ittáani**
final	**ʕinnihááʕi**
semi-final	**ʕábl innihááʕi**
referee	**riff; ḥákam, ḥukkáam**
side-lines	**ʕilxuṭúuṭ ilga(a)nibíyya**
half-way line	**ʕilxáṭṭ ilwiṣṭáani**
goal	**goon, ʕigwáan**
crossbar	**ʒárḍit iggóon**
goalpost	**ʒamúud iggóon, ʒimdáan iggóon**

net	ʃábaka
ball	kóora, kúwar
shin-pad	rúkba, rúkab
score-board	táxtit innatíiga
to shoot	ʃaat, yiʃúut
to kick	ḍárab, yíḍrab ; ʃaat, yiʃúut
to kick off, start	ʔibtáda, yibtídi
to dribble	dáḥrag, yidáḥrag ikkóora
to pass	báaṣa, yibáaṣi
to score	dáxxal, yidáxxal góon ; gaab, yigíib góon
to be on top	báʔa, yíbʔa ʔáḥsan
to draw	ʔitɛáadil, yitɛáadil
to win, to beat	ɣálab, yíɣlib
to lose	ʔitɣálab, yitɣílib

Sentences

Shall we go to the football match next Sunday afternoon ?	tíigi níḥḍar muba(a)ráat ikkóora yóom ilḥádd illi gáay baɛd iḍḍúhr ?
It's an international match.	dí muba(a)ráah dawlíyya.
Are they well-known teams ?	ʔilfíraʔ illi ḥatílɛab maʃhúura ?
Everybody was cheering.	kulli wáaḥid kan biyíhtif.
What a terrific shot !	ʔamma ʃóota faẓíiɛa ʔáwi !
The crowd doesn't seem to agree with the referee.	yíẓhar inn iggumhúur miʃ mittífiʔ maɛa-rríff.
Why is the referee blowing his whistle now ?	ʔirríffi biyṣáffar léeh dilwaʔti ?
He handled.	lámas ikkóora-b ʔíidu.
That's a foul !	di ɣálṭa !
The home team is two up.	faríiʔ ilbaladíyya ɣáalib b-itnéen.
Our team was leading at half-time.	ʔilfaríiʔ bitáɛna káan kasbáan f-ilháaf táayim ilʔawwaláani.
What was the score ?	gáabu káam góon ?
We drew.	ṭilíɛna diróon.
Did Tirsana beat Al-Ahli ?	ʔittirsáana ɣálab ilʔáhli ?
Tirsana won 3—2.	ʔittirsáana ɣálab taláata l-itnéen.
The right back is playing well.	ʔilbáak ilyimíin biyílɛab kuwáyyis.
It was a wonderful goal.	káan góon háayil.
Is your team playing in the next round of the Cup ?	firʔítkum ḥatílɛab ɛa-kkáas f-iddóora-ggáyya ?
How many teams take part in the Cup ?	fiih káam faríiʔ ḥayilɛábu ɛa-kkáas ?
How many does the ground hold ?	ʔilmálɛab yisáaɛi káam ?

TENNIS

Vocabulary

tennis	**tínis**
tennis match	**mu(u)ba(a)ráah f-ittínis**
tennis court	**málɛab tínis**
game	**geem**
set	**sett ; magmúuɛa**
point	**liɛba**
singles	**mu(u)ba(a)ráah fárdi**
doubles	**mu(u)ba(a)ráah záwgi**
mixed doubles	**muxtálaṭ záwgi**
racket	**máḍrab (tínis), maḍáarib**
tennis ball	**kóorit tínis**
net	**ʃábaka**
base-line	**ʕilxáṭṭ ilxa(a)rígi**
service-line	**xáṭṭ isséerv**
server	**ráami-sséerv**
umpire	**ḥákam, ḥukkáam**
linesman	**muláaḥiz, mulaḥzíin**
slice	**katt**
lob	**ʃóota ṭawíila ɛálya**
cannon-ball; drive	**ʃóota qawíyya**
forehand	**ʃóota ʕamamíyya**
backhand	**ʃóota xalfíyya**
professional (player)	**láaɛib muḥtárif**
to volley	**ʕáṭaɛ, yíʕṭaɛ iʃʃóota**
to serve	**ráma, yírmi (-sséerv)**
to spin	**dáwwar, yidáwwar (ikkóora)**
to return	**ɛaḍḍ, yiɛúḍḍ**

Sentences

Do you play tennis?	**bitilɛab tínis ?**
I am not a good player.	**ʕana ma balɛábʃi-kwáyyis.**
Are there any courts in the neighbourhood?	**fiih maláaɛib ʕuráyyib ?**
You can join our tennis club, if you like.	**tiʕdar tinḍámmi-l náadi-ttínis bitáɛna, ʕiza ḥabbéet.**
The subscription is very high.	**liʃtiráak γáali ʕáwi..**
Have you brought your racket with you?	**gibti maḍrábak maɛáak ?**
I need new tennis shoes and half a dozen balls.	**ʕana ɛáawiz gázmit tínis gidíida-w núṣṣi dástit kúwar.**

Throw that ball away, it doesn't bounce any more.	**ʕírmi-kkóora di-bɛʕíid, ma ɛadítʃi bitnúʈʈi-kwáyyis.**
I must have my racket restrung.	**láazim aʂállaḫ ilmáḍrab bitáɛni.**
Let's start with a singles and we can fix some doubles later.	**xallíina nibtídi-lʕáwwil b-ilmu(a)-ba(a)ráah ilfárdi-w baɛdéen nibʕa-ŋwáffaʕ záwgi.**
Your service!	**ʕisséervi-bʈáaɛak!** (or **ʕínta-lli-ḫatibtídi**).
That was a fault! Fault!	**di kanit**[1] **yálʈa! yálʈa!**
The ball touched the net.	**ʕikkóora lámasit iʃʃábaka.**
You should let the ball bounce.	**láazim tisíib ikkóora-tnúʈʈ.**
I only play for fun.	**ʕana bálɛab l-ittasáali** (or **l-ittasliya**) **bass.**
Fifteen-love.	**xamasʈáaʃar — láa ʃéeʕ.**

RIDING AND RACING

Vocabulary

riding	**rukúub ilxéel**
racing	**sibáaʕ**
riding hack	**ḫuʂáan irrukúub**
racehorse	**ḫuʂáan issibáaʕ**
thoroughbred	**ḫuʂáan ʕaʂíil**
thoroughbred mare	**fáras ʕaʂíila**
stallion	**ḫuʂáan, ḫiʂína; xeel**
mare	**fáras, ʕafráas**
foal	**muhr**
bay	**ʕáʃʕar, ʃáʕra, ʃuʕr**
dapple grey	**rumáadi-mnáʕʕaʈ**
white, grey (horse)	**ḫuʂáan ábyaḍ**
black (horse)	**ḫuʂáan íswid**
chestnut (horse)	**ḫuʂáan áʂhab**
rider	**ráakib, rákba, rakbíin**
jockey	**júki** (or **jóoki**)
stud-owner	**ʂáaḫib ilxéel**
stable-owner	**ʂáaḫib liʂʈábl**
riding outfit	**bádlit rukúub ilxéel**
reins	**ligáam**
stirrup	**rikáab, rikabáat**
spur	**mihmáaz, mahamíiz**
saddle	**sarg**
saddle girth	**ḫizáam**

[1] Pronounced **kat** in quick speech.

riding-school	**madrásit rukúub ilxéel**
race-course	**ḥálabit issibáaʕ**
groom	**sáayis, saysíin**
trot	**rakḍ**
gallop	**ɡadw**
canter	**ḥarwála**
flat race	**sibáaʕ**
steeplechase	**sibáaʕ ilḥawáagiz**
trotting-race	**sibáaʕ irrákḍ**
winning post	**ɡaláamit ʕáaxir issibáaʕ**
totalisator	**rihéan mutabáadal**
winner	**kasbáan**
betting	**rihéan**
the front legs	**ʕirrigléen ilʕuddamaníyya**
the hind legs	**ʕirrigléen ilwarraníyya**
horse-shoe	**ḥidw**
by a length	**bi ṭúul**
to ride, mount	**ríkib, yírkab**
to dismount	**nízil, yínzil**
to kick	**ráfaṣ, yúrfuṣ**
to buck	**ʕitbáaha, yitbáaha**
to shy	**gámaḥ, yígmaḥ**
to bolt	**ʃárad, yíʃrid**
to back a horse	**ráahin, yiráahin (ɡa-lḥuṣáan)**
to neigh	**ṣáhal, yíṣhal**
to stamp	**daas, yidúus**
to harness	**sárrag, yisárrag**

Sentences

Is there a riding-school in the town?	**fíih madrásit rukúub ilxéel f-ilbálad di?**
I should like to hire a horse.	**ʕana ɡáawiz aʕággar ḥuṣáan.**
I need some riding-lessons.	**ʕana ɡáawiz áaxud durúus fi-rkúub ilxéel.**
A course of riding-lessons costs a lot of money.	**magmúuɡit durúus rukúub ilxéel bitkállif (filúus) kitíir.**
Where can I hire a riding-outfit?	**ʕáʕdar aʕággar bádlit rukúub xéel minéen?**
Have you any riding-breeches?	**ɡándak banṭalonáat rukúub xéel?**
Where is my whip?	**féen ilkurbáag bitáaɡi?**
The horse is vicious.	**ʕilḥuṣáan ʃíris.**
The mare is lame.	**ʕilfáras ɡárga.**
Do you like going to the races?	**bitḥíbbi titfárrag ɡala-sbáaʕ ilxéel?**

Where is the entrance to the race-course?	**féen báab málɛab issábaʕ ?**
The nearest I was to a win was when I backed the second.	**ʕáʕrub márra kutti ḫáksab fiiha lamma rahínti ɛa-lḫuṣáan illi ṭliɛ ittáani.**
My horse was scratched just before the start.	**ʕilḫuṣáan illi rahínti ɛaléeh ṭallaɛúuh m-issábaʕ ʕablima yibtídi.**
Have you any idea which horse will win?	**tiʕdar tixámmin ʕáyyi-ḫṣáan ḫayíksab ?**
I have an idea the French horse will win.	**ʕithayyáali-nn-ilḫuṣáan ilfaransáawi húwwa-lli ḫayíksab.**
Whose is the winner?	**ʕilḫuṣáan illi kísib bitaɛ míin ?**
Who trained the winner?	**míin illi márran ilḫuṣáan illi kísib ?**
Did you back the favourite?	**ʕinta rahínti ɛa-lḫuṣáan ilmufáḍḍal ?**
Where is the totalisator?	**féen makáan ilmuráhna ?**
There are two race-courses in Alexandria, one called the Sporting, the other Sumuha.	**fiih malɛabéen li-sbáaʕ ilxéel f-iskindiríyya, wáaḫid ismu "spóorting" w-ittáani-smu "sumúuḫa".**

SHOOTING

Vocabulary

shooting	ʕiṣṣéed
marksman, hunter	ṣayyáad, ṣayyadíin
shooting-party	tagámmuɛ iṣṣayyadíin
bird shooting	ṣéed iṭṭuyúur
fox	táɛlab, taɛáalib
deer, gazelle	ɣazáal, ɣizláan
rabbit	ʕárnab, ʕaráanib
hare	ʕárnab bárri, ʕaráanib barríyya
game	ṭuyúur or ḫayawanáat iṣṣéed
partridge	ḫágal, ḫigáal
siluki, greyhound	kálbi-slúuʕi, kiláab silúʕíyya
gun-dog	kálbi ṣéed
the bag	ḫaṣíilit iṣṣéed
rifle	bunduʕíyya, banáadiʕ
shotgun	bunduʕíyyit ráʃʃ, banáadiʕ ráʃʃ
butt	ɣáraḍ, ʕaɣráaḍ
barrel	masúurit bunduʕíyya
trigger	zináad, ʕiznída
shot	ṭálʕa, ṭalʕáat

sight	niʃinkáah, niʃinkaháat
cartridge	xarṭúuʃ, xaraṭiiʃ
snare	ʃábaka, ʃabakáat
trap	maṣyáda, maṣáayid
hunting grounds	ʔárḍ iṣṣéed
to shoot	ḍárab, yíḍrab b-ilbunduʔíyya
to hit	ṣaab, yiṣíib
to miss	ʔiṭṭálʔa xayyíbit[1]
to stalk	ʔitráʔʔab, yitráʔʔab
to hunt, go shooting	ṣaad, yiṣíid

Sentences

Is there any chance of going shooting hereabouts ?	fiih ḥitta múmkin ilwáaḥid yiṣíid fiiha hína ?
Would you like to go shooting hares with me ?	tiḥíbbi tiigi-tṣíid ʔaráanib barríyya-mʕáaya ?
This ground is reserved for shooting.	ʔilʔárḍi di maḥgúuza l-iṣṣéed.
Is the shooting season for birds open ?	múusim ṣéed iṭṭéer ibtáda ?
A brace of partridges and two rabbits.	góoz ḥágal wi ʔarnabéen.
Are you a good shot ?	ʔinta-btiʕraf tiṣíid kuwáyyis ?
I have practised target shooting.	ʔana-tmarránti ʕala ʔiṣá(a)b(i)t ilhádaf.
Did you clean your gun ?	ʔinta naḍḍáfti bunduʔiyyítak ?
I've been shooting in Manzala.[2]	kunti baṣíid ṭéer f-ilmanzála.
Where can I buy a rifle ?	ʔáʔdar aʃtíri bunduʔíyya-mnéen ?
Can you let me have some cartridges ?	múmkin tiddíini-ʃwáyyit xaraṭiiʃ, min faḍlak ?
There are foxes and hares in the desert.	fiih taʕáalib wi ʔaráanib barríyya f-iṣṣáḥra.
We mostly go shooting birds in Egypt.	ʔiḥna-f ʔáɣlab ilʔaḥwáal binṣíid ṭuyúur fi máṣr.

FISHING

Vocabulary

fishing	ṣéed issámak
fisherman	ṣayyáad issámak
fishing-boat	ʔáarib ṣéed

[1] Lit. "the shot missed".
[2] In the north of the Delta.

fishing-fleet	ʕawáarib ṣéed
fishing-tackle	ʕadawáat ṣéed issámak
net	ʃábaka, ʃabakáat
harpoon	ḥárbit iṣṣéed
angler	ṣayyáad b-issinnáara
fishing-rod	bóoṣit (or ʒaṣáayit) issinnáara, boṣáat issananíir
fishing-line	xéeṭ issinnáara
float, bob	ʒawwáama, ʒawwamáat
fish-hook	sinnáara, sananíir
bait	ṭuʒm
worm	dúuda, didáan
fly	dibbáana, dibbanáat
salt-water fish	ṣámaka m-ilmáyya-lmálḥa
herring	rínga, ringáat
cod	sámak bakaláa
sole	sámak múusa
tunny	tóona or sámak tóona
sardine	sardíin
red mullet	búuri ʕáḥmar
grey mullet	búuri
shell-fish	sámak bi maḥáara
octopus	ʕuxṭubúuṭ
crab	ʕábu galámbu
prawns	gambári
lobster	lubístar
salmon	sálamun
fresh-water fish	sámak níili
carp	ʃabbúuṭ
pike	ʕábu ḥárba
eel	tiʒbáan sámak, taʒabíin sámak
fish-bone	ṣáfa (c.), ṣafáaya, ṣafayáat
fish-scale	ʕiʃr (c.), ʕiʃráaya, ʕiʃrayáat
sea	baḥr, buḥúur
lake	buḥáyra, buḥayráat
river	nahr, ʕánhur
stream	tírʒa, tíraʒ
fishpond	bírkit sámak
to fish	ṣáad, yiṣíid sámak
to angle	ṣáad, yiṣíid b-issinnáara
to bite	kal, yáakul

Sentences

Do you like fishing?	**bitḫíbbi ṣéed issámak?**
Do I need a licence to fish here?	**láazim yikúun maṛáaya rúxṣa ṛaʃan aṣíid hína?**
Where can I buy fishing-tackle?	**ʕáʕdar aʃtíri ʕadawáat ṣéed issámak minéen?**
I've forgotten to bring my fishing-rod.	**nisíit agíib ṛaṣáayit issinnáara-btáṛti.**
The bait is no good.	**ʕiṭṭúṛmi miʃ kuwáyyis.**
Have you had a good catch?	**ṣídti [1]-ktíir?**
Can one go out with the fishing-fleet?	**ʕilwáaḫid yíʕdar yíṭlaṛ maṛa ʕawáarib iṣṣéed?**
What bait do you use?	**ʕéeh iṭṭúṛm illi bitṣíid bíih?**
Is angling popular in Egypt?	**ʕinnáas biyḫíbbu ṣéed issámak b-issinnáara-f máṣr?**
Did you fry the fish we caught this morning?	**ʕaléet issámak illi ṣidnáah innahárda-ṣṣúbḫ?**
There is a great variety of shell-fish on the Egyptian coast.	**fíih ʕanwáaṛ kitíira min issámak ʕábu maḫáara ṛala-ʃʃawáaṭiʕ ilmaṣríyya.**

SWIMMING

Vocabulary

swimming	**sibáaḫa**
seaside-resort	**piláaj, pilajáat; máṣyaf, maṣáayif**
swimming-pool	**ḫammáam sibáaḫa**
(lady's) bathing-costume	**mayóo(h) ḫaríimi, mayoháat ḫaríimi**
swimming-trunks	**mayóo(h) rigáali**
bath-towel	**fúuṭit ḫammáam**
bathing-cap	**ṭaʕíyyit ḫúma**
cabin	**kabíina, kabáayin**
attendant	**ɣafíir, ɣúfara**
lifebelt	**ḫizáam innagáah**
artificial respiration	**tanáffus ṣináaṛi**
cramp	**taʃánnug**
diving-board, spring-board	**mináṭṭa**
swimmer	**sabbáaḫ, sabbáaḫa, sabbaḫíin**
breast stroke	**ṛúum sídr**
back stroke	**ṛúum ḍáhr**
butterfly stroke	**ṛúum faráaʃa**

[1] Pronounced ṣítti.

crawl	ʒúum báṭn
dive	ɣáṭsa, ɣaṭsáat
beach	piláaj, pilajáat
sunbathing	ḥammáam ʃáms
wave	moog, ʕamwáag
shower	duʃʃ, ʕidʃáaʃ
to swim	ʒaam, yiʒúum
to dive	ɣíṭis, yíɣṭas
to plunge	naṭṭ, yinúṭṭ
to crawl	ʒáam, yiʒúum ʒala báṭnu(h)
to shiver	ʕirtáʒaʃ, yirtíʒiʃ
to dry	náʃʃif, yináʃʃif; ʕitnáʃʃif, yitnáʃʃif
to float	ʒaam, yiʒúum
to drown	ɣíriʕ, yíɣraʕ
to bathe	ʕistaḥámma, yistaḥámma

Sentences

Shall we go for a swim (bathe)?	tiigi nistaḥámma?
Can we bathe in the river?	níʕdar nistaḥámma f-innáhr?
No, you must go to the swimming-pool.	láʕ, láazim tirúuḥu ḥammáam issibáaḥa.
No bathing!	mamnúuʒ listiḥmáam!
Are you a good swimmer?	ʕinta bitʒúum kuwáyyis?
Let's swim to the opposite bank.	yálla-nʒúum l-iʃʃáṭṭ ittáani.
The current is very strong.	ʕittayyáar ʃidiid ʕáwi.
Can you swim on your back?	tiʕdar tiʒúum ʒala ḍáhrak?
He is floating.	huwwa ʒáayim.
Can you do the crawl?	tiʕdar tiʒúum ḍárbi-dráaʒ?
I've got cramp.	ḥaṣálli taʃánnug.
Swim and help him, he's gone under.	ʒúum wi sá(a)ʒdu(h), láḥsan da yíṭis.
He was nearly drowned.	huwwa káan ḥayíɣraʕ.
Stay in the shallow water.	xallíik f-ilmáyya-lli miʃ ɣariiʕa.
Hang on to the life-line.	ʕímsik fi ḥábli-lʕamáan!
Don't swim beyond the danger sign.	ma-tʒúmʃi baʒdi ʒalámt ilxáṭar.
This part is for swimmers only.	ʕilḥítta di l-illi-byiʒrúfu-yʒúumu báss.
Is there a vacant hut?	fiih kabíina fáḍya?
Can you recommend a nice seaside-resort?	ma tiʒráfʃi máṣyaf kuwáyyis?
The yellow flag means there is no undertow.	ʕilʒálam láṣfar maʒnáah inni ma fiiʃ dawwáama.

Who won yesterday's water-polo match?	míin illi kisib liɛbit ilpúulu-lma(a)ʕíyya-mbáariḥ?
There is an open-air swimming-pool in the town.	fiih ḥammáam sibáaḥa makʃúuf f-ilbálad di.

ROWING AND BOATING

Vocabulary

rowing	tagdíif
boating	ʕittanázzuh f-ilʕawáarib
boat	ʕáarib, ʕawáarib
steamship, launch	ʕáarib buxxáari, ʕawáarib buxxaríyya
rowing boat	ʕáarib tagdíif
punt	pant, pantáat
houseboat	ɛawwáama, ɛawwamáat
rubber boat	ʕáarib maṭṭáaṭ
motor-boat	lanʃ, lanʃáat
skiff	ʕiskíff
oar	migdáaf, magadíif
paddle	bádal, bidáal
rudder	dáffa, daffáat
sliding seat	kúrsi mutaḥárrik
oarsman	mugáddif, mugaddifíin
cox	mudíir iddáffa
crew	baḥḥáara
plank	looḥ, ʕilwáaḥ
starboard	yimíin
port	ʃimáal
to row, paddle	gáddif, yigáddif
to steer	wággih, yiwággih
to float	ɛaam, yiɛúum

Sentences

Boats for hire.	ʕawáarib l-ilʕigáar.
Come to the jetty.	taɛáala ɛa-lmársa.
You can hire a boat for ten piastres an hour.	tiʕdar tiʕággar ʕáarib bi ɛáʃara sáaɣ f-issáaɛa.
There's a strong head wind.	fiih ríiḥ ʃidíid muwagháana.[1]
The boat leaks.	ʕilmáyya-btúdxul ilʕáarib.
Let's go and watch the boat-race.	yálla nitfárrag ɛala-sbáaʕ ilʕawáarib.

[1] muwa(a)g(i)ha + na.

Our club won by two lengths.	nadíina sábaʕ bi ṭuléen.
Are you a member of the Rowing Club?	ʕinta ʕúḍwi-f náadi-ttagdíif?
I should like to join your club.	ʕana ʕáawiz aʃtárik fi nadíiku(m).
I bought a small rubber boat.	ʕiʃtaréet ʕáarib maṭṭáaṭ ṣuɣáyyar.

SAILING

Vocabulary

sailing boat	ʕáarib ʃiráaʕi
sail	ʕalʕ, ʕulúuʕ
yacht	yaxt, yuxúut
mast	ṣáari, ṣawáari
boom	ʕárya, ʕawáari
keel	ʕáʕdit issafíina or qa(a)ʕídit issafíina
flag	ʕálam, ʕaʕláam
lighthouse	fannáara, fannaráat
barge	márkib náʕl, maráakib náʕl
buoy	ʃamandúura, ʃamanduráat
anchor	mírsa (or mársa), maráasi
breeze	riiḥ, ʕaryáaḥ (or riyáaḥ); nasíim, nasáayim
dead calm	háadi[1] gíddan
yachting season	fáṣli-rkúub ilyuxúut
regatta	sibáaʕ ilʕawáarib
course	ṭaríiʕ, ṭúruʕ
to sail	ríkib, yírkab ʕáarib ʃiráaʕi
to strike	ráxa, yírxi (-lʕalʕ)
to manoeuvre	ʕámal, yíʕmil munawráat
to cruise	ṭaaf, yiṭúuf ilbáḥr
to reef	ṭáwa, yíṭwi (-lʕalʕ)
to drift	ʕingáraf, yingírif maʕa-ttayyáar
to put into harbour	rása, yírsi; rássa, yirássi
to reach port	wíṣil, yíwṣal ilbárr

Sentences

There's a sailing boat anchored in the harbour.	fíih ʕáarib ʃiráaʕi ráasi f-ilmíina.
There's a fresh breeze to-day; it's good sailing weather.	fih ríiḥ kuwayyísa-nnahárda; da gáwwi-kwáyyis ʕaʃan rukúub ilʕáarib.

[1] Adjectival form, as in ʕilbáḥri háadi gíddan "the sea is dead calm".

Weigh the anchor.	ʃiil ilmársa !
Help me hoist the sails.	saʕídn(i)-áfrid ilʕulúuʕ.
Let's spend the day on the water.	yálla-nʕáḍḍi-lyóom f-ilmáyya.
Have you enough to eat with you?	maʕáak ʕákli-kfáaya ?
Do you know anything about sailing?	tíʕraf ḥáaga ʕan rukúub ilʕawáarib iʃʃiraʕíyya ?
We've often cruised in the Mediterranean.	ʕiḥna lafféena-ktiir b-ilʕáarib f-ilbáḥr ilʕábyaḍ.
Is this yacht seaworthy?	ʕilyáxti da yistáḥmil ilbáḥr ?
We were overtaken by the storm.	ʕilʕaṣífa fagaʕítna.
The boat's heeling over.	ʕilʕáarib maayil ʕala gámbu(h).
The yacht has capsized.	ʕilyáxt inʕálab.
There's a regatta out at sea this afternoon.	fiih sibáaʕ ʕawáarib f-ilbáḥr innahárda baʕd iḍḍúhr.
Set the course north, we've drifted too far west.	xálli ṭaríʕna ʕala-nnáḥya-lbaḥaríyya, ʕiḥna-nḥaráfna ʕáwi náḥyit ilyárb.

INDOOR GAMES

Vocabulary

indoor games	ʕalʕáab manzilíyya
draughts	ḍáama ; síiga [1]
draughtboard	lóoḥit iḍḍáama
king	málik, mulúuk
man, piece	wáraʕ (c.), wáraʕa, waraʕáat ; kalb, kiláab [2]
chess	ʃaṭaráng
chess-board	lóoḥit iʃʃaṭaráng
queen	ʕilwazíir
king	ʕilmálik
knight	ʕilḥuṣáan
rook, castle	ʕiṭṭábya
bishop	ʕilfíil [3]
pawn	ʕaskári, ʕasáakir
dice	zahr (generic) ; wáḥda min izzáhr (a die)
dice-box	sandúuʕ izzáhr
roulette	rulíit

[1] Kind of draughts played on the ground with pieces of stone in the countryside.
[2] In síiga only.
[3] Lit. "elephant".

lottery	**lutaríyya**
skittles	**kiil**
billiards	**bilyárdu**
cannon	**karambóola, karamboláat**
chalk	**tabaʃíir**
cue	**ɛáṣa [1]-lbilyárdu**
pocket	**geeb, giyúub**
dominoes	**ḍúmina**
pack of cards	**kutʃéena, kataʃíin**
player	**láaɛib, láɛba, laɛbíin**
suit	**ʕilli záyyi báɛḍ ; loon**
spades	**baṣtóoni**
hearts	**kúuba**
diamonds	**dináari**
clubs	**subáati**
ace	**ʕaas, ʕasáat**
ace of spades	**ʕáas baṣtóoni**
king	**ʃáayib, ʃuyyáab**
queen	**bint, banáat**
jack, knave	**wálad, wiláad**
joker	**jóokar**
ten	**ʕilɛáʃara**
deuce	**ʕilʕitnéen**
trump	**wáraʕa rábḥa**
dummy	**ḍámi or moor or máyyit**
to play	**líɛib, yílɛab**
to gamble	**líɛib, yílɛab ʕumáar**
to play cards	**líɛib, yílɛab kutʃéena**
to shuffle	**fánnaṭ, yifánnaṭ ikkutʃéena**
to deal	**fárraʕ, yifárraʕ**
to cut	**ʕáṭaɛ, yíʕṭaɛ**
to ruff, trump	**yálab bi wáraʕa rábḥa**
to take a trick	**kísib, yíksab iddóor**
to follow suit	**wáafiʕ, yiwáafiʕ ; líɛib, yílɛab zayy ilwáraʕa-lʕawwalaníyya**
to take a piece (chess)	**kál, yáakul wáraʕa**
to protect the king	**ḥáma, yíḥmi-lmálik**
to check	**káʃʃ, yikíʃʃ ilmálik**
to mate	**máwwit, yimáwwit ilmálik**
to cast dice	**ráma, yírmi-zzáhr**

[1] Or ɛáṣat.

Sentences

Do you often play draughts?	ʕinta-btilɛab ḍáama-ktíir?
No, I'm more interested in chess.	láa, ʕana baħíbb iʃʃaṭaráng áktar.
It's your move.	ʕiddóor ɛaléek.
I castle the king.	ʕana ħáħmi-lmálik, ħaħúṭṭu makáan iṭṭábya.
I wonder if I can exchange that knight for a rook.	ya tára (a)ɣáyyar ilħuṣáan da bi ṭábya.
Whites to play.	lábyaḍ yílɛab.
If you move that pawn your queen is in danger.	ʕiza ħarrákt ilɛaskári da-lwazíir bitáaɛak ħayinkíʃif.
Check!	kíʃʃ i [1] málik!
Check and mate!	ʕilmálik máat, xaláaṣ!
Will you play me a game of table-tennis?	tilaɛíbni bíngi búng (or kóorat iṭṭáwla).
He's good at billiards.	huwwa-byílɛab bilyárdu-kwáyyis.
Have you ever seen a pool game?	ɛumrákʃi ʃúfti líɛbit bilyárdu ʕamrikáani?
I'll give you ten cannons.	ħaddíilak ɛáʃar karamboláat.
We can play at three cushions.	níʕdar nílɛab fi tálatt irkáan báss.
Shall we play billiards or cards?	tiħíbbi nílɛab bilyárdu walla kutʃéena?
Have you a new pack?	maɛáak kutʃéena-gdíida?
I've shuffled, you cut.	ʕana fannáṭṭ, xúd íʕṭaɛ.
You deal.	fárraʕ.
Who will score?	míin ħayɛídd?
Whose call (*or* turn) is it?	ʕiddóor ɛala míin?
Diamonds are trumps.	ʕilʕawráaʕ iddinaríyya híyya-lli rábħa.
Your play, your turn.	ʕílɛab, ʕiddóor ɛaléek.
You must follow suit.	ʕinta láazim tílɛab wáraʕa-mwáfʕa.
This is my trick.	dí liʕbíti.
I must discard.	ʕana magbúur ármi wáraʕa muxtálifa.
Don't look at my cards.	ma-tbúṣṣiʃ fi wáraʕi.
Lay the cards on the table.	ħúṭṭ ilwáraʕ ɛa-ṭṭarabéeẓa.
I've lost a pound at cards.	ʕana-xṣúrti-gnéeh fi líɛbit ikkutʃéena.
He's won the kitty.	huwwa kísib kúlli ħáaga.
I've five spades in my hand.	ʕana-mɛáaya xámas baṣtonáat.

[1] The expression, like the game, comes from Persia, and **i** here is the Persian so-called "*ezafe*".

THE TIME

Vocabulary

time	ʕizzáman
watch	**sáaɛa, saɛáat**
wrist-watch	**saɛit yádd**
sundial	**mizwála, mazáawil**
clock	**saɛit ħéeṭ** (wall); **saɛit máktab** (mantelpiece, etc.)
alarm clock	**munábbih, munabbiháat**
hand	**ɛáʕrɑb, ɛaʕáarib**
dial, face	**míina**
second-hand	**ɛáʕrɑb issawáani**
minute-hand	**ɛáʕrɑb iddaʕáayiʕ**
hour-hand	**ɛáʕrɑb issaɛáat**
watchmaker	**saɛáati, saɛatíyya**
second	**sánya, sawáani**
minute	**daʕíiʕa, daʕáayiʕ**
hour	**sáaɛa, saɛáat**
day	**yoom, ʕayyáam** (or **ʕiyyáam**)
Sunday	**yóom ilħádd**
Monday	**yóom litnéen**
Tuesday	**yóom ittaláat**
Wednesday	**yóom lɑ́rbɑɛ**
Thursday	**yóom ilxamíis**
Friday	**yóom iggúmɛa**
Saturday	**yóom issábt**
week	**ʕusbúuɛ, ʕasabíiɛ**
month	**ʃɑhr, ʕúʃhur** (or **ʃuhúur**)
January	**yanáayir** [1]
February	**fibráayir**
March	**máaris**
April	**ʕabríil**
May	**máayu**
June	**yúnya** (or **yúnyu**)
July	**yúlya** (or **yúlyu**)
August	**ʕɑɣúsṭus**
September	**sibtámbir** (or **sibtímbir**)
October	**ʕuktóobɑr**
November	**nufímbir** (or **nufámbir**)
December	**disímbir** (or **disámbir**)

[1] It is unlikely that the user of this book will require the different names of the lunar months of the Muslim year.

season	**faṣl, fuṣúul**
spring	**rabíiʕ**
summer	**ṣeef**
autumn	**xaríif**
winter	**ʃíta**
year	**sána, siníin** (or **sanawáat**)
leap year	**sána kabíisa**
century	**qarn, quruun**
working days, week-days	**ʕayyáam ilʕámal ; ʕayyáam ilʕusbúuʕ**
public holiday	**ʕúṭla, ʕuṭláat**
holiday(s)	**ʕagáaza, ʕagazáat ; fúsḥa**
Qurban Bairam [1]	**ʕíid iḍḍiḥíyya** or **ʕilʕíid ikkibíir**
Ramadan Bairam [2]	**ʕíid ilfíṭr** or **ʕilʕíid iṣṣuyáyyar**
New (lunar) year	**ʕíid ráʕs issána-lhijríyya**
10 days after New Year	**ʕaʃúura**
the Prophet's birthday	**ʕíid máwlid innábi**
Easter	**ʕíid ilfíṣḥ** or **ʕíid ilqiyáama**
Christmas	**ʕíid miláad ilmasíiḥ**
morning	**ṣubḥ**
every morning	**kúlli yóom iṣṣúbḥ**
noon, midday	**ḍuhr**
afternoon	**báʕd iḍḍúhr**
evening	**mísa** or **mása**
every evening	**kúlli yóom f-ilmísa**
night	**leel** (c.), **léela, layáali**
midnight	**núṣṣ illéel**
to-night	**ʕilléela** or **ʕilleláadi**
last night	**ʕilléela-lli fáatit**
the night before last	**ʕilléela-lli ʕábl illi fáatit**
to-day	**ʕinnahárda**
yesterday	**ʕimbáariḥ**
the day before yesterday	**ʕáwwil imbáariḥ**
three days ago	**ʕáwwil áwwil imbáariḥ**
some days ago	**díik innahár**
this year	**ʕissanáadi**
last year	**ʕissána-lli fáatit** or **ʕáamin áwwil**
the year before last	**ʕissána-lli ʕábl illi fáatit** or **ʕáwwil ʕáamin áwwil**
three years ago	**ʕáwwil áwwil ʕáamin áwwil**

[1] The feast occurring after the pilgrimage in the Muslim month of pilgrimage.
[2] The feast which takes place immediately after the fasting period of the month of Ramadan.

some years ago	**dfik issána**
moon	**ʔámar, ʔiʔmáar**
star	**nígma** or **nagm, nugúum**
sun	**ʃams**[1]
calendar	**natíiga, natáayig**
sunrise	**ʃurúuʔ iʃʃáms**
sunset	**ɣurúub iʃʃáms**
eclipse	**xusúuf ilqámar** (moon); **kusúuf iʃʃáms** (sun)
full moon	**ʔámar arbaɛṭáaʃar; badr; ʔámar káamil**
new moon	**hiláal**[2]
first quarter	**ʔirrúbɛ ilʔawwaláani**
third quarter	**ʔirrúbɛ íttáalit**
the modern age	**ʔilɛáṣr ilḥadíis**
the Middle Ages	**ʔilɛuṣúur ilwúṣṭa**
the pre-Islamic period	**ʔilɛáṣr ilja(a)híli**
time of the Prophet	**fáṭrit innubúwwa**
time of the three Caliphates	**ɛáṣr ilxulafáaʔ irra(a)ʃidíin**
time of the Umayyad dynasty	**ɛáṣr iddáwla-lʔumawíyya**
time of the Abbasid dynasty	**ɛáṣr iddáwla-lɛabbasíyya**
in olden times	**ʔayyáam zamáan; f-ilɛuṣúur ilqadíima**
nowadays, the present day	**ʔilwáʔt ilḥáaḍir; liyyámdi**
the past	**ʔilʔayyáam illi fáatit**
the future	**ʔilmustáqbal**
summer-time	**ʔittawʔíit iṣṣéefi**
early	**(min) bádri**
punctual	**f-ilmaɛáad**
late	**mitʔáxxar, mitʔaxxára, mitʔaxxaríin**
in good time	**bádri**
in advance	**ʔabl**
to wind up (watch)	**mála, yímla**
to repair	**ṣállaḥ, yiṣállaḥ**
to wake up, get up	**ṣáḥa, yíṣḥa**
to wake (someone) up	**ṣáḥḥa, yiṣáḥḥi**
to go to bed, go to sleep	**náam, yináam; dáxal, yídxul f-issiríir**
to get up early	**ṣáḥa, yíṣḥa bádri**
to go to bed late	**náam, yináam mitʔáxxar**

[1] A feminine noun.

[2] Egyptian terms for " moon " in relation to size are : **hiláal** (new), **badr** (full), **maḥáaq** (no moon). **ʔámar** implies no specific reference to size.

Sentences

Can you tell me the right time?	tiʕdar tiʕúlli-ssaʒa káam b-iẓẓábṭ, min faḍlak?
Is your watch right?	sáʒtak maẓbúuṭa?
It is ten minutes fast.	miʕaddíma ʒáʃar daʕáayiʕ.
It is a quarter of an hour slow.	miʕaxxára rúbʒi sáaʒa.
It always keeps good time.	dáyman maẓbúuṭa.
What time is it?	ʕissáaʒa káam?
It's exactly eight o'clock.	ʕissáaʒa tamánya b-iẓẓábṭ.
It's five past eight.	ʕissáaʒa tamánya-w xámsa.
It's a quarter-past eight.	ʕissáaʒa tamánya-w rúbʒ.
It's half-past eight.	ʕissáaʒa tamánya-w núṣṣ.
A quarter to nine.	ʕissáaʒa tísʒa-illa rúbʒ.
One a.m.	ʕissáaʒa wáḥda ṣabáaḥan.
Eight a.m.	ʕissáaʒa tamánya ṣabáaḥan.
Three p.m.	ʕissáaʒa taláata masáaʕan.
Eleven p.m.	ʕissáaʒa-ḥḍáaʃar masáaʕan.
It is noon.	ʕissáaʒa-ṭnáaʃar.
The train leaves at 2.30.	ʕilʕáṭri biyʕúum issáaʒa-tnéen wi núṣṣ.
You'll have to be at the station half an hour beforehand.	láazim tikúun f-ilmaḥáṭṭa ʕábl ilmaʒáad bi núṣṣi sáaʒa.
Don't be late.	ma titʕaxxárʃ.
I shall be in time/on time.	ḥáagi f-ilmaʒáad.
It's time to get up/to go to bed.	láazim tiʕúum báʕa/tináam báʕa.
Hurry up, it's half-past seven.	bi súrʒa, ʕissáaʒa sábʒa-w núṣṣ.
My alarm clock has stopped.	ʕilmunábbih bitáaʒi wiʕif.
I must take my watch to the watchmaker.	ʕana láazim awáddi sáʒti l-issaʒáati.
It needs cleaning.	ʒáwza titmásaḥ.
The glass is cracked.	ʕilʕizáaz mafiúuʕ.
Set your watch by the station clock.	ʕiẓbuṭ sáʒtak ʒala sáaʒit ilmaḥáṭṭa.
There'll be a concert next month.	(ḥaykun) fiih ḥáfla musiqíyya-ʃʃáhr iggáyy.
I shall be back in a week.	ʕana ḥárgaʒ báʒdi ʕusbúuʒ.
A fortnight ago I was in London.	ʕana kútti-f lándan min ʕusbuʒéen.
It gets dark early.	ʕiddínya bitḍállim [1] bádri.
What is the date to-day?	ʕinnahárda káam (f-iʃʃáhr)?
To-day is the fifteenth of September.	ʕinnahárda xamasṭáaʃar sibtímbir.

[1] Pronounced biḍḍ-.

My birthday is on the tenth of October.	ɛiid miláadi yóom ɛáʃara ʔuktóobar.
Are you going away this year?	ʔinta ḥatsáafir bárra-ssanáadi?
I came back the day before yesterday.	ʔana-rgiɛt áwwil imbáariḥ.
I shall be leaving again tomorrow (the day after tomorrow, next week).	ʔana ḥasáafir táani búkra (báɛdi búkra, ilʔusbúuɛ iggáay).
Don't arrive at the last minute.	ma-tgiiʃ fi ʔáaxir daʔiiʔa.
One moment, please.	daʔiiʔa, min fáḍlak.
At dawn.	ʔilfágr.
At dusk.	ʔilmáɣrib.
Last year was a leap year.	ʔissána-lli fáatit kanit[1] sána kabíisa.
Can you spare me a moment?	tísmaḥ daʔiiʔa.
I have no time.	ma ɛandiiʃ wáʔt.
It's getting late.	ʔitʔaxxárna.
Please call for me early.	taɛáala bádri, min faḍlak.
He left long ago.	míʃi min bádri.
This building is two centuries old.	ʔilmábna da ɛúmru qarnéen (or baʔáalu qarnéen).
How old are you?	ɛúmrak kam sána?
I was thirty-six last January.	kutti sitta-w talatíin yanáayir illi fáat.
He is in his forties.	húwwa f-ilʔarbiɛináat.
She is an old lady.	hiyya sitti ɛagúuza.
He is older than his brother.	huwwa ʔákbar min axúuh.
She is younger than her sister.	hiyya ʔáṣɣar min uxtáha.

THE WEATHER

Vocabulary

the weather	ʔiggáww
climate	manáax
weather	ṭaʔs
air	háwa
heat	ḥaráar
warmth	dáfa
cold	bard
rain	máṭar

[1] Pronounced kat in quick speech.

snow	talg [1]
sun(shine)	ʃams
thunderstorm	zawbáʕa, zawáabiʕ
thunder	raʕd
lightning	barʕ
thunderbolt	ṣa(a)ʕíqa, ṣawáaʕiq
hail	bárad [1]
ice	galíid [1]
thaw	dawabáan ittálg [1]
sky	sáma
cloud	saḥáab (c.), saḥáaba, súḥub
wind	riiḥ, ʕaryáaḥ
gale, tempest	ʕa(a)ṣífa, ʕawáaṣif
hurricane	ʕiʕṣáar, ʕaʕaṣíir
breeze	nasíim
fog	ḍabáab
mist	ḍabáab xafíif
dew	náda
frost	tilíig [1]
horizon	ʕúfuq
rainbow	qáwsu qúzaḥ
cardinal points	ʕilgiháat ilʕaṣlíyya
North	ʃimáal; báḥari
East	ʃarʕ
South	ganúub; ʕíbli
West	ɣarb
compass	búṣla, buṣláat
tide	madd
ebb	gazr
flow	madd
sea, ocean	baḥr, buḥúur
flood	fayaḍáan
atmosphere	gaww
fine weather	gáwwi-kwáyyis
bad weather	gáwwi wíḥiʃ
cold	bard; saʕʕ
chilly	bard
warm	dáafi; ḥarr
hot	ḥarr
it is freezing	ʕiddínya tálg
it is snowing	ʕiddínya bitmáṭṭar tálg

[1] The term is included as useful for talking about weather conditions outside Egypt.

it is raining	**ʕiddínya bitmáṭṭar**
the sun is coming out	**ʕiʃʃámsi ḥatíṭlaɛ ahé(h)**
the sun rises at six	**ʕiʃʃámsi-btíṭlaɛ issaɛa sítta**
the sun sets at five	**ʕiʃʃámsi-btúɣrub issaɛa xámsa**
the sky is overcast	**ʕissáma-myaɣyíma**

Sentences

What is the weather like?	**ʕiggáww izzáyyu-nnahárda ?**
It is fine.	**ʕiggáwwi-kwáyyis.**
It's a lovely day.	**ʕinnahárda yóom laṭíif.**
The weather is beautiful/dull.	**ʕiggáwwi gamíil/miɣáyyim.**
The weather is changeable.	**ʕiggáwwi mutaqállib.**
The weather is settled.	**ʕiggáwwi ṣáafi.**
It's hot/cold.	**ʕiddínya ḥárr/bárd.**
It's rainy.	**ʕiddínya bitmáṭṭar.**
It's foggy.	**ʕiddínya malyáana ḍabáab.**
It's very slippery, be careful.	**ʕiddínya zuḥléeʕa, xud báalak.**
It's a nice evening.	**ʕiggáww illeláadi-kwáyyis.**
It's close, sultry.	**ʕiddínya kátma.**
Do you think the weather will stay fine?	**tiftíkir inn iggáwwi ḥaytínni-kwáyyis ?**
The north wind is cold.	**ʕirríiḥ ilbáḥari báarid.**
It's stormy, windy.	**ʕiddínya ríiḥ.**
The wind has dropped.	**ʕirríiḥ báṭṭal.**
It's raining cats and dogs.	**ʕilmáṭar séel.**
It's pouring.	**ʕilmáṭar ʃidíid ʕáwi.**
I am wet through.	**ʕana mablúul xáalis.**
Where is my umbrella?	**féen ʃamsiyyíti ?** [1]
Take a raincoat with you.	**xúd maɛáak bálṭu máṭar.**
Will there be a thunderstorm?	**ḥaykúun fíih zawbáɛa ?**
It's thundering and lightning.	**ʕiddínya-btúbruʕ wi tirɛid.** [2]
The sky is completely overcast.	**ʕissáma-myaɣyíma tamáam.**
The sky is clear.	**ʕissáma ṣáfya.**
It's clearing up.	**ʕiddínya bitnáwwar; ʕilyéem biyrúuḥ.**
It's too sunny here, let's sit in the shade.	**ʕiʃʃámsi ḥámya ʕáwi hína, taɛáala núʕɛud f-iḍḍíll.**

[1] **ʃamsíyya** is "parasol" rather than "umbrella"; most of this "bad weather" Arabic will not be required in relation to conditions on the spot, but one needs to be able to talk about weather conditions in general.

[2] Notice the different order in comparison with the English.

It's getting chilly.	ʕiddínya bitbárrad.
Are you cold?	ʕínta bardáan?
I feel hot.	ʕana ḥarráan.
It's warm in here.	ʕiddínya dáfa hina.
I can't stand the heat.	ʕana miʃ ʕáadir ʕa-lḥárr.
It's a warm day.	ʕinnahárda dáfa.
It's a warm climate.	ʕiggáwwi dáafi.
What's the temperature?	dáragit ilḥaráara káam?
It has gone up to 22° (Centigrade).	báʕit ʕitnéen wi ʕiʃríin miʕawíyya.
The glass is rising/falling.	ʕiḍḍáyt iggáwwi-byirtáfiʕ/-byinxáfiḍ.
The meteorological station is up on that hill.	maḥáṭṭit ilʕarṣáad iggawwíyya fóoʕ ittallída.
They broadcast the weather report every day.	biyzíiʕu-nnáʃra-ggawwíyya kúlli yóom.
The atmosphere is clear.	ʕiggáwwi ṣáafi.

SOCIAL LIFE

Vocabulary

social life	ʕilḥayáah ligtimaʕíyya
visit, call	ziyáara, ziyaráat
invitation	dáʕwa, daʕawáat
party	ḥáfla, ḥafaláat
appointment	miʕáad, mawaʕíid
meeting	muʕábla, muʕabláat
chat	dardáʃa
reception	ʕistaʕbáal, ʕistaʕbaláat
visiting-card	biṭáaʕit ziyáara, biṭaʕáat ziyáara
acquaintance	maʕrífa, maʕáarif
friend	ṣáaḥib, ʕaṣḥáab ; ṣadíiq, ʕaṣdiqáaʕ
neighbour	gaar, giráan
to invite	dáʕa, yídʕi
to visit, call on	ẓaar, yiẓúur
to ring the bell	dáʕʕ, yidúʕʕ iggáras ; ḍárab, yíḍrab iggáras
to arrive	wiṣil, yíwṣal
to be punctual	wiṣil, yíwṣal f-ilmaʕáad
to be late	ʕitʕáxxar, yitʕáxxar
to welcome	ráḥḥab, yiráḥḥab (bi)
to take leave	xárag, yúxrug

to expect, wait for	ʕistánna, yistánna ; ʕintáẓar, yintíẓir
to meet (a friend in the street)	ʕáabil, yiʕáabil (ṣadíiʕ f-iʃʃáariʕ)
to introduce	ʕáddim, yiʕáddim
to say good-bye	wáddaʕ, yiwáddaʕ (long journey) ; ʕáal maʕa-ssaláama (in the street)
to make an appointment (with)	wáaʕid, yiwáaʕid
to make conversation, to converse	ʕikkállim, yikkállim
to push the door	dáfaʕ, yídfaʕ ilbáab
to pull the door	sáḥab, yísḥab ilbáab

PAYING A CALL

Sentences

Did you ring the bell?	ʕinta ḍarábt iggáras ?
Is Miss (*or* Mrs.) Aziza at home?	ʕazíiza háanim f-ilbéet ?
Please come in.	ʕitfáḍḍal ídxul.
Mrs. Ali would like to speak to you.	ḥáram ilʕustáaz ʕáli ʕáwza-tkallímak.
Show the visitor in.	dáxxal izzáayir.
Very pleased to see you.	fúrṣa saʕíida.
It's a great pleasure to me.	ʕana saʕíid gíddan.
The pleasure is mine.	ʕana ʕásʕad.
Thank you for your kind invitation *or* It was kind of you to invite me.	mutaʃákkir gíddan ʕala daʕwítak iṭṭayyíba.
Make yourself at home.	da béetak, xúd ráḥtak.
You are very kind.	ʕinta karíim ʕáwi.
My parents send their regards.	wáldi-w waldíti biysállim ʕaléek.
Am I late (early)?	ʕana-tʕaxxárti walla ʕéeh ? (ʕana gáyyi bádri ?)
May I introduce my husband?	ʕaʕáddim lúkum zóogi ?
May I introduce my friend Hasan?	ʕaʕaddímlak ṣadíiʕi ḥásan ?
Here are my son and daughter.	da ʕíbni wi di bínti.
Please sit down.	ʕitfáḍḍal úʕʕud.
Have some tea and cake.	ʕitfáḍḍal ʃáay wi xúd káḥki kamáan.
Please help yourself.	ʕitfáḍḍal.[1]

[1] The form is an imperative one; the corresponding feminine form is ʕitfaḍḍáli and the plural ʕitfaḍḍálu.

Do stay to dinner.	xallíik maɛáana l-ilɛáʃa.
Next time you must stay with us.	ʔilmárra-ggáaya láazim tistánna-mɛáana.
Can you put me up for to-night?	ʔáʔdar abáat hína-lléela ?
I'm sorry but I must go.	ʔana ʔáasif, ʔana láazim ámʃi.
Do stay a little longer.	xallíik maɛáana kamáan ʃuwáyya.
I have to meet a friend.	láazim aʔáabil wáaħid ṣáħbi.
I mustn't miss my train.	láazim álħaʔ ilʔáṭr.
I hope you'll come again soon.	ʔaħíbb aʃúufak táani-ʔráyyib.
Come whenever you like.	ʔitfáḍḍal fi ʔáyyi wáʔt itħíbb (or tiɛgíbak).
Many thanks for your hospitality.	mutʃákkir gíddan ɛala kárumak.
Could we meet for lunch to-morrow?	níʔdar nitʔáabil ɛa-lɣáda búkra ?
Sorry, I have an engagement.	ʔáasif, ʔana maʃɣúul f-ilwaʔtída.
I've nothing on the day after to-morrow.	ma ɛandiiʃ ħáaga (or ʔana fáaḍi) báɛdi búkra.

N.B. We most of us say what is expected of us in given circumstances. This not only involves a host, for example, in the expression of typical greetings but his guest also in appropriate responses. Such exchanges tend to be even more ritualistic and closely bound together in Arabic than in European languages. The following are examples of typical Egyptian exchange between friends or acquaintances, host and guest, etc.

Lit. "Peace be on you" (said by newcomer).	ʔissaláamu ɛaléekum.[1]
Peace be on you, the mercy of God and His blessings.	ɛaléekumu-ssaláam wi raħmátu-lláah wi barakáatu(h).
Greetings (by host).	ʔáhlan wi sáhlan.[2]
Greetings.	ʔáhlan wi sáhlan bíik.
Greetings (by non-Muslim host).	saɛíida.[3]
Greetings.	saɛíida-mbáarak (or -mbárka).
Do sit down. How are you?	ʔitfáḍḍal istaráyyaħ. ʔizzáyyi ħaḍrítak/ʔizzáyyi ṣiħħítak/ʔizzáyy ilħáal/ʔizzáyyak ?[4]

[1] This general greeting between Muslims or Christian and Muslim is not used by women. Notice the plural suffix **-kum**, a common feature of the language of personal address.

[2] Less formal than **ʔissaláamu ɛaléekum**, it may be used when passing an acquaintance in the street and translates "hullo"; **ʔáhlan** alone is even less formal.

[3] **saɛíida** and the reply are not used between Muslims.

[4] The alternatives are given in descending order of formality.

Very well, thank you.[1] How are you?	**ʕilḥámdu li-lláah, ʕalláah yiḥfáẓak (or ṣiḥḥíti-kwayyísa). ʕizzáyyi ḥaḍrítak ínta?**
Very well, thank you.	**ʕilḥámdu li-lláah.**
How is the family?	**ʕizzáyy ilɛéela?**
Very well, thank you.	**ʕilḥámdu li-lláah, kuwayyisíin.**
Lit. "You have honoured us" (i.e. I'm very pleased to see you).	**ʃarraftína.**
Lit. "May God honour you".	**ʕalláah yiʃárraf ʕádrak** (or **ʕalláah yiʃarráfak**).
Lit. "You have given us light".[2]	**nawwárti bétna** (or **nawwartína**).
Lit. "God give you light".	**ʕalláah yináwwar ɛaléek.**
Lit. "You have cheered us".[3]	**ʕanistína.**
Lit. "May God cheer you".	**ʕalláah yiʕánsak.**
Lit. "Blessing has come".[3]	**ḥáṣalit ilbáraka.**
Lit. "God bless you".	**ʕalláah yibáarik fíik.**
Do have a cup of coffee.	**ʕitfáḍḍal fingáan ʕáhwa.**
Lit. "May you always have coffee".[4]	**ʕáhwa dáyman.**
Lit. "May your life be everlasting".	**dáamit ḥayáatak.**
Please excuse me, I've an appointment.	**ʕaḥíbb astáʕzin/ʕastáʕzin baʕa/ ʕismáḥli, ɛándi maɛáad.**
Stay a while, it's still early.	**xallíik ʃuwáyya, líssa bádri.**
Thank you (but I must go).	**ʕaʃkúrak.**
Remember me to the children.	**sallímli ɛala-lʕawláad.**
Thank you, I will (lit. "God give you peace").	**ʕalláah yisallímak.**
Good-bye.	**maɛa-ssaláama.**
Good-bye.	**ʕalláah yisallímak.**

The following examples, for which there is usually no very appropriate English translation, relate to occasions as indicated.

Good wishes on the occasion of the big feast **ɛíid iḍḍiḥíyya** or Qurban Bairam.	**ʕin ʃáaʕ alláah issána-ggáyya-tkun ɛala gábal ɛarafáat.**[5]

[1] The literal translation is "Praise be to God, may God protect you".

[2] An alternative to **ʃarraftína.**

[3] A further alternative to **ʃarraftína,** but also commonly used at the end of a visit.

[4] Said after the coffee has been drunk.

[5] Lit. "If God wills, may you be at Mount Arafat next year".

Response.	(ʔíḥna w-íntu) gámʕan, ʔin ʃáaʔ alláah.[1]
On other festival occasions, including the important Ramadan Bairam.	kúllĭ sána w-inta ṭáyyib/kúllĭ ʕáam w-antum bi xéer.
Response.	w-ínta ṭáyyib/w-ínta b-iṣṣíḥḥa w-issaláama.
To pilgrim returning from Mecca.	ḥággĭ mabrúuk (or mabrúur) or ḥággĭ mabrúur wi ẓámbĭ maɣfúur.
Response by pilgrim.	ʕuʔbáal ʕandúkum or ʔalláah yibáarik fíik.
Congratulations to groom or bride after wedding.	mabrúuk, ʕuʔbáal ilbakáari or mabrúuk, ʔin ʃáaʔ alláah zurríyya ṣálḥa.
Response.	ʔalláah yibáarik fíik.
Bon voyage!	ʔin ʃáaʔ alláah tikun ríḥla-kwayyísa.
Response.	ʔin ʃáaʔ alláah, wi-nʃúuf wiʃʃúkum bi xéer.
Welcome to one returning from a journey.	ḥamdílla b-issaláama (or ʕa-ssaláama).
Response by traveller.	ʔalláah yisallímak.
When visiting a sick person.	salámtak.
Response by invalid.	ʔalláah yisallímak.
Invitation to join you (eating, drinking, etc.).	ʔitfáḍḍal.
Declining the invitation.	láʔ, mutaʃákkir or ʕiʃt.
Congratulations!	mabrúuk.
Thank you.	ʔalláah yibáarik fíik.
Congratulations on your success.	ʔahanníik bi nagáaḥak.
Thank you.	ʔaʃkúrak.
Beggar's request for alms.	ḥásana li-lláah.
Refusal.	ʔalláah yiʕṭíik or ʕal-alláah or ʕal-álla.

[1] Lit. "we and you (*sc.* you and I) together, I hope".

PASSING THE TIME OF DAY,[1] ETC.

Good morning.	**ṣabáaḥ ilxéer** or **ṣabáaḥ innúur.**
Good morning (reply).	**ṣabáaḥ ilxéer** (or **innúur**) **ʕaléek** or **ʕalláah yiṣabbáḥak b-ilxéer.**[2]
Good day.	**naháarak saʕíid.**[3]
Good day (reply).	**naháarak saʕíid mubáarak.**
Good evening.	**misáaʕ ilxéer** (or **mísa-lxéer**).[4]
Good evening (reply).	**misáaʕ ilxéer** (or **mísa-lxéer**) **ʕaléek** or **ʕalláah yimassíik b-ilxéer.**
Good evening.	**léltak saʕíida.**[5]
Good evening (reply).	**léltak saʕíida-mbáarak** (or **mbárka**).
Good night (on parting at night).	**tíṣbaḥ ʕala xéer.**
Good night (reply).	**ʕalláah yiṣabbáḥak b-ilxéer** or **w-ínta min ʕáhl ilxéer** or **w-ínta min ʕáhlu(h).**
Haven't seen you for a long time.	**ma ʃuftákʃi b-ʕáali** (or **min**) **múdda ṭawíila.**
What a pleasant surprise to see you.	**ṣúdfa ṭayyíba gíddan inn aʃúufak.**
Pleased to see you.	**kuwáyyis inn aʃúufak.**
Delighted (to meet you).	**mabṣúuṭ.**
We must keep in touch with each other.	**láazim niṭṭíṣil bi baʕḍína.**
Good-bye, see you again soon.	**maʕa-ssaláama, ʕaʃúufak ʕuráyyib.**
Pleasant journey.	**ríḥla saʕíida.**
Good luck. All the best.	**maʕa-ssaláama. ʕatmannáalak kúlli xéer.**
Keep well; look after yourself.	**xud báalak bi náfsak.**
Cheerio.	**maʕa-ssaláama.**
Don't forget us.	**ma tinsanáaʃ.**

[1] **ʕissaláamu ʕaléekum, ʕáhlan wi sáhlan,** and **saʕíida,** together with their appropriate responses, are used as general greetings at any time of day.

[2] **ṣabáaḥ innúur** may also be used as a somewhat less formal response to **ṣabáaḥ ilxéer.**

[3] This exchange is used between Christians, or between Christian and Muslim.

[4] **ʕásʕad alláahu misáak,** with the reply **ʕalláah yimassíik b-ilxéer,** is also in use.

[5] Again, unlikely to be used by Muslims.

REQUESTS

Please . . .	min fáḍlak . . . ʕiɛmil maɛrúuf . . . walláahi tiɛmílli-lxídma di . . . walláahi tixdímni . . . ʕargúuk . . .
A cup of coffee, please.	fingáan ʕáhwa, min fáḍlak.
May I trouble you for a match (a light)?	maɛáak kabríit, min fáḍlak? or tísmaħ tiwalláɛli.
May I ask you to do me a favour?	múmkin tiɛmílli xídma, min faḍlak?
I've a favour to ask you.	ʕana líyya ɛándak rága.
Excuse me.	ɛan íznak or ʕismáħli.
Would you be good enough to post this letter for me?	tísmaħ tírmi-ggawábda f-ilbúṣṭa?
I've a request to make.	ʕana ɛáawiz mínnak ħáaga.
I don't want to be disturbed.	ʕana miʃ ɛáawiz ħáddi yiʕlíʕni (if sleeping)/yiɛaṭṭálni (if working).
Can you help me?	múmkin tisaɛídni?
Your request will be granted.	ṭalabáatak maqḍíyya or ṭalabáatak.
Have you applied for your passport?	ʕaddímti ṭálab ɛaʃan paṣpóorak?
May I open the window?	múmkin áftaħ iʃʃibbáak?
Do you mind if I close the door?	tísmaħ áʕfil ilbáab?
May I apply for the job?	múmkin aʕáddim ṭálab l-ilwaẓíifa di?
I should like to hear your opinion.	ɛáawiz áɛraf ráʕyak.
What do you want?	ɛáawiz éeh?
Can I help you?	ʕáyyi xídma?
Don't bother.	miʃ muhímm or ma titɛíbʃi náfsak

THANKS

Thank you.	ʃúkran/maɛa-ʃʃúkr/ʕaʃkúrak/mutaʃákkir/mutaʃakkiriin/káttar xéerak.
Don't mention it.	ʕilɛáfw.
Many thanks.	mutaʃákkir gíddan/ʕálfi ʃúkr.
I'm very grateful (to you).	mamnúun gíddan.
Much obliged.	maɛa-ʃʃúkr.
I am deeply indebted to you.	da fáḍli-kbíir mínnak.
You are very kind.	xéerak ɛaléena (or ɛaláyya).
You've done me a great favour.	ʕafḍáalak ɛaláyya-ktíir.

I wish I could repay you.	nixdímak f-ilʔafráaħ or rabbína yiɛaddárni ɛala ráddi maɛrúufak (or gamíilak).
Please accept my sincere thanks.[1]	wa tafaḍḍálu bi qabúul fáaʔiq ittaħiyyáat.[1]
Thank you very much for the present.	mutaʃákkir gíddan ɛa-lhadíyya.

REGRETS, APOLOGIES

I am sorry you are not well.	la báʔsi ɛaléek.
I am sorry for you.	ʔana zaɛláan ɛaʃáanak.
I am sorry about the misunderstanding.	ʔana ʔáasif ɛala súuʔ ittafáahum da.
May I express my regrets.	ʔana ʔuqáddim ʔiɛtiza(a)ráati.[2]
It is very regrettable.	ħáaga muʔsífa gíddan.
Let me express my condolences.	ʔáxlaṣ ittaɛáazi[2]; ʔilbaʔíyya-f ħayáatak.
Pardon. Sorry.	ʔáasif. la muʔáxza.
I beg your pardon.	la muʔáxza.
Excuse me a minute.	ɛan ʔíznak.
Please forgive me.	ʔiɛzúrni, min faḍlak.
I didn't want to hurt your feelings.	ʔana ma ʔaṣádtiʃ[3] aʔzíik.
It was not my fault.	ma kaníitʃi[4] ɣalṭíti.
I didn't do it on purpose.	ʔana ma kúntiʃ[5] ʔáaṣid.
Don't be angry.	ma tizɛálʃ.
Please don't take offence.	ma tifhamníiʃ ɣálaṭ.
Don't think me impolite.	ma tiftikírʃ inn ána ʔalíil izzóoʔ.
Please put it down to my ignorance.	ʔáṣl ana ma kúntiʃ[5] fáahim.

INQUIRIES

Where is the station?	ʔilmaħáṭṭa féen?
Can you direct me to the post-office?	tiʔdar tiwarríini máktab ilbaríid/ilbúṣṭa?
Is this the way to the theatre?	ʔilmásraħ innaħyáadi?
Is there any bus-stop near here?	fiih máwʔaf ʔutubíis hína-ʔráyyib?

[1] Written language only.
[2] May be said or written (e.g. in telegram).
[3] Pronounced ʔaṣáttiʃ.
[4] Pronounced ma katʃi in rapid speech.
[5] Pronounced ma kúttiʃ.

Where is the booking-office?	féen ʃibbáak ittazáakir?
Where can I change money?	ʔaláaʔi fákka féen?
Where can I leave my luggage?	ʔasíib ʕáʃʃi féen?
Can you get me a taxi?	tiʔdar tigíbli táksi, min fáḍlak?
Which is the best hotel in this town?	ʔéeh ʔáḥsan lukánda f-ilbálad di?
Can I have a room for one night?	ʕáawiz áḥgiz ʔóoḍa l-illéela?
Where is the lift?	ʔilʔaṣanṣéer féen?
Are there any letters for me?	fíih gawabáat ʕaʃáani?
Where does Mr. Usman live?	ʔilʔustáaz ʕusmáan sáakin féen?
Does Dr. Tammam live here?	ʔidduktúur tammáam sáakin hína?
Has anybody called?	fíih ḥáddi sáʔal ʕaláyya?
Was there any telephone message for me?	ḥáddi ḍarábli tilifóon?
Could you tell me about/recommend me . . .?	tiʔdar tiʔúlli ʕala . . . ?

PUBLIC NOTICES

Caution!	xáṭar!
Look out!	ʔiḥðar![1]
Danger! Do not touch!	xáṭar! mamnúuʕ illáms!
Danger of death!	xáṭar mumíit!
Private! No entry!	xaaṣṣ! mamnúuʕ idduxúul!
Keep off the grass.	mamnúuʕ lmáʃy ʕala-lḥaʃíiʃ.
Trespassers will be prosecuted.	mamnúuʕ idduxúul.
Wet paint.	ʔiḥðar ilbúuya.
Stick no bills.	mamnúuʕ láṣq ilʔiʕla(a)náat.
Beware of the dogs.	ʔiḥðar ilkiláab.
Beware of pickpockets.	ʔiḥðar innaʃʃa(a)líin.
No hawkers.	mamnúuʕ ilbéeʕ hína.
You may telephone from here.	tilifonáat ʕumumíyya.
Entrance; way in.	duxúul; mádxal.
Exit; way out.	xurúug; báab ilxurúug.
Emergency exit.	báab ilxáṭar.
Toilet.	dáwrat miyáah; mara(a)ḥíiḍ.
Vacant.	xáali.
Engaged.	maʃɣúul.
Road up.	taṣlíiḥ.
Keep to the right (left).	yamíin (ʃimáal) fáqaṭ.
Drive slowly.	háddiʔ issúrʕa.

[1] ð as *th* in "the".

Diversion.	ʕiṭṭaríiʕ maʃɣúul.
No thoroughfare.	ʕiṭṭaríiʕ masdúud.
One-way street.	ʕittigáah wáaḥid.
Main road ahead.	ʕaṭṭaríiq almuqáaṭiɛ raʕíisi.
Pedestrians only.	l-ilmuʃáah fáqaṭ.
No traffic.	mamnúuɛ murúur issayya(a)ráat.
No parking.	mamnúuɛ wuqúuf issayya(a)ráaṭ.
Red.	ʕáḥmar.
Amber.	ʕáṣfar.
Green.	ʕáxḍar.
Traffic lights.	ʕiʃa(a)ráat ilmurúur.
No smoking.	mamnúuɛ ittadxíin.
Private.	xaaṣṣ.
Open from 8 to 2.	mawaɛíid ilɛámal min tamánya l-itnéen.
For hire.	l-ilʕi(i)gáar.
No bathing.	mamnúuɛ listiḥmáam.

BOOKS, NEWSPAPERS, AND MAGAZINES

Vocabulary

books, newspapers, and magazines	kútub wi súḥuf wi magalláat
bookshop	maktába, maktabáat
public library	maktába ɛáamma, makáatib ɛáamma
volume	mugállad, mugalladáat
edition	ṭábɛa, ṭabɛáat
binding	taglíida, taglidáat
guide-book	kitáab siyáaḥi, kútub siyaḥíyya
novel, story	qíṣṣa, qiṣaṣ
bookstall	kúʃk iggaráayid
press	ʕiṣṣiḥáafa
newspaper	garíida, garáayid ; gurnáal, garaníil [1]
daily	garíida yawmíyya, garáayid yawmíyya
weekly	garíida (magálla) ʕusbuɛíyya
monthly	magálla ʃahríyya, magalláat ʃahríyya
illustrated paper	garíida (magálla) muṣawwára
technical (professional) journal	gurnáal fánni, garaníil fanníyya
trade journal	gurnáal tugáari, garaníil tugaríyya
official bulletin	náʃra rasmíyya, naʃaráat rasmíyya

[1] Sometimes gurnáan, garaníin.

comic paper	**magálla mudḥíka** or **magálla fuka(a)híyya**
fashion magazine	**magállit ilʕazyáaʕ** [1]
review, periodical	**magálla, magalláat**
leader	**ʕilmaʕáal irraʕíisi**
news	**ʕilʕaxbáar**
short story	**qíṣṣa qaṣíira**
column	**ɛamúud, ɛawamíid**
cartoon	**karikatéer**
review (book, film, theatre)	**naqd ; taɛlíiq**
headlines	**ɛanawíin**
advertisement	**ʕiɛláan, ʕiɛlanáat**
publisher	**náaʃir, na(a)ʃiríin**
editor	**muḥárrir, muḥarriríin**
journalist	**ṣáḥafi, ṣaḥafiyyíin**
reader	**qáariʕ, qurráaʕ**
printer	**ɛáamil iṭṭibáaɛa, ɛummáal iṭṭibáaɛa**
print	**maṭbúuɛ ; ṭibáaɛa**
bookseller	**bayyáaɛ kútub, bayyaɛíin kútub ; ṣáaḥib maktába, ʕaṣḥáab makáatib**
newspaper vendor	**bayyáaɛ garáayid**
to publish	**náʃar, yínʃur** (or **yun-**)
to print	**ṭábaɛ, yíṭbaɛ**
to read	**ʕára, yíʕra**
to skim through	**ʕiṣṣáffaḥ, yiṣṣáffaḥ**

Sentences

Have you any modern literature?	**ɛándak kútub f-ilʕádab ilḥadíiθ ?** [2]
Can you recommend a good guide-book?	**tiʕdar tiʕúlli ɛala kitáab siyáaḥi-kwáyyis ?**
Please show me some illustrated books on Egyptian architecture.	**warríini min fáḍlak báɛḍ kútub muṣawwára ɛan fánn ilɛimáara-lmáṣri.**
Haven't you a bound copy of this novel?	**ma ɛandákʃi núsxa-mgallída min ilqíṣṣa di ?**
I want a good Arabic–English pocket dictionary.	**ʕana ɛáawiz qamúus géeb ingilíizi ɛárabi-kwáyyis.**
Is there a good library here?	**fiih maktába-kwayyísa hína ?**
Please bring me the morning paper.	**min fáḍlak hátli-ggaríida-ṣṣabaḥíyya.**

[1] A written form; sing. **ziyy.**
[2] **θ** as *th* in English "think".

Have the evening papers come out?	ʕiggaráayid ilmasaʕíyya ʕíliʕit ?
Are these the latest periodicals on economic matters?	ʕilmagallátdi ʕáaxir magalláat ẓáharit f-ilʕiqtiṣáad ?
Have you read the leader?	ʕaréet ilmaʕáal irraʕíisi (or ilmaʕáal liftitáaḥi) ?
What's the news?	ʕéeh ilʕaxbáar ?
The late news is at the bottom of the first page in Al-Ahram.	ʕáaxir xábar fi ʕásfal iṣṣáfḥa-lʕúula f-ilʕahráam.
Please let me have a weekly paper.	ʕana ʕáawiz garíida ʕusbuʕíyya, min faḍlak.
Let me have a comic paper, please.	min fáḍlak ʕiddíini magálla faka(a)híyya.
Do you stock English papers?	ʕandúku garáayid ingilíizi ?
Could I borrow your paper for a minute?	múmkin astílif garídtak daʕíiʕa ?
Have you read the advertisements?	ʕaréet ilʕiʕlanáat ?
I've read the "Situations Vacant" ("Situations Wanted") section.	ʕaréet qism "waẓáayif xálya" ("waẓáayif maṭlúuba").
Which is the best fashion magazine?	ʕéeh ʕáḥsan magálla l-ilʕazyáaʕ ?
Have you a map of Cairo?	ʕándak xaríiṭa l-ilqahíra ?
The bookstall at the corner has them.	tilaʕíihum f-ilmaktába-lli ʕa-lʕímma.
Do you read the national and international Press?	bitiʕra-ggaráayid ilmaḥallíyya w-iggaráayid ilʕa(a)lamíyya ?

THE HOUSE

Vocabulary

house	beet, biyúut
building	mábna, mabáani; ʕimáara, ʕimaráat
flat	ʃáʕʕa, ʃúʕaʕ
storey	door, ʕadwáar
basement	badróom, badromáat
cellar	máxzan táḥt ilʕárḍ, maxáazin táḥt ilʕárḍ
attic	ʕóḍt[1] issuṭúuḥ
roof	saṭḥ, suṭúuḥ
wall	ḥéeṭa, ḥeṭáan
window	ʃibbáak, ʃababíik

[1] Pronounced ʕoṭṭ.

balcony	balkóona, balkonáat
glass-covered balcony	vɑrɑ́ndɑ ʕizáaz, vɑrɑndɑ́ɑt ʕizáaz
door	baab, bibáan
key	muftáaḥ, mafatíiḥ
room	ʕóoḍɑ, ʕíwɑḍ
floor	ʕɑrḍ ; door, ʕadwɑ́ɑr (storey)
ceiling	saʕf, ʕúsʕuf
drawing-room	ʕóḍt[1] iggulúus
dining-room	ʕóḍt[1] iṣṣúfrɑ
bedroom	ʕóḍt[1] innóom
dressing-room	ʕóḍt[1] ittasríiḥa
study	ʕóḍt[1] ilmáktab
nursery	ʕóḍt[1] ilɛiyáal
hall	ṣɑ́ɑlɑ, ṣɑlɑ́ɑt
bathroom ; bath(-tub)	ḥammáam, ḥammamáat
wash-basin	ḥooḍ, ʕiḥwɑ́ɑḍ
lavatory	kabinée(h), kabineháat
stairs	síllim, saláalim
banisters	dɑrɑbzéen
furniture	ɛafʃ
stove	furn, ʕifrɑ́ɑn
air-conditioning	takyíif háwa
radiator	radyéetɑr, radyetɑrɑ́ɑt
curtain	sitɑ́ɑrɑ, satáayir
blind, shutter	ʃiiʃ
sunblind	tánda, tandáat
brazier	mánʕad, manáaʕid
switch	muftáaḥ innúur ; kubs,[2] kubsáat
lamp	lɑ́mbɑ, lɑmbɑ́ɑt ; lɑ́nḍɑ, lɑnḍɑ́ɑt
carpet	siggáada, sagagíid
table	ṭɑrɑbéeẓɑ, ṭɑrɑbeẓɑ́ɑt
chair	kúrsi, karáasi
easy-chair	futáyy, futiyyáat
mirror	miráaya, mirayáat
sideboard	bufée(h), bufeháat
cupboard	duláab, dawalíib
bed	siríir, saráayir
couch	kánaba, kanabáat
bedside table	ṭɑrɑbéeẓɑ-ṣɣayyɑ́rɑ ; kumudíinu, kumudináat
pillow	mixádda, mixaddáat
blanket	bɑṭṭɑníyya, bɑṭṭɑniyyáat

[1] Pronounced ʕoṭṭ.
[2] Pronounced kups.

sheet	miláaya, milayáat
eiderdown	liḥáaf, ʕilḥífa
bedspread	máfraʃ siríir
kitchen	máṭbax, maṭáabix
kitchen range	wabúur iṭṭábx, bawabíir iṭṭábx
cooker	(gas) fúrni b-ilɣáaz; (electric) fúrni kahrabáaʕi [1] (or fúrni b-ikkahrába)
shelf	raff, rufúuf
coal fire	náar fáḥm
pan	ḥálla, ḥílal
saucepan	kasaróola, kasaroláat
frying-pan	máʕla, maʕlayáat; ṭáaẓa, ṭaẓáat
pots and pans	ʕadawáat ilmáṭbax
cutlery, silver	faḍḍíyya
crockery, china	ṣíini
teapot	barráad ʃáay, bararíid ʃáay
coffee-pot	barráad ʕáhwa, bararíid ʕáhwa
gas (electricity, water) meter	ʕaddáad ɣáaz (kahrába, máyya)
pantry	(ʕóḍt ik)kaẓáar
to cook	ṭábax, yúṭbux
to live	síkin,[2] yúskun; ʕaaʃ, yiʕíiʃ
to move in (out)	náʕal, yínʕil fi (min)
to lease, to rent	ʕággar, yiʕággar

Sentences

Flats to let.	ʃúʕaʕ l-ilʕi(i)gáar.
Have you taken a furnished flat?	ʕaggárti ʃáʕʕa b-ilʕáfʃ (or bi ʕafʃáha)?
I want a room with service.	ʕáawiz ʕóoḍa maʕa-lxídma.
I want full board.	ʕana ʕáawiz ʕóoḍa b-ilʕákl.
I want to buy a house with a garden.	ʕáawiz aʃtíri béet bi-gnéena.
Where do you live?	ʕinta sáakin féen?
I live on the second floor, to the right.	ʕana sáakin f-iddóor ittáani, ʕa-lyimíin.
I live on the top floor.	ʕana sáakin f-iddóor ilʕaxráani.
The stairs have (just) been painted.	ʕissaláalim madhúuna búhya.
Is your friend upstairs?	ṣáḥbak fóoʕ?

[1] Or kahrabáaʕi.
[2] Or sákan.

He's downstairs in the dining-room.	huwwa táḥti-f ʕóḍt iṣṣúfra.
I want a large, airy room.	ʕana ɛáawiz ʕóoḍa háwya-w wásɛa.
This room looks on to the park.	ʕilʕóoḍa di bitṭúlli ɛa-lmuntáza.
This building has a lot of floors with four flats on each.	ʕilɛimáara di fiiha-dwáar kitíira, wi kúlli dóor fiih ʕárbaɛ ʃúʕaʕ.
I need a writing-desk and book-cases.	yilzámni máktab wi dawaliib kútub.
Is the bed comfortable?	ʕissiriir muriiḥ?
It is too hard (soft).	gáamid (láyyin) ʕáwi.
Switch on (off) the light.	wállaɛ (ṭáffi) innúur.
The lamp on the bedside table has no bulb.	ʕilʕabajóora-lli gámb issiriir ma fihúaʃ lámba.
Can I have a bath?	múmkin áaxud ḥammáam?
There's no hot water to-day.	ma fiiʃ máyya súxna-nnaharda.
Where is the maid?	féen ilxaddáama?
The boy (*sc.* servant) is nowhere to be found.	ʕana miʃ láaʕi-lfarráaʃ (or ʕilfarráaʃ miʃ mawgúud).
The table is laid for lunch.	ʕiṣṣúfra gáhza l-ilɣáda.
The knives, forks, teaspoons, and tablespoons are in the side-board drawer.	ʕissakakíin, ʕiʃʃíwak, maɛáaliʕ iʃʃáay w-ilmaɛáaliʕ fi dúrg ilbuféeh.
This crockery is chinaware.	ʕilʕiṭbáaʕ di ṣíini.
This flat is air-conditioned.	ʕiʃʃáʕʕa di fiiha takyíif háwa.
Bring another chair to this corner.	háat kúrsi táani f-irruknída.
This door needs a new lock.	ʕilbáab da ɛáawiz ṭábla-gdiida.
The key is lost.	ʕilmuftáaḥ ḍáaɛ.
There's an iron bolt on the front door.	fiih tirbáas ḥadiid ɛa-lbáab ilbarráani.
What's the monthly rent for this flat?	ʕiʃʃaʕʕáadi-b káam f-iʃʃáhr?
Must I pay in advance?	láazim ádfaɛ muʕáddam?
Could I move in next month?	múmkin ánʕil hína-ʃʃáhr iggáay?
When did you move out of your old flat?	naʕálti ʕímta min ʃaʕʕítak ilʕadiima?
Are you the owner of this house?	ʕinta ṣáaḥib ilbéet da?
I've only a lease for one year.	ʕana-mʕaggáru sána wáḥda báss.[1]

[1] Lit. "I've leased it (*sc.* house), etc.".

GEOGRAPHICAL DIVISIONS

COUNTRIES AND NATIONS

Vocabulary

countries and nations	**ʕaddúwal w-alʕúmam** [1]
Africa	**ʕafríiqya**
African	**ʕafríiqi, ʕafriqíyya, ʕafriqiyyíin**
Albania	**ʕalbá(a)nya**
Albanian	**ʕalbáani, ʕalbaníyya, ʕalbaniyyíin**
America	**ʕamríika**
American	**ʕamrikáani, ʕamrikaníyya, ʕamrikáan or ʕamríiki, ʕamrikíyya, ʕamrikiyyíin** [2]
Arabia	**ʕilmamláka-lɛarabíyya-ssuɛudíyya**
Arabian	**suɛúudi, suɛudíyya, suɛudiyyíin**
Argentine	**ʕilʕarjantíin**
Argentinian	**ʕarjantíini, ʕarjantiníyya, ʕarjantiniyyíin**
Asia	**ʕásya**
Asian, Asiatic	**ʕasyáawi, ʕasyawíyya, ʕasyawiyyíin**
Australia	**ʕusturálya**
Australian	**ʕusturáali, ʕusturalíyya, ʕusturaliyyíin**
Austria	**ʕinnímsa**
Austrian	**nimsáawi, nimsawíyya, nimsawiyyíin**
Belgium	**baljíika**
Belgian	**baljíiki, baljikíyya, baljikiyyíin**
Brazil	**barazíil**
Brazilian	**barazíili, barazilíyya, baraziliyyíin**
Bulgaria	**bilɣárya**
Bulgar, Bulgarian	**bilɣáari, bilɣaríyya, bilɣariyyíin**
Canada	**kánada**
Canadian	**kánadi, kanadíyya, kanadiyyíin**
Chile	**ʃíili**
Chilean	**ʃíili, ʃilíyya, ʃiliyyíin**
China	**ʕiṣṣíin**
Chinese	**ṣíini, ṣiníyya, ṣiniyyíin**
Czechoslovakia	**tʃikusluvákya**
Czech	**ráagil, ḫáaga, etc., min (or bitáaɛ) tʃikusluvákya**
Denmark	**ʕiddinimárk**
Dane, Danish	**dinimárki, dinimarkíyya, dinimarkiyyíin**

[1] Written form.

[2] **ʕálam ʕamrikáani** "American pen(cil)" but either **ráagil ʕamrikáani** or **ráagil ʕamríiki.**

Egypt	maṣr[1]; bárri máṣr; ʕilqúṭr ilmáṣri
Egyptian	máṣri, maṣríyya, maṣriyyíin
England	ʕingiltíra
Englishman, English	ʕingilíizi, ʕingilizíyya, ʕingiliziyyíin, ʕingilíiz
Eritrea	ʕaritríya
Eritrean	ráagil, ħáaga, etc., min ʕaritríya
Ethiopia	ʕilħábaʃa
Ethiopian	ħábaʃi, ħabaʃíyya, ʕaħbáaʃ
Europe	ʕurúbba
European	ʕurúbbi, ʕurubbíyya, ʕurubbiyyíin
Finland	fillánda
Finn, Finnish	fillándi, fillandíyya, fillandiyyíin
France	faránsa
Frenchman, French	faransáawi, faransawíyya, faransawiyyíin
Germany	ʕalmánya
German	ʕalmáani, ʕalmaníyya, ʕalmáan
Ghana	ɣáana
Ghanaian	ráagil, etc., min ɣáana
Great Britain	biriṭáanya-lʕúẓma
Briton, British	biriṭáani, biriṭaníyya, biriṭaniyyíin
Greece	ʕilyunáan
Greek	yunáani, yunaníyya, yunáan
Holland	hulánda
Dutchman, Dutch	hulándi, hulandíyya, hulandiyyíin
Hungary	ʕilmágar
Hungarian	mágari, magaríyya, magariyyíin
Iceland	ʕayislánda
Icelander, Icelandic	ráagil, etc., min ʕayislánda
India	ʕilhínd
Indian	híndi, hindíyya, hanádwa
Ireland	ʕayirlánda
Irishman, Irish	ʕayirlándi, ʕayirlandíyya, ʕayirlandiyyíin
Israel	ʕisraʕíil
Israeli	ʕisraʕíili, ʕisraʕilíyya, ʕisraʕiliyyíin
Italy	ʕiṭá(a)lya
Italian	ṭalyáani (or ṭul-), ṭalyaníyya, ṭaláyna or ʕiṭáali, ʕiṭalíyya, ʕiṭaliyyíin
Japan	ʕilyabáan
Japanese	yabáani, yabaníyya, yabaniyyíin
Jugoslavia	yuɣusláfya
Jugoslav	yuɣusláafi, yuɣuslafíyya, yuɣuslafiyyíin

[1] maṣr is generally used in Egypt itself in the sense of "Cairo".

Kenya	**kínya**
Kenyan	**ráagil**, etc., **min kínya**
Luxemburg	**luksumbúrg**
Luxemburger	**ráagil**, etc., **min luksumbúrg**
Mexico	**ʕilmaksíik**
Mexican	**maksíiki, maksikíyya, maksikiyyíin**
New Zealand	**niwzi(i)lánda**
New Zealander	**niwzilándi, niwzilandíyya, niwzilandiyyíin**
Norway	**ʕinnurwéeg**
Norwegian	**nurwéegi, nurwegíyya, nurwegiyyíin**
Pakistan	**pakistáan**
Pakistani	**pakistáani, pakistaníyya, pakistaniyyíin**
Persia	**fáaris** or **ʕi(i)ráan**
Persian	**fa(a)rísi, farisíyya, farisiyyíin** or **fársi, farsíyya, farsiyyíin** or **ʕi(i)ráani, ʕiraníyya, ʕiraniyyíin**
Poland	**bulánda**
Pole, Polish	**bulándi, bulandíyya, bulandiyyíin**
Portugal	**ʕilburtuɣáal**
Portuguese	**burtuɣáali, burtuɣalíyya, burtuɣaliyyíin**
Roumania	**rumánya**
Roumanian	**rumáani, rumaníyya, rumaniyyíin**
Russia	**rú(u)sya**
Russian	**rúusi, rusíyya, ruus**
Scotland	**(ʕi)skutlánda**
Scotsman, Scottish	**ʕiskutlándi, ʕiskutlandíyya, ʕiskutlandiyyíin**
Spain	**ʕasbánya**
Spaniard, Spanish	**ʕasbáani, ʕasbaníyya, ʕasbaniyyíin**
Sweden	**ʕissuwéed**
Swede, Swedish	**suwéedi, suwedíyya, suwediyyíin**
Switzerland	**suwísra**
Swiss	**suwísri, suwisríyya, suwisriyyíin**
Turkey	**turkíya**
Turk, Turkish	**túrki, turkíyya, ʕatráak** (or **tarákwa**)
United States of America	**ʕilwilayáat ilmuttáḫida-lʕamrikíyya**
North American	**ráagil**, etc., **min ʕamríika-ʃʃamalíyya**
South America	**ʕamríika-lganubíyya**
South American	**ráagil**, etc., **min ʕamríika-lganubíyya**
Wales	**weelz**
Welshman, Welsh	**ráagil**, etc., **min wéelz**

REGIONS, TOWNS, ISLANDS

Vocabulary

regions, islands, towns	ʕalʕaqaliim, ʕalgúzur, ʕalmúdun
Ankara	ʕanqára
Athens	ʕaθíina
Balearic Isles	gúzur ilbilyáar
Bavaria	bavárya
Bethlehem	béet láḥm
Biscay	biskáay
Bordeaux	burdóo
Bombay	bumbáay
Brussels	birúksil
Burgundy	birgándi
Canary Islands	gúzur ilkanáari
Ceylon	sayaláan
Corsica	kursíika
Crete	kiríit
Cyprus	qúbruṣ or ʕúbruṣ
Dunkirk	dankírk
Edinburgh	ʕadímb(i)ra
Genoa	jíniwa
Geneva	jinéev
Greenland	girínland
(the) Hague	la(a) háay
Haifa	ḥíifa
Istanbul	ʕisṭambúul
Jerusalem	ʕurʃalíim or ʕilqúds
Karachi	kará(a)tʃi
London	lándan
Malta	málṭa
Marseilles	marsílya
Mediterranean (Sea)	ʕilbáḥr ilʕábyaḍ ilmutawáṣṣiṭ
Moscow	músku
Naples	náapuli
Netherlands	ʕilʕaráaḍi-lmunxáfiḍa
Newfoundland	niwfáwndland
New York	niwyóork
Nairobi	nayrúubi
Nice	niis
Pekin	pikíin
Philippine Islands	gúzur ilfiliplíin
Pyrenees	ʕilpirinlíz
Rhodes	róodis

Rome	róomɑ
Sardinia	sardínya
Scandinavia	ʔiskandinéevya
Sicily	ṣiqilíyya
Teheran	ṭɑhrɑ́ɑn
Tel Aviv	tálli ʔabíib
Thames	ʔittéemz
United Kingdom	ʔilmamláka-lmuttáħida
Venice	viníis
Vienna	viyánna
Warsaw	wársu
Zanzibar	zangibɑ́ɑr

COUNTRIES AND CAPITALS OF THE ARAB WORLD[1]

Vocabulary

Aden (protectorate and town)	ʔádan
Algeria	ʔilgazáaʔir
Bahrein	baħréen or ʔilbaħréen
Hadramaut	ħɑḍrɑmóot
Iraq	ʔilɛirɑ́ɑq or ʔilɛiráaʔ
Jordan	ʔilʔúrdun
Kuwait	ʔikkuwéet
Lebanon	libnáan
Libya	lí(i)bya
Cyrenaica	bɑ́rqɑ
Tripolitania	ṭɑrɑ́ɑblus
Morocco	murrɑ́ɑkiʃ
Oman	ɛumáan
Persian Gulf	xalíig ilfa(a)rísi
Sudan	ʔissudáan
Syria	súrya
Tunisia	tɑ́unis
United Arabic Republic	ʔilgumhuríyya-lɛɑrɑbíyya-lmuttáħida
Yemen	ʔilyáman
Algiers	ʔilgazáaʔir
Aden	ɛádan
Aleppo	ħálam
Amman	ɛammáan
Baghdad	baɣdáad
Basra	ʔilbɑ́ṣrɑ

[1] ʔilbiláad ilɛɑrɑbíyya-w ɛawaṣímha.

Beyrut	**bayrúut**
Benghasi	**báni ɣáazi**
Casablanca	**ʕiddáar ilbayḍáaʕ**
Damascus	**dimáʃq**
Fez	**faas**
Homs	**ḥims**
Khartoum	**ʕilxarṭúum**
Kuwait	**ʕikkuwéet**
Marrakesh	**murráakiʃ**
Mecca	**mákka**
Medina	**ʕilmadíina**
Mosul	**ʕilmáwṣil**
Muscat	**másqaṭ**
Port Sudan	**bursudáan**
Oran	**ʕu(u)ráan**
Rabat	**ʕirrabáaṭ**
Riyadh	**ʕirriyáaḍ**
Tangier	**ṭánja**
Tetuan	**taṭwáan**
Tripoli (Libya)	**ṭaráablus (ilɣárb)**
Tunis	**túunis**
the Arab League	**ga(a)míɛit iddúwal ilɛarabíyya**
the Arab world	**ʕilɛáalam ilɛárabi**
the Maghrib	**ʕilmáɣrib**
the Near East	**ʕiʃʃárq ilʕádna**
the Middle East	**ʕiʃʃárq ilʕáwsaṭ**

REGIONS AND TOWNS OF EGYPT[1]

Vocabulary

administrative divisions	**ʕilʕaqalíim ilʕidaríyya**
governorate	**muḥáfẓa, muḥafẓáat** (or **mi-**)
province	**mudiríyya, mudiriyyáat**
Eastern Province	**mudiríyyit iʃʃarʕíyya**
Western Province	**mudiríyyit ilɣarbíyya**
Munufiyya Province	**mudiríyyit ilmunufíyya**
district	**márkaz, maráakiz**
Ashmun District	**márkaz ʕaʃmúun**
geographical divisions	**ʕilʕaqalíim ilguɣrafíyya**
Lower Egypt *or* the Delta	**ʕilwágh ilbáḥari** or **ʕiddílta**
Upper Egypt	**ʕilwágh ilʕíbli** or **ʕiṣṣiɛíid**
Western Desert	**ʕiṣṣaḥráaʕ ilɣarbíyya**

[1] **ʕaqsáam wi múdun máṣr.**

Eastern Desert	ʕiṣṣaḥráaʕ iʃʃarqíyya
Sinai	síina or ṣaḥráaʕ síina
Qattara Depression	munxáfaḍ ilqaṭṭáara
Gulf of Suez	xalíig issuwées
Gulf of Aqaba	xalíig ilɛáqaba
Red Sea	ʕilbáḥr ilʕáḥmar
Nile	ʕinníil
Rashid branch (of the Nile)	fárɛi raʃíid
Damietta branch (of the Nile)	fárɛi dumyáaṭ
Siwa Oasis	wáaḥit síiwa
Suez Canal	qanáat issuwées
Lower Egyptian	baḥráawi, baḥrawíyya, baḥárwa[1]
Upper Egyptian	ṣiɛíidi, ṣiɛidíyya, ṣaɛáyda
Bedouin	bádawi, badawíyya, badw
countryside	ʕilʕaryáaf
town	bálad, biláad ; madíina, múdun
Cairo	ʕilqa(a)híra ; maṣr
Alexandria	ʕiskindiríyya
Damietta	dumyáaṭ
Port Said	burṣaɛíid
Suez	ʕissuwées
Fayoum	ʕilfayyúum
Asyut	ʕasyúuṭ[2]
Qena	qína
Luxor	lúʕṣur
Aswan	ʕaṣwáan
Giza	ʕiggíiza
Marsa Matruh	márṣa maṭrúuḥ
quarter (of town)	ḥayy, ʕaḥyáaʕ
Old Cairo	máṣr ilʕadíima
New Cairo	máṣr iggidíida
the Citadel	ʕilʕálɛa
Azhar Mosque	ʕilʕáẓhar
places of interest	ʕamáakin muhímma
the Pyramids	ʕilʕahráam
the Sphinx	ʕabu-lhóol
Pharaonic remains	ʕasáar ilfaráɛna
Muhammad Ali Mosque	gáamiɛ muḥámmad ɛáli
Ibn Talun Mosque	gáamiɛ íbni ṭulúun
Amr Ibn al-As Mosque	gáamiɛ ɛámr ibn ilɛáas
the Antiquities Museum	dáar ilʕasáar ilmaṣríyya or ʕilʕantikxáana

[1] Or baḥárwa.
[2] Or ʕasyúuṭ.

Karnak	**kárnak**
the High Dam	**ʕissádd ilɛáali**
Sakkara	**saʕʕáara**
the Barrages	**ʕilʕanáaṭir**[1] **ilxayríyya**
the Zoo	**ginént ilḥayawanáat**
Literary Museum	**dáar ikkútub** or **ʕikkutubxáana**
the Muski	**xáan ilxalíili**
St. Catherine's Monastery	**díir san(ta) katríin**
the Bitter Lakes	**ʕilbuḥayráat ilmúrra**

Sentences

What is your nationality?	**ʕínta min ʕáyyi ʕúṭr ?**
I am English (Egyptian, French, German, Ghanaian).	**ʕana-ngilíizi (máṣri, faransáawi, ʕalmáani, min ɣáana).**
Have you any identification papers?	**maɛáak ʕawráaʕ taḥʕíiʕ ʃaxṣíyya ?**
I have a British passport.	**ʕana-mɛáaya paṣpóor (or gawáaz sáfar) ingilíizi.**
How long have you been here?	**baʕáalak hína ʕaddéeh ?**
Here is my identity card.	**biṭáaʕit taḥʕíiʕ iʃʃaxṣíyya-btaɛt(i ʕ)ahéh.**
I am Egyptian by birth.	**ʕana mawlúud fi máṣr.**
I am English by marriage.	**ʕana góozi-ngilíizi.**[2]
I am stateless.	**ʕana maliyyáaʃ wáṭan.**
I am a refugee.	**ʕana muháagir.**
Can I claim British nationality?	**ʕáʕdar áṭlub ilʕinsíyya-lbiriṭaníyya ?**
Are you a naturalized Britisher?	**ʕinta xádt ilʕinsíyya-lbiriṭaníyya ?**
I want to travel to Iraq.	**ʕana ɛáawiz asáafir ilɛiráaʕ.**
Can I enter Italy without a special visa?	**múmkin ádxul ʕiṭálya min ɣéer víiza ?**
My mother tongue is French.	**lúɣati-lʕaṣlíyya faransáawi (or ʕilfaransáawi lúɣati-lʕaṣlíyya).**
Are you a foreigner?	**ʕinta ʕagnábi ?**
I've been through Egypt (*sc.* without stopping).	**ʕana ɛaddéet ɛala máṣri w-ana-msáafir.**
I've been down the Nile.	**ʕana safírti f-inníil.**
He has just returned from Syria.	**ya dóob rígiɛ min súrya or huwwa líssa ráagiɛ min súrya dilwaʕti.**
Do you speak English (Arabic)?	**bitikkállim ingilíizi (ɛárabi) ?**

[1] Or **ʕanáaṭir.**
[2] Lit. "my husband is English".

I only speak a little Arabic.	ʕana bakkállim ɛárabi bagíit (or ʃuwáyya).
I can read Arabic but I cannot speak it fluently.	ʕan-áʕdar áʕra ɛárabi ʕinnáma ma (ʕa)ʕdárʃ akkállim kuwáyyis.
I shall have to take Arabic lessons.	ʕana láazim áaxud durúus ɛárabi.
Can you recommend a good Egyptian teacher?	tiʕdar tiʕúlli ɛala mudárris másri kwáyyis?
Can you understand me?	ʕinta fa(a)hímni (or ʕinta fáahim)?
You have an accent in Arabic.	ʕilɛárabi-btáaɛak mikássar ʃuwayya.
Do you understand the Sa'idi dialect?	ʕinta-btífham kaláam issaɛáyda?
Do you speak colloquial Arabic?	ʕinta-btikkállim ɛárabi dáarig?
Do you know Classical Arabic?	bitíɛraf ɛárabi faşíiḥ?
I've studied Arabic.	ʕana-tɛallímti ɛárabi.
I don't understand (you).	ʕana miʃ fáahim.
I don't understand your meaning.	ʕana miʃ fáahim ʕáşdak.
Please speak (more) slowly.	ʕikkállim ɛala máhlak, min fadlak.
What does that word mean?	ʕikkilmáadi maɛnáaha ʕéeh?
Could you please translate this sentence for me?	múmkin titargímli-ggumláadi?
How do you spell this word?	bitistahágga-kkilmáadi-zzáay?
I'll spell it (out) for you.	ʕana ḥastahaggáalak.
You have a good (bad) pronunciation.	nútʕak kuwáyyis (wíḥiʃ).
They have their own dialect.	biyikkallímu láhga maxşúuşa.
Would you act as interpreter for me with this gentleman?	múmkin titargímli kaláam issáyyid?